Nevada's Paul Laxalt
A Memoir

Paul Laxalt

Nevada's Paul Laxalt

A Memoir

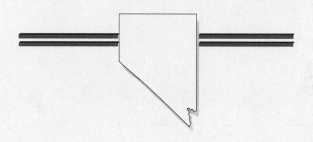

BY

Senator Paul Laxalt

Jack Bacon & Company
Reno, Nevada
2000

Library of Congress Card Number: 99-067639
ISBN 0-930083-09-1

Jack Bacon & Company
516 South Virginia Street
Reno, Nevada 89501

First Edition

For Carol

❖ *Table of Contents* ❖

❖ *Preface* ❖

In the late Reagan years, when memoirs by insiders became all too common, I was contacted by various book agents who said I had a compelling story to tell.

In late 1986, my last full year in the United States Senate, the exercise became so serious that outlines were submitted by an agent to publishers in Manhattan. I soon learned about literary reality: No one in the hierarchy of the New York publishing world was interested in Paul Laxalt except as a vehicle to "tell all" concerning the Reagans.

In short, they wanted a "kiss and tell" book or no book.

In the dozen years since then, I've been busy doing other things and only recently considered writing about my experiences.

Nowadays, with the gradual melding of many major publishing houses into large corporations, more than ever, publishing is a "bottom line" game. Unless the book is written by a Tom Clancy-type with potential for both huge book sales and good prospects for television or the movies, chances of someone like me having a book published by a major house are nil.

So, with full recognition that I won't retire on the proceeds of this book, I've decided to return to my roots and work with my friend Jack Bacon, a Nevada publisher. And with no unrealistic commercial goals to meet, I have the luxury of not having to write it to fill someone's prescription for gossip, sex or scandal.

In the following pages, I tell the story of a first-generation Basque kid from a small town, in a sparsely-populated state, who through circumstance and good fortune was privileged to be a participant in many important state, national and international events of the last 30 years, including major events in the 1980s, perhaps one of the most significant periods in our history.

My respite from public life has enabled me to recall these events fairly free of the accompanying high emotion. I hope that improves its objectivity.

If this book inspires just one person, however modest in circumstance, to arrive at the conclusion that public office is indeed a high calling and a noble profession and then decides, as I did, to run for office, the effort will have been worth it.

❖ *Introduction* ❖

Kenny C. Guinn
Governor of Nevada

Being elected Nevada's 28th Governor in 1998 was the greatest honor bestowed upon me during my life. I had served in important positions before, such as superintendent of a school system, chairman of a bank, chairman of a utility, and president of a university. But to be elected by my fellow Nevadans as chief executive of this great state was incomparable – both an incredible privilege and an extraordinary responsibility.

One thing that I have kept constantly in mind is to do well by those Governors who came before me. Although I have personally known and respected my predecessors, one in particular stands out because of our close friendship over the past three decades. I am referring to my good friend Paul Laxalt.

Paul's public service career is well known to many, but his family's story is equally compelling. Perhaps one reason I relate so well to Paul is that we have similar backgrounds. Indeed, neither Paul Laxalt nor Kenny Guinn was born into wealth or privilege.

My father worked in the farmlands of central California from morning until night so that his children could enjoy the opportunities that he did not have. My parents couldn't give us much, but they made sure we had a home and an education.

Likewise, Dominique Laxalt, who came to America in 1906 from the Basque region of France with virtually nothing, worked for decades as a sheepherder in the lonely deserts and mountains of Nevada.

Because Dominque's occupation required him to be away from home for long periods of time, the job of raising the six Laxalt children fell in large measure to Paul's mother, Theresa, who also ran a small restaurant and hotel in Carson City.

Like my parents, Paul's "Mom and Pop" sacrificed in ways largely unheard of today. They devoted themselves completely to the goal of instilling in the Laxalt children qualities that last a lifetime — hard work, devotion to family, education, personal responsibility, and community service.

While his father might have preferred that he join him in the shepherding business, Paul heard a different calling. After graduating from Carson High, where he was a top student and star athlete, Paul attended Santa Clara University. When Pearl Harbor was attacked, Paul enlisted along with many other Nevadans. During his service, he saw combat action in the Philippines.

When he returned, Paul attended law school and eventually went into practice with his father-in-law, John R. Ross, who later became a federal judge.

Paul entered elective politics for the first time in 1954, when he was elected District Attorney of Ormsby County. Eventually, he would be elected Lieutenant Governor (1962), Governor (1966), and United States Senator (1974, 1980). When he retired in 1987, he was one of the most popular figures in Nevada political history.

Paul's governorship fell at a critical time for our state. His accomplishments attest to that fact: He repaired badly damaged relations between the state and federal government over Nevada's legalized gaming industry; he helped pass a law that allowed corporations, for the first time, to hold gaming licenses; he expanded the state parks system, while taking steps to protect Lake Tahoe;

and he improved the quality of education by, among other accomplishments, creating a community college system and medical school.

As a U.S. Senator, Paul fought tirelessly on behalf of the conservative principles in which he, and many other Nevadans, believed so deeply. He became one of the most respected members of the U.S. Senate, which accrued to the benefit of his constituents over and over.

Paul was also one of Ronald Reagan's closest and most trusted friends. He served three times as the President's national campaign chairman and was also the President's indispensable link to the Senate.

Although he rose to greater and greater prominence, Paul never forgot his roots in Nevada. Perhaps it was his ability to maintain the "common touch" that made him such a memorable figure in Nevada's history. I hope that I, too, never forget my own humble beginnings and my early years of struggle as a young husband and father in Las Vegas.

This book tells Paul's life story. But in some ways it tells my story as well — and the stories of millions of other Americans who were fortunate enough to be born in this great land of opportunity.

One of Paul's memorable campaign slogans succinctly told the secret of his political success: "One of us."

Paul Laxalt truly is one of us — a Nevadan, a patriot, and a believer in the American dream. My wife Dema and I are proud to call Carol and Paul Laxalt "friends." We also feel fortunate to have called him Governor.

❖ *Acknowledgements* ❖

Although this effort has been on my mind since 1986, I didn't get serious until some three years ago. After digging out old outlines, I started writing.

Janene Assuras, my trusted assistant who came with me from the Senate, did the typing. Since she is a devoted Democrat, I detected some clenched teeth at times when I discussed politics. But Janene never took issue with me on any aspect of the book. Great lady! Sadly, she suffered a severe stroke in early 1998, which caused her to have to leave the office.

Janene, many thanks for your loyal service over the years, including the work on this book.

After Janene left, Tom Loranger assumed full responsibility. Tom has been with me since my Senate days, rising from being an intern to being my administrative assistant. Tom had previously helped me with research and organization of the reams of materials I had accumulated over the years. He was also invaluable in terms of fact checking and touching base with the many people mentioned in the book. After all this time, I'm convinced that Tom knows more about my record than I recall myself.

Tom, you've been absolutely essential to this effort. I shall always be so grateful to you.

When it came to selecting a publisher, I turned to my old

friend in Reno, Jack Bacon. During my Senate days — on his own — Jack had published a small book about my nominating speeches on behalf of President Reagan, naming it "The Nominating of a President." It was warmly received. Jack eagerly accepted this project, and he has worked ever since with Tom and me on a "hands-on" basis. The final product is the result of his creativity and professionalism.

Jack, many thanks.

From the beginning, I was constantly told to select a top editor. Peter Hannaford, a good friend whom I have known since the early Reagan days, kindly consented to do the editing. A Californian, Peter knows Nevada well, has followed my career and is quite familiar with "the Washington scene." His suggestions were incorporated and, as a result, the final product is immeasurably better than it would have been otherwise.

Peter, thanks for all your help. I will always appreciate the fact that you did absolutely no violence to what I was attempting to do.

Bill Martin, back in the Senate days, did some drafts for me on the "Reagan period." They were most helpful to me, and I thank him for his good work.

Paul Laxalt
October 1999

CHAPTER I

❖ Growing Up in Carson City ❖

THE EARLY YEARS

How did the son of immigrant Basque parents, who disliked large social functions, who had a strong penchant for privacy, who once dreaded the prospect of making a speech, who had six young children, who was engaged in a successful law practice in a delightfully parochial small town, who had a disdain for politics and politicians, end up in politics?

Unlike others whom I met later in public life, I had no "grand plan" – the right schools, the right profession, gradual elevation into the social and business world, laying the right foundation for the inevitable plunge. None of that happened to me.

Indeed, in my high school days when I was an unreconstructed "jock," moving from one sport to the other as the weather changed, I would dream of one day being a coach, which to me would indeed be the summit.

Looking back, what may have launched and continued my career in politics was a sense of obligation, a sense of "paying back" through public service to a state and country which had treated an "old country" family such as ours so well.

In 1906, as a lad of 18, my father – "Pop" – came to the American West, as many other Basques did in those days, to herd sheep. It was their ticket to the "Sweet Promised Land," the title of the beautiful book published in 1957 that my brother Bob wrote about our father.

Thousands left their homes in the Basque Country, in the Pyrenees Mountains of France and Spain, because the tradition and the law there were that the eldest child would receive the family's properties upon the death of the parents. The younger ones, like my father, were shut out of any inheritance. For many years, I had felt he had been wrongfully dispossessed of some handsome inheritance – that is, until I visited his birthplace in Tardets when I was Governor.

The "homestead" consisted of an old stone house with a few acres of land, upon which a family could barely subsist. People there had simply come to grips with the grim reality that their property could only support the eldest son and his family; the rest had to leave.

I've often thought how gut-wrenching it must have been for Pop to leave a close-knit family, travel thousands of miles on ships and trains, not knowing a word of English, and end up in some God-forsaken sheep camp in the deserts of Nevada.

I guess the human critter is amazingly flexible, and if a person has the requisite will and courage, he'll eventually prevail. And I suppose, too, that the natural excitement of a young man in going to America, making a fortune in a few years, and returning home as the "Master of the Basque Universe" was a real motivation.

Later, as Governor, when I was delivering commencement addresses all over Nevada, I used to tell high school graduates that by modern standards Pop's work was modest and humble. After all, he was a sheepherder, but he was a damned good one!

Like most Basques, he combined hard work with entrepreneurial spirit. As he accumulated a few dollars, he bought sheep. Before long, he owned thousands of sheep.

By about 1920, he was one of the major figures in the sheep business in the West. He was dashing, handsome and drove a resplendent Cadillac. His forays into the city of Reno (population 15,000) became legendary.

In many respects, the 1920s were free-wheeling years. Whatever you wanted to borrow from the banks, they were ready to lend – with a hefty rate of interest, of course. Although the analogy is a bit loose, Dominique Laxalt in the '20s had the same kind of cozy relationship with the banks (which he would greatly regret later) that Donald Trump enjoyed in New York in the '80s.

Momma and Poppa Laxalt on their wedding day – October 8, 1921. *Nevada Historical Society*

It was in 1921 that Mom innocently visited Reno. She had been on a mission of mercy to pick up her younger brother, Michel, a French officer, who had been gassed in World War I. Michel had been sent to Letterman's Hospital at the San Francisco Presidio for treatment. When his condition worsened, he was sent to a medical facility in Colfax, California. Mom moved to Reno and commuted back and forth to visit Michel there. He died, and Mom started to return home to the French officer to whom she was engaged at the time.

In Reno, she met my father. From that point on, the French officer's stock sunk out of sight. Ever strong-willed, well-educated and cultured (the Cordon Bleu School in Paris), she succumbed to Dominique's charms and — perhaps to a lesser extent — his Cadillac.

On October 8, 1921, they were married at a festive wedding in a Basque gathering place in Reno called the Indart Hotel. (Reports of many broken female hearts at the time were exaggerated.)

Ten months later, I was born. They tended to be rather efficient souls.

Mom was a woman no one — including Pop, me, the Governor, the President, the Pope — would or should trifle with. She was without a doubt the strongest-willed person I've ever known. She combined that with a great tenderness toward those she loved.

I've always felt that fate dealt the Laxalt family a fantastic hand when Momma Laxalt decided to make Carson City our home. What has always been intriguing to me was not so much the landing, but the course that brought us there.

Pop

Pop came to America, as his older brothers had before him, to make a living for himself. As I noted earlier, the law of primogeniture in the Basque country, which is still followed today, is that the family property passes to the eldest male upon the death of the parents. Pop, as the youngest in a family of seven, saw the handwriting on the wall and came to this country in 1906.

For many years, he herded sheep on lonely ranges in Northern California and Nevada. Equipped with a tent, a trusted donkey that carried his camp supplies, a sheep dog, which exhibited almost human skills in handling the sheep, Pop would spend months on end in near isolation, tending to the sheep.

Pop was a gregarious man, which has always made me wonder

how he endured those years. Many didn't, as evidenced by the high suicide rate among young herders.

Poppa (standing) and friends next to his Cadillac, circa 1918. *Nevada Historical Society*

But endure he did!

Year after year, he would take his "wages" and with anything left after bare essentials and the dollars he sent home, he would buy sheep. It wasn't long before he was an owner himself, hiring others like him.

The years around 1920 were boom years everywhere, but particularly in the sheep and cattle industries. Prices were high and so was the demand for meat and wool. "The sky was the limit," and, of course, the bankers saw their chance to have a piece of the killing. They constantly pressed young Basques such as my dad to increase their flocks and holdings, all with highly leveraged financing.

Before long, Pop was involved in a huge livestock operation known as the Allied Land and Livestock Company, which was located on a ranch near Yerington, Nevada. People told me later that they were one of the biggest outfits in Western Nevada, eventually accumulating about 20,000 sheep and 1,000 cattle.

And, of course, all this quick wealth turned heads, including Pop's. Before long, Pop, who wasn't the least bit materialistic, was sporting his Cadillac and became quite the bon vivant in Reno, spending much of his time at the Indart Hotel.

As noted, it was there that Pop met Mom. And what an unlikely event that was. The odds are probably better in a lottery.

Pop, who was born in 1887, came from the mountainous area on the French side of the Pyrenees, where his people lived hard-working, simple lives.

In later trips to visit Pop's home in Tardets, I never could figure out how in the world so many people could live in such a relatively small house. And, as I was to learn later, my grandparents never owned their home property. They were always renters.

Momma as a young woman.

Mom

Mom, whose maiden name was Theresa Alpetche, was born and raised in St. Etienne de Baigorry, a small Basque village about an hour's drive down the mountain from where Pop was raised. Today, it's much the same as it was during Mom's days there as a child and as a young woman.

One of my greatest joys is to go to the same church that Mom did. The women sit on the main floor, the men in the balconies. Sunday masses there have a musical quality unlike anything else I've ever seen or heard. To hear all those beautiful Basque voices join as one in chanting centuries-old hymns is a thrilling experience.

Mom's background was quite different from Pop's. Her family had the means to expose her to educational and cultural opportunities that resulted in a beautiful, sophisticated young woman. She attended and graduated from the Cordon Bleu, the premier cooking school in all of France in those days, and still numbered among the best.

Yes, Mom's beginnings were a lot different from Pop's. As he would at times comment, particularly when Mom would be critical: "That woman is sure high-toned." Of course, when such verbal dueling took place, Mom wasn't the least hesitant about reminding Pop of his humble origins "living with the sheep and the pigs."

Had it not been for the injuries her brother suffered in World War I, Mom probably never would have come to America. She was comfortably situated, living at the family hotel in Bordeaux, and happily engaged to the French Major.

Unfortunately for the Major, fate intervened when Mom's father directed her to travel to the States to provide her brother Michel with company and thereafter to bring him home. As noted, Michel died shortly after her arrival.

While she was in Reno, she met Pop. After their marriage, Pop took Mom to live at the spacious ranch house near Yerington. It served as the headquarters for the Allied outfit.

She quickly undertook her duties as lady of the house. Just as quickly, she "became with child," as the saying went.

On August 2, 1922, she gave birth to a nine-and-a-half pound son and tried to name him Paul Dominique. I say "tried" because, as I learned years later, she and her nurse had a communications problem. The nurse's boyfriend's name was Arthur and Laxalt was a strange name to her. Besides, Rene Lacoste was then a world renowned French tennis player.

The Laxalt clan *(L. to R.)* John, Robert, Momma, Peter, Poppa, Marie, PL and Sue.

So, on the official records of St. Mary's Hospital in Reno, and the records of the State of Nevada, Theresa Laxalt gave birth to a son whose name was "Arthur Lacoste." I had the darndest time sorting this out many years later! The birth certificate was finally corrected in 1942.

After me came Robert in 1923, Suzanne in 1925, John in 1926, Marie in 1928 and Peter in 1931.

Did Dominique and Theresa live happily ever after? I guess the answer depends on your perspective. If "happily ever after" meant reigning over the ranch in "Gone With the Wind" style, it didn't quite work out that way.

Around the time of my birth (and I hope the events weren't connected), economic depression struck in the West. Overnight, Pop was wiped out. All the money he'd sweated and worked for was gone!

Over-extended on their bank loans, people like Pop were unable to keep up their payments when revenues fell. Then came the inevitable foreclosure, and Pop and Mom were literally out in the streets, or, to be exact, out in the sheep camps.

Pop returned to sheepherding, and Mom found herself in a primitive camp, cooking for several sheepherders, ranch hands and cowboys.

Several months of that were enough for Mom.

Somehow, through the Basque "grapevine," she learned that a small Basque hotel in Carson City could be purchased.

Quickly, Mom, who, looking back, must have been one of the first feminists, bought the hotel for one hundred dollars. Thereby, in 1926, Mom, brother Bob (who had been born in the sheep camp days in Alturas, California) and I became full-fledged residents of Carson City, Nevada.

It was the smallest capital in the country, with a population of a little more than 1000 people, almost all of whom were dependent on state government.

Pop, who never really enjoyed "living inside" — as he called town life — stayed in the hills herding sheep. Occasionally, he came to town, which, over the course of a few years, accounted for the Laxalt family's increase from two to six kids.

Lest the reader think the "Hotel" was of Bellagio proportions, it wasn't. It consisted of a two-floored wooden structure, a virtual firetrap, which had been built in the 1870s during the Comstock Lode gold and silver rush. It was, as I recall, about 40 feet wide and 100 feet long. The ground floor was divided in half lengthwise. On one side was the dining room and kitchen. On the other, the bar.

In the back were our living quarters, in an area no more than 30 by 40 feet. On the second floor were a half dozen small rooms, all served by one bathroom. Sheepherders, Virginia & Truckee Railroad employees and highway department workers were our main patrons.

Mom somehow managed to raise us, working 16 to 18 hours a day.

The "French Hotel" was an instant success. Mom was a fabulous cook, and word of her culinary skills spread rapidly through the area. It was truly a family enterprise. As soon as we kids were old enough, we worked in the kitchen, served in the dining room and bar and kept the upstairs in livable condition (although I don't recall "turned down" beds to be part of the service).

Meals were served family style at long rectangular tables. There were no preferred places. As soon as the bell rang, the rush for seats began. Nor did it make any difference what position you might have in the community, the state or country — save for one, the Honorable Pat McCarran, Nevada's senior United States Senator.

Senator McCarran was like a deity in our household. The fact that he was a man of international renown and highly controversial in some circles was of no moment when compared to his real achievement: He was the champion of young Basque sheepherders immigrating to the U.S. At a time when his powerful voice was closing the door to many newcomers, he kept the "Basque door" wide open.

This led later to an ironic political development for me. When I became interested in politics, I found that almost every Basque in the West was a registered Democrat. Some cynics suggested that a McCarran condition for entry to the U.S. by a Basque was that he become a Democrat. So what about Pop, a staunch Republican? He was "pre-McCarran."

On those rare days when the Senator would grace our table, he would hold court while he spoke at length (helped a bit by our good bourbon) on subjects that hardly anyone in Carson City knew or cared about. Yet, he always sounded so good, and he was so well-informed that his audience listened raptly to everything he said.

We had other political figures in from time to time, and whenever "brandy time" came, the political discussions started.

Those occasions may have been the awakening of my political interest — sort of a process of "osmosis."

Eventually, Pop decided to leave the range and move to Carson City.

What a tough decision that must have been for him! Most all his life, Pop had been an "outdoorsman" with no walls to confine him, no roof to hide the sky. He must have keenly felt that Mom was working too hard, and the time had come for him to give up his beloved sheep and help out.

People told me later that he fit in well — for awhile. He was very good with people. Everyone loved Dominique. And we kids loved having a full-time Pop.

But, as time passed, he felt increasingly trapped. Inside life simply wasn't for him.

One day it all came to the surface in a violent way. And I was there to witness it all as a young boy.

Most every small town has its bully. At least it seemed so in those days. In Carson City, the town bully was a big, strapping Irishman whom everyone tried to avoid, particularly when he was boozing.

One evening, unfortunately for him, he wandered into the

French Hotel "three sheets to the wind." That was his first mistake. Mom was tending bar that night with Pop playing cards at a nearby table with some of his Basque pals.

I don't know what "Irish" said to Mom, but whatever it was, it was his next mistake. Pop overheard something that he thought was insulting, and like a switch flipping on, he went into a white-hot rage.

I was next door cleaning up the dining room when all hell broke loose. I ran into the bar and saw Pop beating and kicking "Irish" unmercifully. Before he knew it, and probably to his complete relief, "Irish" found himself in the middle of Carson Street, his pride badly damaged, but at least he was alive. He never darkened the door of the French Hotel again.

The only other time I saw Pop lose his cool was a few years later when he and I were riding our sheep range together. Suddenly, we observed a huge band of sheep on our range that shouldn't have been there. Herding them was a young man who had no idea what deep trouble he was in.

As soon as Pop spotted him, he spurred his horse into a gallop, with me trailing behind. Before I knew it, he was off his horse, his face and eyes blazing, with his trusty 30-30 rifle in hand heading straight for the young man. I almost passed away on the spot. So did the herder. In no uncertain terms, he was advised to "get the goddamn hell off my range…now!" In record time, the young man was gone with his sheep, never to trespass Dominique's range again.

Lest the reader gain the impression that Pop was some kind of brutish animal given to frequent temper tantrums, he was anything but that.

He was soft-spoken, gentle and loved people. Above all, he loved to talk to them — at length. Often I would accompany him to Reno and would wait seemingly forever for him to say goodbye to his friends. Reflecting on this, I think he was making up time for those lonely years when he had no one but his dog and donkey to talk to.

Despite the fact that he was away so often, he was a good father. I don't recall him ever saying that he loved us. Had he done so, I am sure that we would have been embarrassed. He displayed his care for us in other ways. We always knew he was there. We also knew that we should never "sass" him. We wouldn't dare think about showing disrespect to either of our parents. They didn't demand respect; they commanded it by their innate dignity and example. Besides, "Irish's" experience was always buried not too deeply in our consciousness.

Pop was one of the most curious people I've known. His appetite for knowledge was insatiable. Each time I took provisions to him at his sheep camp, his first question was how many newspapers and magazines had I brought with me. He had a fourth-grade education, yet spoke several languages and was fully conversant with public affairs. What a career he might have had if he had been exposed to a full education.

Despite his love of people, Pop hated social events if they were the least bit formal. He loved sitting in a Basque hotel, drinking wine and jawboning with his friends.

But birthdays, graduations, weddings, baptisms — forget it. When any such thing loomed on the calendar, he simply disappeared.

He even ducked my inauguration as Governor.

When I asked him to attend — not so much for me, but for the family and the people of the State — he simply and firmly said, "No."

It was only after sensitive negotiations, headed by brother Robert, that he reluctantly agreed to a compromise. He would attend if it was "private." So, we family members — with a few close friends, and nine other recently-elected state officials — ended up in the Supreme Court of Nevada with Chief Justice Gordon Thompson administering the oath and Dominique Laxalt as the principal witness.

Poor Pop! If he hated two groups in the world, they were lawyers and politicians. And here his eldest son had turned his back on the sheep business and became both a lawyer and a politician!

On the other hand, he wasn't all that enthusiastic about my sheepherding abilities. He often said later that he'd sent me to law school in self-defense, for each time I tended the flock alone, I'd lose at least a hundred sheep!

School Days

We grew up exposed to foreign languages. French, Basque, Italian and Spanish were used almost interchangeably with English. By the time I went to school, I was a linguist of sorts, but my knowledge of English left much to be desired. That led to my being teased by my "American" classmates, which in turn led to my addressing that problem head on with my fists. After a couple of victories — first-grade style — the criticism waned, then stopped.

I've watched with interest the efforts of certain minority groups to establish "bilingual rights" in America. They wouldn't have had any support from Momma Laxalt. From the time we started school, we Laxalts spoke only English. She felt strongly that if her children were to live in America and enjoy its benefits, it was essential that we make an all-out effort to speak English.

Since that time, I have had occasion to wish we had kept up our other languages as well. Many times in Europe, particularly in France, the Basque Country, Spain and Italy, I've yearned to be able to speak the native language. To speak through another diminishes the quality and intensity of the conversation. Until I went to school, I had a conversational knowledge of each, but over the years, alas, I've lost it.

School in Carson City consisted of the usual 12 grades, but all 12 were housed in one building! It was just three blocks from home. When I see the difficulty these days that my grandchildren have in just getting to school, I harken back to our "good old days" when school was three short blocks from home.

Our class, which averaged about 30 students, went to school in that same building for 11 years, all the way from the ground floor to the second floor as "mighty" Juniors.

Carson City as it looked when I was growing up. *Courtesy Nevada State Museum*

In 1937, the school board decided to open a new high school a couple of blocks up the street. I remember our first visit to our new school. For us athletes, the high point was a new gym that could seat as many as 500 people. No longer would we have to play in the old armory across town, which had long since outlived its usefulness.

If I were to describe my school in those days from my present perspective, I would use the words "stability and constancy." The teachers often spent their entire careers teaching the same grade in the same school. They taught traditional subjects in the traditional style. Reading, writing and arithmetic, and variations thereof, were the order of the day.

Whatever those old-timers did served us well. In later years, at the university, in law school, and later in professional life, we Laxalts were always able to compete. Our early training in English under a young teacher named Grace Bordewich was invaluable. My brother Bob, the writer, would be the first to credit Grace for spawning his later career as an author.

In the 1930s, Carson City proclaimed itself "the smallest capital in the world." And it was! In those days, its population was a little more than a thousand people.

Since it was the seat of government where the Capitol and various state buildings were located, most of the residents were directly or indirectly connected to the state government. A large percentage from Carson High took state jobs after they graduated. Most then served until they retired. Many never left the Carson City area.

Looking back, life was so simple in those days. Perhaps too simple. As in all small towns, the general lament among the young was, "I can hardly wait to get out of this one-horse town."

Horizons were very limited. So was access to outside information. There was no television. I don't recall any of the news magazines or any discussion about them. Certainly, no one had heard of The New York Times or The Washington Post.

If we wanted to find out what was going on in the outside world, information had to be gleaned from "Movietone News," "Current Events" at school or from our radios. In any case, living in an informational wasteland didn't bother us any. We really didn't give a damn what happened outside of Carson City. It was pretty much our whole world.

Even though it was the state capital, Carson City had few paved streets. Carson Street, the main drag, was paved and had diagonal parking. In the early days, we had bike races on Carson Street. Any motorist who interrupted them was greeted with contempt.

We had one movie house, the Carson Theater. Admission: 25 cents. It was there that I first suc-cumbed to hero worship, consisting mainly of Western stars such as Tom Mix, Buck Jones, Hopalong Cassidy and Roy Rogers. I don't re-member any women making the list, mainly, I'm sure, because they seemed so remote and unattainable. What in the world would a kid from Carson City do with a fancily dressed, bejeweled beauty who wanted to dine at "21" in New York City?

When I was 15, I became a golf caddy at Glenbrook, Lake Tahoe, a bastion of "old wealth." For me, it was a new world hearing wealthy golfers talk about strangers such as Hitler and Mussolini, and what a "son-of-a-bitch" President Roosevelt was.

With my volunteer tennis coach, Helen Wills Moody, in the summer of 1937 at Glenbrook, Lake Tahoe. She was the world's tennis champ at the time and a world-class lady.

It was also at Glenbrook that I had the great fortune of play-ing tennis with Helen Wills Moody, one of the greatest women tennis players of all time. During her illustrious career, she won 31 major titles, including eight Wimbledon and seven U.S. Open singles titles.

In 1937, Mrs. Moody had come to Glenbrook to establish residence for a Nevada divorce. She asked the locals for some names of people with whom she might practice. Since I had just won a junior tournament, I was recommended.

For several weeks, I had the privilege of playing almost daily with Mrs. Moody. As a result, she completely overhauled my tennis game, and I went on to play in high school and college and still enjoy playing competitively to this day.

Momma standing in front of the home where we all grew up at 402 N. Minnesota Street in Carson City. *Laxalt Family Collection*

LIFE AT HOME

After a few years of living in the back of the hotel, Momma Laxalt decided to buy a house at 402 North Minnesota Street. As I remember, it cost about $3000. It had some historical significance, which was lost on me as a child and remains so now.

Compared to our cramped quarters in the hotel, the house seemed immense. It had a huge living room adjoining an equally large dining room, which in later years proved to be the center for family get-togethers. We also "brought in" the 1962 Lieutenant Governor, 1964 Senate and 1966 Governor races in those rooms.

The house was short of bedrooms for our brood. Two bedrooms didn't do it. Mom solved the problem by having a screen porch attached to the back of the house. This became a dorm of sort for us four boys. Great in the summer, but a killer in the winter. Considering there were no windows, only screens, sleeping out there was quite a challenge — or so it seems in retrospect. Yet we youngsters didn't think it was any big deal.

Our home was across the street from Judge Clark Guild's stately house, replete with turrets. The neighborhood was in what is now the heart of the historical district with large frame houses with porches, most of which were built in the late 19th Century.

The location couldn't have been better: Three blocks from school and church; four blocks from downtown; four blocks to an open pasture of ranches to the west of Carson where we could roam wild and free from the stress and tension of "city life."

When I have told my children and later my grandchildren how we fared under Theresa "The Warden" Laxalt, I've had the impression they thought I was spinning tall tales.

She was the unquestioned "boss." Pop was making his family contribution by herding sheep in some distant range. It was Mom's responsibility to raise six kids.

And raise us she did...in "old country" fashion. There were no guests for dinner. Certainly no overnight guests. Come to think of it, I don't recall in the years I was in school staying overnight at any house.

Mom subscribed to the early-to-bed-early-to-rise school of

thought. This was just as well, for there wasn't much to do at night except listen to the radio (such shows as "The Shadow" and "Jack Armstrong," which were over early in any case).

There were no disciplinary problems in our house, at least none that I recall. There were no problems because no one would dare challenge Mom. Her word was the absolute law. There certainly weren't any "Come, let us reason together" sessions. She didn't believe in democracy when it came to family matters.

Her administration was an iron-handed dictatorship with no semblance of "due process." Authority was to be respected, never challenged, whether in school, in church or at home. I suppose that in these so-called enlight-ened days of parenting, her approach would be regarded as harsh and outdated. I won't discuss that here, but I do know that Mom's hard-line approach worked.

Mom was intensely religious. We lived only a short distance from St. Theresa's Catholic Church, which was like a second home.

The "Rock of Gibraltar" of the Laxalt family, our parish priest, Monsignor Henry Wientjes.

The church was presided over by Monsignor Henry J. Wientjes, a Dutch priest who served his parishioners in Carson City un-selfishly for 24 years until his retirement in 1959.

He believed that parishioners should carry their share by contributing handsomely to his many collections. Realizing that some might need a little nudge once in a while, he would on certain occasions read the contributions from his pulpit. As kids, we were always proud to see Mom top the list with a contribution of $10.

As the eldest, I was quickly drafted by Monsignor and Mom to be an altar boy. In the winter, I also served the Lord as the "furnace man" by lighting the church furnace at three or four in the morning. That duty, as much as anything, tested my faith in the Roman Catholic Church.

I did my work so well that by the time I was about 14, Monsignor and Mom conspired that I should become a priest. They wanted to send me to a seminary in California the next fall.

Now, I didn't mind being an altar boy or even the "furnace man," but becoming a priest was going too far, in my opinion.

A few days before my dreaded departure for the seminary, I really started to feel "the noose tightening." Going to Mom and Monsignor would, I was sure, be a waste of time. They weren't about to thwart "God's will." So, I went to Pop, who fortunately was home from the hills.

Never had I gone to him to "appeal" any decision of Mom's. Because his work with the sheep kept him away from home so much, he simply didn't intrude and backed Mom completely when it came to family decisions.

"Pop," I said, "Mom and Monsignor want me to go to a school in California to become a priest. I know that it would be an honor for the family, but I don't think I'm cut out to be a priest. Do I have to go?"

He said, "No, you don't, Paul. It would be wrong for you, and the church, if you haven't been called. Don't worry about it. I'll talk to Momma."

He did — and the idea never surfaced again.

Mom never held it against me, but Monsignor was different. He was decidedly cool toward me for awhile, but eventually he got over it. He probably figured that the church's loss was his gain. After all, how would he find such a highly-qualified "furnace man"?

I didn't know until much later that the recruiting of new priests had extended to Reno. There, Maurice Welsh agreed to go to the seminary and later became an excellent priest. He took great delight in telling people in later years: "And there I was at the train station waiting to go to the seminary in California with Paul Laxalt. But he never showed!"

High School

I'll never know what seminary life was like, but life at Carson High School couldn't have been more enjoyable.

In 1937, our class was the first to go into the new high school. In addition to new classrooms, we had a brand new gym and a football field — with grass, no less.

From the time we were able to throw a ball, each of us Laxalt boys loved athletics. Name the sport, we tried it. We boxed, played basketball, football and even indulged in track. Later, we became golf and tennis addicts.

In the winter, when we were small, we often moved the furniture in the living room to the walls so we could play a game of indoor football. I've often thought how patient Mom was for allowing her living room to be turned into a gridiron. As a father, I doubt I would have!

Of all the sports, basketball was the most popular in Carson City. I've heard about Indiana high school basketball being a "religion," but it couldn't have been more important to a community than it was to Carson City.

We were blessed with a coach, George McElroy, who could motivate youngsters better than anyone else I've ever met. Quiet and soft-spoken, he nonetheless was a strict disciplinarian. In the 1930s, little Carson High School was the team to beat in all of

Nevada. During one period, Coach McElroy led Carson to three straight state championships. I was honored to play on the 1938 championship team.

Over the years, I've been blessed to be a part of many momentous and exciting events. But nothing will ever match the sheer joy and excitement of the evening we won it all. The fans, the cheerleaders, our teammates — all of us screamed our lungs out. Even Coach "Mac" managed a wan smile. And to top it all off, Momma Laxalt enjoyed every minute of it — and was she ever proud!

1938 Carson High basketball team — Nevada State champs. I'm seated in the first row on the far left. Behind me is Coach George McElroy. Holding the basketball is our "hero," Caesar Congdon.

Graduating from high school and going to college was so much easier then than it is now. Although Santa Clara was a top school, all it took to get me in was a presentable transcript, a "sign off" by Monsignor Wientjes, plus a trip with Momma Laxalt to Union Federal Savings to float a loan for $500 for my first year's expenses.

Now, after recently going through the experience with my grandson, Adam — entrance exams, interviews, endorsements by prominent alumni — I pine for those "good old days."

We never thought about it much then, but the education we Laxalts received at Carson High must have been a very good one. Later, we went to prime colleges throughout the country. We all owe our teachers like Grace Bordewich and Coach McElroy a huge debt of gratitude.

CHAPTER 2

❖ *On to College; On to War* ❖

SANTA CLARA DAYS

If I'd had my way, I would happily have gone to the University of Nevada in Reno. Mom would have none of it.

"You just want to go to Reno to drink beer and not do your studies." (Little did she realize that while we weren't beer drinkers at Santa Clara, we became avid California wine drinkers — at $1.00 a gallon!)

Instead, she decided that her boys would be enrolled — some would say incarcerated — at Santa Clara University in Northern California. Santa Clara, at that time, was an all-male school with about 500 students. It was run by the Jesuits, an order which was founded by a Basque — St. Ignatius. The school was well-walled, and local lore was to the effect that in the "old days," before I arrived, they even had dogs to make certain the students wouldn't drift away from campus.

Mom, in order to insure that I'd make it, decided that the family should hand-deliver me to the Father President. The whole clan (Mom and six kids) loaded into Pop's truck, with the back open, for our ride from Carson City to Reno, where a train would carry us to Santa Clara. Pop, of course, took a pass. It was the first train trip for us kids.

And so it was on a September day in 1940 that Theresa Laxalt entrusted me to the safekeeping of the Jesuits of Santa Clara. Although Mom's entourage seemed perfectly natural at the time, I suspect that Father President thought that he had just been visited by the Beverly Hillbillies.

Santa Clara provided me with a marvelous academic education. I quickly became exposed to such exotic subjects as philosophy, epistemology, world history, political science and religion. To this day, I can almost hear my old professors whispering in my ears.

But my real education came from exposure to my fellow students. Santa Clara then enjoyed, as it does now, an excellent reputation. As a result, it attracted students from around the country. We even had several students from foreign countries. For a small town kid who thought that his horizons were broadened by meeting someone from Reno, Santa Clara was a world-widening experience.

There I met students who became life-long friends.

Stan Patrick was my roommate after my first year. He was an All-American high school basketball player from St. Leo's on the Southside of Chicago, who, although only 6'1", could jump like a deer. At Santa Clara, he set many scoring records.

He was such a marvelous all-round athlete that one day Buck Shaw, Santa Clara's outstanding football coach, who would later coach the Eagles to the NFL championship, saw Stan punting and promptly drafted him. After a few pratfalls, initiated by our opponents, Stan lost interest in football and concentrated on the more genteel game of basketball.

Aside from our mutual athletic interests, Stan and I hit it off because we were both "first generation" – the children of immigrant parents. His dad's name was Patrickus, but as so often happened in those days, in an effort to be "Americanized," Patrickus became Patrick.

After the war, Stan went on to graduate from the University of Illinois and marry his beautiful wife, Betty.

He later became one of the originals in the Basketball Association of America, the forerunner to the NBA.

Thereafter, he taught school and coached in his wife's hometown of Belvedere, Illinois, until he retired. To this day, we stay in touch, although Betty passed away while I was writing this book.

Wally McGovern also became a close friend. He was an all-star basketball player from Seattle. At Santa Clara, he became the playmaker, equivalent to a point guard these days.

All heart, he invited Stan and me to be his guests at the McGovern family home in Seattle, where we worked as longshoremen for one of our college summers. That experience convinced us that a comfortable job involving inside work, with much less heavy lifting, was the way to go.

Wally went on to become a Naval officer, a lawyer and a highly-respected federal judge in Seattle. He and his wife, Rita, continue to be close friends of ours.

For an athlete like me, Santa Clara was heaven.

Buck Shaw, the fabled "Silver Fox," was the football coach. In the late 1930s, he had the best five-year football record nationally of any major university. At the time, Santa Clara was called "the Notre Dame of the West."

Of particular pride to Nevadans like me was the fact that Frank Petersen of Reno High School became a first-string halfback under Shaw. Frank, who later became a Reno lawyer, was for many years one of Nevada's greatest football players.

For a youngster from Carson High where a "crowd" at a football game would be fewer than a thousand fans, I was thrilled with my first visit to Kezar Stadium in San Francisco, which was filled with 60,000 shouting fans. It was a spine-tingling experience for me.

Santa Clara also excelled in basketball. By the time I arrived, they had a national reputation, even playing in New York's famed Madison Square Garden. After the war, such stars as Bruce Hale, Bob Feerick, Marty Passaglia and others went on to make their marks with professional teams.

But in the small town of Santa Clara, football was king. One day attending Mass, I heard the parish priest refer to the twelve apostles as the Santa Clara football team and one substitute!

Despite the fact that we were under a near-constant curfew, we had an adequate social life. Although most of us were nearly always broke (my allowance was five dollars a month, which I usually shared with Patrick and McGovern), we managed to go to an occasional movie (25 cents) and have a milkshake at the local creamery (10 cents). As a result of our constant hitch-hiking, which was a relatively safe and benign activity in those days, transportation was never a problem. An "S.C." letter sweater was a cinch to get a ride to nearby San Jose.

Pearl Harbor

Several of us went to a movie in San Jose on December 7, 1941. As we left the theater, all hell had broken loose. Newspaper "Extras" were everywhere, announcing that Pearl Harbor had been bombed by the Japanese.

Our first reaction, like that of most Americans, was, "Where the hell is Pearl Harbor?" Beyond that, I don't recall any hand-wringing among the students. For all we knew, this would all be over far before any of us would be called up.

Being totally non-political, we had no idea that Pearl Harbor would trigger a war that would change our lives forever. Before it was over, many of our fellow students would go to war and never come home.

As the months wore on, it became clearer that it was not "if," but "when," we would all go into the service. More and more, we made it our business to be educated about the various services. The question became: "Should we go into the Army, Navy, Air Corps or Marine Corps?"

Not once did I hear anyone discuss how he could avoid service. If anyone had questioned our involvement in the war or even thought about leaving for Canada or anyplace else, he would have been strung up on the nearest yardarm. Different war; different times.

In the summer of 1942, the Army had done a full-court press on those Santa Clarans who hadn't already committed. Their pitch was that if we signed up, we'd be able to complete our junior year before being called. Many of us signed up and became members of the Army Enlisted Reserve Corps (E.R.C.).

The year 1943 seemed oddly peaceful — at first. We knew we'd be leaving for military service by the end of the school year, but at the moment that seemed far off. Studies, athletics and life went forward as if we were insulated. In the spring, we even conducted our school elections, knowing full well that if elected there was no way we could serve.

You're in the Army now

Our E.R.C. unit was "mustered in" at Fort Ord, California, on the coast near Monterey. We arrived from Santa Clara by bus. It was a far cry from our school vacations when we traveled to the Monterey and Carmel beaches to stay at one of the summer homes of the parents of our Santa Clara friends.

In those carefree days, we looked forward to a few "beach days" with good friends. Now, we were headed toward a new life in the Army. With all the "horror stories" we'd heard about basic training and overseas combat, our future didn't seem too appealing.

Fort Ord gave us a first look at what our lives would be like in the service of our country. We were quickly issued clothing and other essentials. And, of course, we had to have our "shots."

Many had never had a vaccination before. To see in line ahead of me big, hulking men the size of football players, keel over like falling timber was not reassuring.

Reminding myself that having a needle stuck into my arm was no big deal, that the fear was all in my head, when my turn came, I stepped up bravely, thrust my arm forward, took the shot like a man — and promptly passed out.

Ord included various tests to determine our strengths and weaknesses, both physically and emotionally. That testing resulted in each of us being "classified" for assignment to the "proper" unit.

Since my phobias included not being able to stand the sight of blood or shots in the arm, the Army, in its wisdom, assigned me to the Medical Corps.

As a result, I was soon off on a long, rainy ride to Camp Barkeley, in central Texas near Abilene. Camp Barkeley was activated in 1941 as an infantry division training center, specializing in basic training. At Barkeley, our quarters consisted of pyramidal tents. Each tent had a senior noncommissioned officer from the regular Army assigned to it. Wisely, the powers that be had decided that we college "slobs" needed someone to maintain order.

We learned all about footlockers and how to pack them properly. With six men to a tent, there was no place for strewn clothes. Everything had to be carefully hung and stored. Since then, I've often thought that service life caused millions of young Americans to be far more tidy and organized than they would have been otherwise.

I guess that "basic" was good for us in a perverse way. Our routine — reveille at dawn, forced marches up to 25 miles, overnight bivouacs, obstacle courses, lengthy and tedious lectures given by bored lecturers (which tested fully our ability to stay awake) — made life so miserable that we thought combat would be a welcome relief.

After basic, we trainees went in several directions. Many went straight to combat units. Most went, as did I, for further training.

Since I was classified as a "medic," I was assigned to Fort Sam Houston in San Antonio, Texas.

After "Tent City" at Barkeley, "Fort Sam" seemed like checking into the Plaza Hotel in New York City. At the time, Fort Sam was one of the old Army military bases with immaculate grounds, buildings, golf courses and tennis courts. Of particular importance were the barracks assigned to us — as big and comfortable as barracks can be. It seemed like heaven to us recent basic trainees.

Then the humidity hit! Coming from Nevada and Northern California, I'd never experienced humidity. To leave the post in a bus, freshly laundered and pressed, and arrive in downtown San Antonio a soaking mess was a shock. This was all before air conditioning was generally available. It was so hot and wet during the summer that three or four showers per night were not uncommon.

I was assigned to the 18th Medical General Laboratory, a brand new outfit, whose purpose was to bring lab facilities into the field and to conduct battlefield research, such as the effect of a flame-thrower on the human skin and other pleasant subjects.

The outfit was small (fewer than 100 men) and composed almost exclusively of doctors, lab technicians and other research types who probably wondered what they'd done to deserve getting into such an unmilitary outfit. It bore a striking resemblance to television's "MASH" unit.

Although long, forced marches weren't required of us, the medical training for me was harrowing. It seemed that each phase resulted in at least one complete "pass out."

Keep in mind that here was a guy who couldn't stand the sight of blood or who dissolved even at the prospect of being shot with a needle. Having that same guy walk into an autopsy room where some GI in a white jacket is calmly sawing the skull of another GI, recently departed, as part of an autopsy — well, you can guess the result.

The "pecker parade" was another winner. We were assigned for a period to Brooke General Hospital to observe the genitals of our fellow GIs, and treat them for syphilis and gonorrhea. These poor guys who had contracted a venereal disease really suffered. I'm sure that try as we might, we didn't look very professional in treating them.

Early in our training, a gruff old sergeant who delighted in rattling wimps such as us would happily proclaim: "Listen up. I know that some of you have problems with the needles. Hell, some of you can't even take a shot in the arm without passing out. (Boy, did he have me figured!) You'll soon be in combat situations where you'll be drowning in the blood of the wounded. During the next few weeks, we'll try to make half-ass medics out of you, including how to draw blood. On graduation day — a few weeks from now — we'll divide you into pairs, and each of you will draw blood from the other."

His merely saying it caused me to go into a cold sweat. The thought of not only sticking a needle into one of my buddy's veins, but also drawing blood, was more than I could bear. I learned later that quite a few others had reacted the same way.

On graduation day, the dreaded moment came. We drew lots to see who would stick whom. Bill White and I drew one another. Bill was aptly named. He was a skinny kid with a ghostly look about him. We flipped a coin to see who would go first.

Unhappily, I won. I summoned all the courage I could so that Bill, who sensed my fear, wouldn't panic. I applied the tourniquet and asked him to pump his hand. Then I picked up the needle and syringe and shakily pointed it at a decent sized vein that even I couldn't miss.

During training we'd been instructed that the needle should be inserted laterally. I tried but failed. Instead of slipping into the vein, I went through it, causing a hematoma. Blood started to ooze slowly over Bill's arm. His eyes rolled back, and he keeled over in a dead faint. Instantly, so did I! We awoke on the floor — to uproarious laughter from our classmates. Who would have thought that in a few months, I'd be in combat with blood everywhere, and I didn't pass out once.

After graduation, the 18th received orders for us to be shipped overseas — through Seattle. After a few weeks of orientation at Fort Lewis, we were assigned to a troop ship headed to Oahu in the Hawaiian Islands. We didn't know it then, but for some of us, Oahu was just a stopping-off place en route to General Douglas MacArthur's invasion of Leyte in the Philippines.

The trip from Seattle to Oahu was no fun. One unforgettable memory was the sight of thousands of GIs in heavy seas, heaving with seasickness for a good portion of the trip. After that, the sight of Diamond Head on Oahu looked like the gates of Heaven.

We were billeted in a delightful place in the interior of the island called Ekahanui, where an Army camp had been established in the midst of pineapple fields.

Labs were quickly established so that our researchers could do their work. We support troops tried to look busy (an Army preoccupation). In between, we had frequent trips to Waikiki Beach and to Schofield barracks for basketball games between college all-stars now in the service.

In spring 1944, a few of us were notified that we had been selected to join the 7th Infantry Division.

Soon, we were in jungle training preparing for combat in the

Pacific. We thought we were in pretty good shape until we went into training on Oahu. Quickly, we recognized that being "combat ready" was a level we'd never reached before or after.

After a few weeks, the expected orders came. We shipped out for Asia. Several thousand of us GIs boarded the "President Hayes," which had been a luxury liner.

We spent some three months at sea, traveling from Oahu to New Zealand, to Hollandia, Biak and eventually north to Leyte in the Philippines.

I wish I could say now — some 50 years later — that life on the Hayes was a pleasant experience. It wasn't, by a long shot.

I suppose there were luxury suites somewhere, but we "dogfaces" didn't see them. Our quarters were on deck. The whole deck was allocated, in sections, to groups of six or seven. Each group was allocated one cot, without a mattress. But a feather bed couldn't have felt better! For the rest of the week, we slept on steel decking.

If it rained, and it often did, we put on our ponchos and waited out the storm. Boredom was our biggest problem. We played cards by the hour.

Occasionally, we'd stop off at some isolated island for a "beer break." Beer and coconuts were the order of the day.

Considering the ship was full of combat infantry troops — many of whom had already fought in such places as Guadalcanal and Tarawa — everyone got on fairly well. But those who had been in combat had a particular stare that was frightening.

I've often thought of that ship. Considering the circumstances, a crowded boat full of trained killers waiting anxiously to go into combat, it is a credit to the discipline of the troops that there weren't any serious confrontations.

In early October 1944, we were told that the 7th and the 96th Infantry Divisions were going to lead the invasion of Leyte,

General Douglas MacArthur's first target in the Philippines. It was at Leyte that the famous picture of MacArthur was taken where he and his top aides are seen walking ashore in knee-deep water.

Never in history have so many ships been assembled in one area as there were in Leyte Harbor. MacArthur later described it as "one of the greatest Armadas of history." In total, there were about 700 carriers, battleships, cruisers, destroyers, transports and landing craft. It was an amazing display of American power.

It also demonstrated how well the Navy had recovered after the Pearl Harbor disaster less than three years earlier.

The battle plan, as explained to us, was to soften up the invasion area with Naval shellfire prior to the actual invasion. Our intelligence reports indicated the Japanese were "dug in" and would be formidable opposition. We'd learned that lesson the hard way in previous Pacific island invasions where we'd suffered huge casualties.

Since General MacArthur had promised in 1942 when he was forced to leave the Philippines that "I shall return," the Leyte invasion had enormous implications, not only militarily but also psychologically. For MacArthur to return successfully to the Philippines meant that the momentum of the Pacific War would be seen as having moved in our direction.

After an awesome pounding of the Leyte coastal areas, the word came down that we would be invading the next day, October 20, 1944.

The most difficult area was a place called Catlan Hill. The 96th Division was to assault the hill. It was composed mainly of college students. The naval fire had swept the hill mercilessly. During the shelling, there was so much dust and dirt that we couldn't even see the hill. Everyone felt that there couldn't be many Japanese left. Everyone was wrong — very wrong. When the

96th went in, they were met with fierce opposition, and casualties were high.

The 7th went in at dawn. The night before, when the order came down, the troops grew quiet. Those who had been in prior invasions knew well that the casualties could be even worse than what they had seen before.

To everyone's surprise, our troops landed and established a foothold without great difficulty. Compared to the invasion of Normandy, it was a "cakewalk." There was scattered small arms fire, but nothing heavy.

October of 1944, at the Battle of Leyte in the Philippines. I'm the skinny one fourth from the left. I lost almost 40 pounds during less than two months of combat.

After we landed, there began for me the most miserable and depressing 53 days of my life. All I can remember now is a blur of rain, mud, foxholes, broken bodies, blood, gore and death. In 40 days, it rained 34 inches.

Everyone was constantly dog-tired, physically and emotionally. If anyone out there might think that war is somehow glamorous, that surely was not my experience. It was awful.

We used tents to make a rough field hospital. One early morning, I just couldn't function any longer and finally crashed in a vacant cot in a tent full of wounded soldiers.

After a few hours of sleep, I woke to find that the soldiers on either side of me had died during the night. At some time months before, an experience like that would have given me the "willies," but by that time I was so inured to horrible injuries and death that I had become numb to it, which was a necessity. Otherwise, my sanity would have been endangered.

Over the years, I've blotted out most of my ugly Leyte memories. But one incident still remains with me.

One day the litter carriers brought in a young private who had suffered one of the toughest wounds one can suffer in war — he'd been slashed by a bayonet from his stomach to his throat. Apparently, he'd been caught in a foxhole by a Japanese soldier the night before.

As I was tending to his horrible wound, he looked up at me, and in a voice wracked with pain, said, "Sergeant, do you suppose I'll get a Purple Heart for this?" He died shortly thereafter.

On another morning, I couldn't believe it when I ran into a couple of wounded infantry officers — Bill Cassinelli of Reno and Leon Etchemendy of Gardnerville — both of whom I'd known in Nevada. Fortunately, Bill and Leon survived, although Bill lost a leg.

One morning, our commanding officer advised those of us from the 18th that we were being shipped back to our outfit on Oahu. Talk about joy!

Within days, during Christmas time, 1944, we returned "home" to Ekahanui. My "Leyte trip" had cost me 40 pounds!

We returnees noticed right away that our buddies in the outfit treated us differently. We were now "combat veterans."

Within a few months, I decided that I'd try to become an officer. I was shipped to Fort Sill, in Oklahoma, and was in the midst of training when the war in the Pacific ended, thanks to President Truman's courage in authorizing the use of the atom bombs in Japan.

A few months later, in late 1945, I was discharged.

It was one of the happiest days of my life!

Not that the Army years weren't helpful to me. The discipline, the organization, the travels, the people, and above all, the satisfaction I derived from serving my country in wartime, these were all things that gave me needed perspective in the years ahead.

But from the day I enlisted, I had lost my freedom. During my years in the service, I felt too often that I was in a form of confinement. My joy reflected the fact that that was no longer the case.

For a boy whose father was a sheepherder, whose home was the hills and mountains of Nevada, not being able to be fully in control of my life was at times a heavy burden.

CHAPTER 3

❖ *Post-War Euphoria* ❖

I observed with regret the shoddy treatment accorded the Vietnam veterans when they returned home in the 1960s and 1970s. Was it their fault that they served honorably in an unpopular war? Did that make their unselfish service for their country less meaningful? I don't think so.

When we World War II vets returned home, we were treated as conquering heroes. Everywhere we went, people thanked us for our service. We had helped save the world from the Nazis, the Fascists and the Japanese militarists.

After my discharge, I went home to Carson City. For months, there was a holiday atmosphere. It was the same, I'm sure, throughout the country. Each time a vet came home, it gave rise to a series of parties. They were boisterous, happy occasions — and very "wet."

Hardly anybody had trouble getting a job. Those of us who had their educations interrupted marked time until the fall of 1946.

In June that year, I married Jackie Ross, the daughter of the city's most prominent lawyer, at St. Theresa's Catholic Church. I'm afraid the groom brought nothing to the marriage but good will and good intentions. I was so broke that I even borrowed my wedding suit from one of my friends. Our honeymoon trip was to a mountain cabin in the Sierra Nevada. The Rosses even furnished the car for the trip. Obviously, no one could say that Jackie Ross married Paul Laxalt for his money.

Marrying into the Ross family was a huge turning point in my life. John R. "Jack" Ross, in addition to being a top lawyer, was one of the most prominent Republican politicians in the state. He had served previously as a District Attorney in Lyon County, Nevada, and had run a good but losing race for Nevada Attorney General in 1942 against Alan Bible, who thereafter served with distinction in the U.S. Senate.

Aside from elective politics, Jack thoroughly enjoyed Republican party politics. He and his wife, Margaret, were staunch Taft supporters in the Presidential race of 1948. The Rosses even traveled by car all the way to Philadelphia for the national Republican convention.

Exposure to the Rosses and their friends — leading political figures of Nevada — broadened my horizons considerably and contributed later to my decision to go into elective politics.

Jack was one of the most brilliant men I've ever known. It's a shame that his destiny wasn't Washington, D.C. He would have been a giant there.

Instead of political office, he became a federal judge, and served with distinction for many years until he died prematurely in 1963 from a stroke.

What Do We Do Now?

After our marriage, Jackie and I had to decide upon our future. I was ambivalent. Medical school in Saint Louis, where my Army C.O. was a dean, was a possibility. But it was clear that my history major at Santa Clara didn't help much to qualify me for medical school. To qualify would require a couple of more years of undergraduate studies, and we were too impatient to wait.

We finally decided on Santa Clara Law School.

I'm sure the "Ross influence" had much to do with that call. Besides, Santa Clara, like most universities, permitted veterans to enter law school after three years rather than fulfill the usual four years of undergraduate work.

So, in fall 1946, off we went to Santa Clara for me to become a lawyer.

If it hadn't been for the GI Bill, law school would have been out of the question financially. In later years, when I decried excessive federal spending, guess which program was always excepted?

I'm not sure if Santa Clara was ready for the returning vets and their wives. The law school was heavily influenced by Ivy League-types who were as traditional as they come. They felt that the practice of law was for the select few, and students should come from established "legal families."

World War II changed all that. As a result, the legal profession became fully democratized.

For a school that had only been for men since its inception, Santa Clara did its best to accommodate the influx of married couples. They developed an area within the campus for "married housing."

This consisted of several prefabricated Quonset huts, with three or four couples assigned to each building. There was no soundproofing. For a complex full of recently-returned vets with their newly acquired wives, all operating at a hormonal high, it made for many interesting situations.

For the GIs who had served overseas, the huts seemed not so bad, but our poor wives must have done a lot of quiet suffering.

Returning to the books, particularly at a tough school, was difficult. In my own case, after years of not reading anything heavier than a comic book or a detective novel, school was sheer hell. For one who hardly ever had to crack a book before, it was wrenching to read and re-read and read yet again the cases before they sunk in.

Added to that was the old law school philosophy of scaring the hell out of the new students from the first day. One of the favorite tactics of terrorization was to assemble all first-year students. A grim faced dean would announce, "Look to either side of you. Before this first year is over, only one of you will be left." Needless to say, this approach wasn't too welcome for a bunch of grizzled vets.

Another source of pressure was the fact that the school had a policy of making grade "77" almost sacred. If you made 77, you were "in." If you managed only a 76, you were "out."

Despite all the irritation and pressure, I managed to squeak through that first year. So did most of my classmates, although some withdrew.

That summer I ran into Walt Schwed, one of my undergrad classmates before the war. He was from Denver and had been going to law school at Denver University. His father was one of the leading lawyers in Colorado.

When I told Walt about my first year at Santa Clara, his reaction was instant. "Hell, man, why go to a bullshit school like that? Denver's different. Instead of trying to push you out, they do everything possible to keep you in." Walt noted that D.U. recognized that vets were far more mature than typical students and were serious about both school and graduating.

That's all I needed to hear. Jackie agreed that a move to Denver was right for us. Her father wasn't so sure. He wasn't used to law school students transferring after one year. He probably wasn't sure whether his new son-in-law was a "rolling stone flake." But he didn't stand in the way and even furnished us with a new Fraser automobile for the long journey from Carson City to Denver.

So in the fall of 1947, the Paul Laxalts went to Denver. Before long, we found a one-room apartment on the top floor of an old house in East Denver. The postage stamp-size kitchen had been created out of an old closet. When the in-laws came to visit, they were aghast, but we convinced them we were doing fine.

Many years later, when we lived in the Governor's Mansion, we'd harken back to our "closet" days in Denver and with some wonderment tried to understand why we were so content there. Perhaps it was because we were living such basic lives, living "without" in order to achieve our goal of obtaining a law degree.

D.U. law school in those days was operating out of various storefronts downtown. It had just the bare necessities — classrooms, a small library and a dedicated faculty, most of whom had other jobs in order to make ends meet. But what a marvelous education they gave us in the most positive environment any student could want!

D.U. was progressive in its approach, too, and far ahead of most traditional law schools. The school was located in the same area as the state courts. If we were studying criminal law, for example, and a comparable case was being tried in the court there, off we'd go to the courtroom to see justice in action.

Seeing it live was far more meaningful than simply reading about it in some casebook. This early courtroom experience served me well when I started trying cases in Nevada. When I graduated, as the old saying went, I "knew where the courthouse was," and what went on there, unlike most law school graduates who had spent their school days almost wholly in the world of "academic cases" with little or no attention given to the practicality of actually practicing law.

In later years, I became a good friend of John Love, who became Governor of Colorado, and Pete Domenici, who became a U.S. Senator from New Mexico. As fellow alumni, both shared my positive sentiments about the D.U. Law School.

Many years later, our oldest daughter, Gail, graduated from

D.U. and successfully practiced law in Denver until she opted to become a full-time wife and mother.

After a couple years, working right through the summers, I graduated from law school. After flirting briefly with staying in Colorado, we decided to go home to Nevada. A strong motivator was the fact that my father-in-law, Jack Ross, said that I could practice with him.

Next came the bar exam. After years of college and law school, a law student's professional future still is very much in doubt until he successfully concludes his or her "baptism of fire" — the bar exam.

Since the exam covered three years of material, most of us took a refresher course. Mine was in San Francisco and was conducted by a legal genius by the name of Witkin. It lasted several weeks and was as tedious as law school.

In fall 1949, I took the Nevada Bar Exam. The bar exam in those days took three days. It consisted of hours of answering questions based upon various subjects of law. Three long days of unshirted hell! Then came the "sweat period," which lasted several days.

Finally, in November 1949, the great news came!

I had passed! All I had to do was take the oath, and I'd be a full-fledged lawyer! For a kid who came from the most humble beginnings, this was pretty heady stuff.

It took my practical Mom, as usual, to bring me down to earth. While proud of her eldest, she pointed out that all I had was a license to practice law. It would be years before I really became a real lawyer. How right she was!

INSTANT FAMILY — ALMOST

Jackie and I, in true Catholic fashion, had tried for some five years to have children. After some heartbreaking miscarriages, we received the sad news that Jackie probably would not be able to have children.

We decided to adopt. Adoption in those days was far less complicated than it is now. We simply applied to the Catholic Welfare people in Reno. After an investigation, we were approved. Within weeks, we received word that a beautiful baby had been born on October 12, 1951, in San Francisco, and was ready to be hand-delivered to us.

What joy is was holding Gail in our arms for the first time (tempered a bit by the fact that she wet all over my lap right off the bat)! The experience was so beautiful that we soon adopted John Paul as a newborn, too, also born in San Francisco. Thereafter, we adopted Sheila, Jackie's niece, whose mother had died.

Then, as so often happens, the floodgates opened.

In short order, Jackie gave birth to Michelle, Kevin and Kathleen.

Within a few short years, the Paul Laxalt family had grown from two to eight!

Practicing Law

John R. "Jack" Ross announced in November 1949, that he had a new associate in his law office by the name of Paul D. Laxalt. Under his careful and competent tutelage, I started to learn the basics of practicing law.

Before long, I had completed my first brief, which he proudly presented to me at a family dinner, drafted my first complaint, completed my first title search, made my first court appearance (carried Jack's books) and had my first client interview and collected my first fee ($150).

I couldn't have served a more productive internship. To break in under Jack's watchful eye was so valuable to me in later years. For that, and his friendship and support, I shall be forever grateful.

CHAPTER 4

❖ *The New District Attorney* ❖

CATCHING THE BUG TO RUN

After a few months, my "internship" was drawing to a close, and I decided in 1950 to take the political plunge by running for District Attorney of Ormsby County in which the capital, Carson City, was located.

Since that time, people have often asked, "Why did you take that first plunge?"

I know it wasn't part of any long-range political plan. I didn't have one. In all probability it was my independent Basque nature speaking out. My father-in-law had treated me wonderfully, but I wanted to accomplish something on my own so that I could be free. That trait surfaced, I fear, from time-to-time in my later career in public service.

My first campaign photo when I was running for District Attorney of Ormsby County in 1950.

Had I then known the political pros I knew later, I'm sure I would not have made the race for District Attorney, a position which had been held for years by Dick Waters.

Here I was, a green young lawyer with no political experience, no campaign team, no money, taking on an experienced, respected incumbent with all the funding he'd need. How could I possibly win?

The key, I guess, was that I was a political novice.

I didn't know I couldn't win.

From the time I declared, hard campaigning was the order of the day. By the time the campaign was over, I had personally visited each house in the county at least twice.

Amazingly, on election night, when the votes were counted, I had won by a vote of 1107 to 827! No one was more surprised than I, except perhaps for Dick, whose political advisers told him I couldn't possibly win.

The District Attorney of Ormsby County was the attorney for the county commissioners. Also, he served as the city attorney for Carson City. This entailed meetings with the commissioners on the fifth of each month, and interminable meetings with the city council at night.

More often than not, after listening to citizen complaints of all types, I didn't make it home until well past midnight. It was here that I learned what grassroots politics was all about.

Also, of course, the DA was the chief law enforcement officer of the county, responsible for any criminal prosecutions that arose.

For the most part, I tried to play the part of the objective lawyer trying to see both sides of a controversy.

Most of the time, I stayed out of trouble. But on one issue, I found myself squarely in the center of a local fight that at times almost spun out of control. Let me explain.

Carson City was the "smallest capital" in the country, composed of less than a couple thousand hardy souls, most of whom worked for the State of Nevada. In short, it was a "company town" where the status quo was revered.

The last thing they wanted in Carson City was change. Nonetheless, flushed with my overwhelming victory at the polls, I launched into my version of reform.

WHY NOT PAVED STREETS?

From the time I came home from the war, I could not understand why a capital city didn't have paved streets. At that time, there were only two or three in the whole town.

In the summer, Carson City was a cloud of dust. In the winter, there was mud, lots of it. Surely, I thought, my fellow citizens would want to be extricated from this horrid problem.

So, at a city council meeting shortly after I was elected, I proposed that the time had come for Carson City to pave its streets. I had done my homework and concluded that the way to do it was to create special assessment districts which, under state law, had bonding authority. We'd simply sell bonds and the property owners would redeem them over a period of time.

Now, one would think that this was as close to a "motherhood" issue as one in office could get. Who could possibly object? Laxalt, overnight, would become a hero — "the king of paved streets in Carson City" — or so I thought.

Boy, was I wrong! All hell broke loose. I had committed the cardinal sin of local politics. That is, never surprise your people with any proposal without first properly "conditioning" them. Had I done that, I would have quickly discovered that many of the old-timers were perfectly happy with the unpaved streets and felt there was nothing wrong with a little dust and mud.

To make matters worse, the most vocal and effective leader of the opposition was my own father-in-law!

A quick political assessment indicated that unless there was a change in strategy, both the paving district and the new city attorney could quickly become "endangered species."

So, to cut my losses, I suggested to the city fathers that it would be prudent if we scaled back the district to include only a small test area. We then targeted an area near the center of town, well beyond my in-laws' house. The strategy worked. Within weeks, the district was formed. The curbs and gutters were installed, and the streets were paved.

My family and I (minus my father-in-law) proudly rode down the first paved street.

After the town's citizens had an opportunity to experience the value of a dust and mud-free street, they, of course, wanted one of their own. Then, the battle was over the priority order of the new paving districts to be created.

Future administrations, profiting from my near-death experience, compelled developers to pave their own streets.

THE RUBBER WAR

You'd think the paving fiasco would have tempered my desire for reform in Carson City. It should have, but didn't.

One day, a delegation of concerned mothers came to my office. In no uncertain terms they advised me that we had a serious crime problem in Carson City, and it was my duty to take care of it.

They informed me that although it was illegal, there were several prophylactic machines throughout town, in bars and gas stations. As mothers, they felt their sons were being wrongfully exposed to these nefarious devices, and that the morality of young Carson City could be destroyed beyond repair. (The fact that my buddies and I had from time-to-time been consumers was a bit troubling, but duty is duty.) If such machines are illegal, they must be stamped out, I so informed the mothers.

Immediately, the full force of the sheriff's office (one sheriff and a deputy) was unleashed. Before the day was out, the machines were confiscated, and a strong statement issued to the local newspaper denouncing the machines.

Again, I had miscalculated. Within days, I had become the laughing stock of the county. I found out quickly that the "pro-rubber" constituency far exceeded the "antis" in Ormsby County. Over time, the devices were quietly returned, and the "war" against rubbers dissipated – for which I was thankful.

The local newspaper – The Nevada Appeal – runs a column about events that occurred "25 years ago... ," "50 years ago... ," etc. Even now they refer to my "rubber" misadventure, and one of my buddies will send me a clipping with a smartass note attached.

Prohibition taught us that booze is here to stay.

My little war taught me that "rubbers" are here to stay, too.

JUDGE GUILD

Judge Clark J. Guild lived across the street from us in a beautiful Victorian house with sweeping porches. Today, it houses several professionals.

When we were growing up, he was as exalted to us as the Governor and Monsignor Wientjes. Mom impressed on us that he was a very important man, and that his property was off limits.

For kids who never had a new car in the family, we were most impressed by the fact that he had a new Buick every year. He also always wore a coat (with a carnation in the lapel) and a tie, which was not very common in our social circles.

Nevada District Judge Clark J. Guild, a great (and sometimes feared) jurist. *Nevada Historical Society*

He also had a wooden leg from the knee down with a steel peg so that when he walked there was an unmatched dignity about him. It was said that he lost his leg in a railroad accident.

He was one of the last lawyers who didn't go to formal school but studied under an admitted lawyer. He had presided over many important matters and enjoyed the respect of all.

He was a widower with two grown children, Marjorie and Clark. Both went to private schools, which were foreign to us "public schoolers." We did know that Marjorie went to Mills College, an exclusive school in Oakland, California. All the guys, including me, had crushes on her.

She eventually married future Nevada Governor Charles Russell, thus becoming Nevada's First Lady. The Russell family was one of the most distinguished and respected in the state. Clark, their eldest son, was in my gubernatorial administration and later became my indispensable manager in operating our family hotel, Ormsby House.

Clark, Jr., Judge Guild's son, is a contemporary. During our youthful years, we were like brothers, and that valued relationship has continued over the years. He became and remains one of the most respected citizens of Nevada.

When it came to business in his court, Judge Guild terrorized most of the lawyers, young and old, who appeared before him. Some felt it was his way of getting even with those "high falutin" college types. Everyone knew that if you were going to be in Judge Guild's court, you'd better be fully prepared or you'd pay the consequences — even in open court in the presence of your clients. It wasn't hard to understand why time in Judge Guild's court was described by the lawyers as "pucker time."

During my school years in Carson City, I don't recall ever having a conversation with the judge. A polite "hello" was about it. He was really out of our class. Having a bull session with him would be like having one with the Governor. It just wouldn't happen.

The situation did not change even after I went to law school.

But I'll never forget being in his house with his son Clark after I'd made my first court appearance before him. I don't even recall what the matter was, but it had to be perfunctory, else I wouldn't have been there.

That day, he strode into the room and said, "Son, you did well today. Keep it up!" I was bowled over. Even the President of the United States couldn't have flattered me more.

After I was elected DA, I was in regular contact with the judge. The nature of my duties, particularly as a prosecutor, were such that it became almost routine for me to be before him. But knowing his reputation, I never indulged in personal conversations with him, and I always made it a point to be completely prepared.

At times, I thought the Bar's fear of him had been overblown and unfair. But one day in court, when I was in my second year as DA, I presented a pro forma quiet title matter to him. My clients were present. (DAs then were permitted to have private practices.)

Everything was going well until suddenly he exploded: "Mr. Laxalt, where is the verification to your complaint?" I pointed out deferentially that it was in his file, whereupon he proceeded to rebuke me for being so derelict and to dare contradict him in his court. Then, summarily, he proceeded to dismiss my matter, to my complete mortification and the chagrin of my clients.

I went back to my office, which adjoined his. The more I thought about what he'd done, the more steamed I became. A check of the court file revealed the verification was there but had been filed by the clerk out of order.

An agonizing period followed in which I tried to cool off and decide what, if anything, I should do. Finally, I did what could have been one of the stupidest things of my young lawyer's life. I decided to confront him.

Sucking in my breath, I went down the marbled hall and knocked on his door. He gruffly said, "Come in."

"Judge," I said haltingly, "may I speak to you?" Without looking up, he said, "Go ahead." "Judge, respectfully, you had no right to embarrass me in front of my clients. I was prepared. The verification was in the file, if only you had looked for it."

Without saying another word, I left and half ran to my own office.

For the next several minutes, there was an eerie, scary silence. I thought to myself, "He's probably preparing contempt of court papers. I'm a dead duck! How stupid can I get?"

Then I heard his door open, and his steps headed in my direction. The steel plate on the bottom of his wooden leg resounded through the building. I felt as though the executioner was on his way.

Then the knock on my door. Shakily, I said, "Come in." The Judge came to the front of my desk, and to my total surprise and relief, said, "You're right, Paul. I checked the file. The verification is there. I'm sorry for what happened, and I'll make it right with your clients. It will never happen again."

My mouth must have been hanging wide open.

For years thereafter, I practiced in his court. Most matters were minor and routine, but I also had several major trials before him. And he always treated me firmly but fairly.

In many ways, I think I became a second son to him.

Terry

The job of a small town District Attorney is many-faceted, I found out quickly. One becomes, whether he wishes to or not, a "jack-of-all-trades" in human relations.

Since there was no separate juvenile division in those days (as there is now), I was the "juvenile division." It became my sorry lot to bring in parents when their kids had screwed up and urge them to keep a closer eye on them.

It was grueling work, since I knew most of the parents, but they seemed to appreciate my feeble attempts to help. As a result, we were able to handle juvenile problems very often in my office, rather than the courtroom. Our home at times became sort of a juvenile detention center.

Most of the time, our "TLC" — tender loving care — worked. Having them at the house was far better than shipping the kids, who weren't criminal types, off to the reformatory in Elko.

Then along came Terry Shugold, a personable, tow-headed 10-year-old. His mom, a single mother, came to me in desperation. She loved the boy deeply, but without a man around the house, she said, Terry was "out of control." She asked if perhaps Jackie and I couldn't take him for awhile. She felt that exposure to other kids and "male influence" might redirect his energies. Today, he'd be a prime candidate for Prozac.

After a long talk with him and with Jackie, we decided to take him into our household. For a few days, he fit in beautifully. He got along well with the kids, was helpful with the chores, and most respectful of us.

Then one morning, I went outside to go to work in my car, but the car was gone! And so was Terry! Witnesses later said it was quite a sight to see a ten-year-old navigating my car down the street standing up on the seat!

Before long, my car and Terry were recovered. Thankfully, neither suffered any damage. That was the end of the Laxalt Juvenile Detention Center.

THE PROSECUTOR

My first murder trial was unforgettable. It resulted in a conviction, but the irate defendant scared the hell out of us years later when he escaped while I was Governor. His various threats against my family while he was imprisoned had been passed on to me. Fortunately, he was quickly captured, much to the relief of all concerned.

I also remember the heartbreak I felt after learning that an old friend, as city clerk, had misplaced a good deal of scarce city funds and mixed them with his own. He went to trial, ably defended by my predecessor as DA, Dick Waters, but the case against him was overwhelming. After we presented our case, he saw the light and pled guilty. He did some time and left the state. Tough duty!

The fact is, I almost always felt sorry for the poor defendant I was prosecuting – not exactly a prime requisite for a crusading young DA.

During my District Attorney days, I became familiar with the workings of the city and county governments, and felt I was able to do some measure of good for the people.

JUDGE ROSS

Near the end of my third year as District Attorney, my father-in-

Federal Judge John R. Ross, my father-in-law, had a great influence on my life.

law told me he was going to seek the open federal judgeship in Nevada. He had given up any thought of running for Governor or U.S. Senator. He reasoned that since Eisenhower was President, the vacancy should go to a Republican.

Jack had already secured the support of our Republican Senator, George Malone. But even in a Republican period, Nevada's Democrat Senator, Pat McCarran, the all-powerful former chairman of the Senate Judiciary Committee, had, as a practical matter, a veto.

Jack asked if I would consider visiting with McCarran while he was in Reno. Frankly, I didn't know how I could help, particularly with Nevada's political God, Pat McCarran. But after the paving adventure, I couldn't say no. (Besides, even Jack had consented to have his street paved by that time.)

In Reno, Senator McCarran would at times hole up at St. Mary's Hospital, where he was treated almost as if he were the Baby Jesus. The nuns would minister to his every want. The Senator's guests in Reno were handled in much the same fashion, I imagine, as guests in Rome who meet the Pope.

Jack's rationale for requesting my assistance was that he didn't know Senator McCarran well. He hoped that some of his partisan references to the Senator hadn't reached McCarran's ears. Therefore, Jack thought it would be safe to send "Momma Laxalt's son" for a bit of reconnaissance. Further, my brother John had worked for McCarran in Washington. That should help, too.

On the appointed day, I was ushered into the great man's "office," a large private room in the hospital.

Having been briefed by his staff, he opened by asking how "Momma Laxalt" was. He still remembered those great evenings at the French Hotel. He then sincerely told me that my mother was "one of the grandest ladies" he'd ever met. Since this was in the early 1950s, before feminism and political correctness became fashionable, I considered this to be a high compliment, and still do.

He then asked about my father-in-law. I told him why I was there and what he already knew — that Jack would be honored to be the next federal judge for Nevada.

Without tipping his hand, he asked if Jack had any "problems," which could hinder his Senate confirmation. Jack had already advised me that I could level with McCarran.

I told the Senator that, from time to time, as a good Irishman, Jack had become overly friendly with the bottle. He wouldn't hurt anybody but himself, but he'd worry the hell out of his family when he'd disappear for days at a time. He usually sought refuge in some nearby Indian reservation, where he and his Indian buddies would commiserate about the problems of the day.

I noted that Jack sought treatment and had been "dry" for years. I asked the Senator if this would be a problem, whereupon

he responded, "Hell, no! If a problem with booze was disquali-
fying, the halls of Congress would be near empty and so would
the federal bench, for that matter. The fact is," the Senator said,
"Jack had guts enough to be treated, and I'm told he's a damned
good lawyer."

"One other thing, Senator," I said, "My father-in-law is a
private man. Although he's active in politics, he has very few close
friends. You won't be
hearing from throngs
of people in his sup-
port, although we
could marshal a cam-
paign if necessary."

To that, he practi-
cally thundered, "The
fact that he doesn't have
a lot of close friends
means to me that he's
been selective." Mc-
Carran, who died later
that year, added, "Do
you know, Son, that
I can count on one
hand my real, trusted

U.S. Senator Patrick A. McCarran, a political giant
not only in Nevada but also throughout the world.
Just as importantly, one of our valued customers at
the French Hotel. Shown here (left) with President
Franklin Roosevelt. *Nevada Historical Society*

friends? I have plenty of acquaintances, but damn few friends!"

How sad, I thought.

But as I progressed through public life, I came to the conclusion that after Pat McCarran's storied and controversial career, if
he had five loyal, trusted friends, he was a fortunate man indeed.

When I communicated to Jack that the "McCarran decks are
clear," he was elated. Shortly after, on May 13, 1954, John R. Ross
was confirmed by the United States Senate and became a truly
great federal judge.

CHAPTER 5

❖ *Back to Private Life* ❖

Jack's elevation to the bench meant that I had to resign from the DA's office in 1954. His practice was just too big to try to handle, along with the duties of the District Attorney.

Cam Batjer, a good friend, succeeded me. Thereafter, as Governor, I had the honor of appointing Cam to the Nevada Supreme Court. While in the Senate, I recommended him to President Reagan, who appointed him to the U.S. Parole Commission, from which he eventually retired.

So off to the Sweetland Building in Carson City I went. My first job was to touch base with the clients to give them the choice of staying on or selecting other counsel.

I must admit to being a bit jolted when I advised one of Jack's rancher clients that Jack was moving on, to which he replied nonchalantly, "Oh, yeah, I heard he got another job." Just then, I got my first inkling that a lifetime of breaking your ass for a client, as Jack had done, would often go unappreciated.

Overall, the transition went well. The clients, most of whom were ranching and mining types, were willing to take a chance on the "new son-in-law" (even though he had a thing for paved streets!).

The next nine years were the most demanding, the most hectic, the most frustrating of my entire life. But all the while, as difficult as it was, it was a rewarding experience, personally and professionally.

That was due in great part to a supportive family, with whom we were in constant contact trading stories of our respective "gifted children."

Kay and Addison Millard, who for years lived across the street, were also raising their family, and they couldn't have been closer or more loyal friends. Later, when I was elected Governor, I had the pleasure of appointing Add to be Nevada's Adjutant General.

The same applied to Ruthe and Swede Swanson. They, too, were raising kids at the time, which meant we had a lot in common. Swede and I regularly played golf, too, which was a relaxing diversion from the stresses and strains of the law and the courtroom.

GROWING FAMILY

As our family grew, so did our housing needs.

Starting with a one-bedroom house across from Jackie's uncle, we moved to two other houses. Finally, we decided to build a ranch-style house "in the country," which in our context meant just outside the city limits on King Street, the street leading to the Capitol (if the old Supreme Court building weren't in the way).

My distinction quickly changed from "up-and-coming lawyer" to "the guy whose house has five toilets," which was a record for Carson City.

The King Street house proved to be a family blessing. With an adjacent field for riding horses, a swimming pool and tennis court, it quickly became Carson's country club. It delights me even now to hear the children speak glowingly of their King Street days.

We quickly moved from a "no children family" to a family of six — five girls and one boy, John. When people used to ask me what I hoped for the five girls, I would say: "I really don't know, but I push convents and elopements a lot."

As I write this, these children are all now in their late 30s and 40s. They've all experienced the ups and downs of life. Collectively, they've given me twelve beautiful grandchildren.

I've never figured out what success really means, but if it's defined by being hard working, true to themselves and others, and being just good people, each of them is a great success in life.

I'd proudly recount what's happened to them, but they're all very private people who have carefully guarded their privacy over the years. I respect that, and will thereby refrain from a glowing father and grandfather statement, as tempting as it is.

Unfortunately, after the Governorship, my wife Jackie and I, after 25 years of marriage, decided to call it quits.

The divorce couldn't have been more amicable. The same for the years thereafter. In all that time, she's never made any unreasonable demands on me. We have a common, continuing interest in the kids, and we'll never jeopardize that.

I shall never forget the enormous contribution she made to me in the tough "law school" days and the trying political years. For all that, I'll always be grateful.

On My Own
Professionally, for such a new lawyer, my days were over-full taking care of a practice which had been built up over 40 years by Judge Ross.

He had a number of clients, mostly ranchers, who had major water interests, which almost inevitably bred litigation. Some of the water suits were decades old and seemed to be never-ending. After months of intense activity, there would be a lull of several years.

From working these files, I gained invaluable knowledge concerning the often-violent histories of the Carson, Truckee and

Walker Rivers. It gave me a valuable background for dealing with water issues later in public life.

One basic fact was deeply ingrained in my psyche. In western farming areas, water is the lifeblood of the business. If you want to get into serious trouble, just mess with someone's water rights.

Our principal water account was the Walker River Irrigation District. The Walker drops from the Sierra Nevada mountains into Western Nevada and is the basic water supply in the valleys there. Without the Walker River water, the area would be sagebrush.

Working with the district, I learned about "duty" of water, dates of water rights, the difference between Riparian and Appropriative water rights, and all the rest. These terms would be Greek to most, but are part of the rancher's day-to-day vocabulary.

Even today, whenever I see a western "water story," I'm drawn to it. Today, the right to water doesn't attract the attention it once did, but the importance of water to the West can never be minimized.

Judge Ross had also represented the Nevada Industrial Commission (NIC) for many years. With his leaving, I assumed responsibility for the account. The NIC — the forerunner to the State Industrial Insurance System — was the agency for processing workmen's compensation claims. Mainly, the claims originated with injuries suffered on the job. It gave me an understanding of how powerful and, at times, how oppressive an agency like this can be. All in all, though, it was composed of people who tried to deal fairly with the claimants.

When Grant Sawyer was elected Governor, his people decided that the NIC counsel job would be an attractive "political plum" to dispense. And although the NIC people went to Grant asking that I be kept on, I was asked to leave and did.

Ironically, if I'd stayed on at NIC, which was a major account,

I doubt that I would have even sought state office. I was content where I was, but perhaps it was a bit of "payback" four years later when I decided to run for Lieutenant Governor and later Governor. Continuing to represent a state agency such as NIC would have constituted a conflict, thus precluding me from running.

I guess the moral of this story is that if you have a potential political opponent "on the shelf," for heaven's sake, leave him there so he won't be running against you in the future.

DICK GRAVES

As a practicing lawyer, the most unique matters that came my way involved the founder of the Nugget in Sparks, Nevada, Dick Graves. Dick came to Nevada in the early 1950s via Idaho. He had been in the gambling business in that state, which permitted slot machines on a "local-option" basis. He had operations in Coeur d'Alene, Sandpoint and Garden City, a small town just outside Boise, the capital.

He was hugely successful in Idaho until a wave of Puritanism hit the state, and slot machines were made illegal.

Dick came to Nevada with his Basque wife, Flora, and their four children. Considering what Dick Graves was able to do in Nevada, many Idahoans told me thereafter that declaring slots illegal in Idaho was the worst decision they ever made.

Dick bought one of the majestic, old houses in Carson City, across from the Governor's Mansion, and promptly proceeded to prospect for "Nevada gold."

He decided to open "Nuggets" in a couple of places to test the market.

In 1954, Dick opened Nuggets in Reno, Carson City and Yerington and, in 1955, he opened the Sparks Nugget.

And for some reason that I still don't fully fathom, he came to me for legal advice. When I later asked him "Why?", Dick simply shrugged his shoulders and said, "I felt that we were both 'comers' and would work well as a team."

After the test period, he decided that Carson City and Sparks were his best potential markets. The Carson City operation was an instant success and the forerunner of the successful operation it has been over the years. He eventually sold the Reno Nugget in 1955 and the Carson City Nugget in 1956.

His pride and joy was the operation in Sparks, a town just east of Reno. When he built the first expanded Nugget there in 1958 — the cornerstone of the present operation — its success was no sure thing. At that time, many of the "old gambling pros" thought that Dick had seriously miscalculated in going to Sparks, which they still considered a "hick town."

He was one of the first to recognize that slot machines were the wave of the gambling future. He kept the other casino games, of course, but from the beginning it was apparent that "slots were king." Later, the same phenomenon occurred throughout Nevada and, even later, throughout the country.

He also recognized that a loss-leader such as inexpensive, good food, was like a magnet in attracting people who, on their way to or from his many restaurants, might drop a few coins in the machines.

One of my many interesting legal experiences with him was when he decided to put a South Seas Polynesian restaurant in the Sparks plant and promptly named it "Trader Dick's." That seemed innocuous enough, but "Trader Vic's," the famous Bay Area restaurant, didn't see it that way. Their lawyers threatened us with everything but legal mayhem. After months of jockeying, they decided to cool it after we convinced them we didn't intend to go the franchise route or worse yet, set up shop in San Francisco.

The day before the "new" Sparks Nugget's grand opening in March 1958, Dick walked me through the facility and said, "This is quite a plant, but what if nobody comes?"

He needn't have worried. From the moment he opened the doors that evening, it was like a huge breath of fresh air to have a Dick Graves' Nugget in operation. Instead of the dark, gloomy, seedy, almost depressing "gambling houses" of the time, Dick's were light, airy and cheerful places.

Over the years, I've seen my share of marketers, but none to match Dick Graves. He was a genius at marketing. He'd say, "You've gotta send out winners to get players." He also brought into play the catchy phrase "Awful, Awful sandwiches." The public loved it.

In the early 1960s, the Circus Room opened in the Nugget. As a promotion, Dick purchased, of all things, an elephant for $8000 from a Wisconsin businessman. The elephant, named "Bertha," became an overnight sensation.

Shortly after Dick bought Bertha, she appeared in the Nevada Day parade in Carson City. Afterward, I held an open house at our King Street residence. I arrived a little late to find Bertha "taking a dip" in our swimming pool! Her trainer was trying frantically to get her out, but she was enjoying her swim too much. Finally, much to my relief, they coaxed her out with a loaf of bread.

Sometimes, Dick was fallible. When he started the Golden Rooster Room at the Nugget, he franchised with none other than the original Colonel Harlan Sanders of Kentucky Fried Chicken fame.

They even worked out a deal whereby Dick used the colonel's recipe for the chicken at the price of five cents per chicken. As part of the arrangement, the colonel was supposed to promote the chicken for Dick by doing radio spots and speaking appearances, but the good colonel didn't show.

Finally, paying the five cents for a "no-show colonel" frustrated Dick to the point that he developed his own seasoning for the chicken and dropped the franchise agreement.

I've wondered what would have happened if the Colonel Sanders Kentucky Fried Chicken marriage had lasted, particularly after KFC went into economic orbit.

By far the greatest legal challenge Dick dumped in my lap was the "Golden Rooster" case.

Dick, ever the master marketer, decided he'd like to have a Golden Rooster restaurant. It featured fried chicken which tasted by pure coincidence, of course, much like the Colonel's. It also featured a 15-pound solid gold rooster which he proudly displayed near the entrance of the Golden Rooster restaurant.

In having the rooster made, Dick decided to go "top of the line." In early 1958, he went to Shreve and Company, the venerable San Francisco jeweler, and ordered the fabrication of an 18-karat, solid gold rooster.

When completed, it was presented with much fanfare to the public. It met with universal acclaim, save for two United States Treasury Department agents, who concluded, in December 1958, that fabricating the rooster without a permit was a violation of the 1934 Gold Reserve Act.

They demanded a meeting in the U.S. Attorney's office the very afternoon they contacted Dick, and they suggested that he bring his lawyer, which meant me. We were notified we were in violation of the Gold Reserve Act, which limited private holdings of gold to 50 ounces.

After we referred them to Shreve's, who told them that they had received permission from the U.S. Mint to make the rooster, we thought the matter was closed.

Eighteen months later, however, in July 1960, the full force of the federal government came down on our rooster. The Treasury Department filed a complaint in federal court in Carson City, charging us with various dastardly things and asking that an extreme penalty be exacted upon one Richard Graves. They also issued a warrant for the rooster's arrest, and the U.S. Marshal promptly confiscated the rooster!

Normally, one would retreat into the shadows in such circumstances, but not Dick Graves. He immediately seized on this as a public relations opportunity. Quickly, he cast this as a David v. Goliath case, with the poor rooster squarely in the middle.

When the federal marshal came sheepishly to pick up the rooster, Dick was fully prepared to capitalize on the sordid event. He made it a major media circus, with the onlookers (volunteers, of course) hissing and jeering at this colossal miscarriage of justice.

Later, he bought a brass replica of the rooster, dressed it in prison garb and displayed it in the golden rooster's "roost" at the Nugget. It was great theater!

The rooster's incarceration paved the way for one of the most "significant" legal events in Nevada's history.

Relying on the precedent of an old maritime case where the owner — pending a confiscation proceeding — applied to have his ship released, we decided that if it was good enough for a ship, it should be good enough for the rooster. So we did what any red-blooded, freedom-loving Nevadan would do: We applied for bail for our rooster!

The hearing to decide whether to grant bail was memorable. Some of the cynics thought that applying the maritime precedent to a rooster was a stretch, but I pressed on with the ardor of a Clarence Darrow.

Unfortunately, on September 9, 1960, Judge Sherrill Halbert of Sacramento, who was brought in because the federal judge in Nevada happened to be my father-in-law, sided with the cynics and denied our application for bail. Rooster lovers throughout Nevada went into mourning.

Here We Crow Again

The Solid Gold Rooster has at last come home to roost. Home is the Sparks Nugget and the Solid Gold Rooster is its current hero—a battle-scarred but crowing symbol of victory over bureaucracy.

The story goes back to May 1958, when Dick Graves, who was just seeing the gleam in Spark's eye for a big casino and restaurant, motel deal, decided he'd create a solid (not hollow) 18k rooster for public display. Nice symbol of the state, he thought, and of gambling. So he commissioned silversmiths in Reno and San Francisco to create this masterpiece of artristy and get permission from the U. S. Mint in San Francisco to go ahead. Let it be said here and now, only the vaguest thoughts of publicity ever entered Dick Graves' mind.

Within a month the SF Mint said okay and the rooster was ready, a spectacular objet d'art in 18k gold weighing 15 pounds, solid all the way through, valued and insured for $40,000. Wow, all bureaucracy broke loose. Why, said the Treasury people, this is obviously a violation of the law which says no private person may own more than 50 ounces of gold unless it is proven to be a "work of art". Rooster was 190 ounces overweight.

And so the battle started. Was Rooster a "work of art" or a [vio-]lation of the law? In November 1958, the U. S. Treasury warned the Sparks Nugget that possession of Rooster was in violation of the Gold Reserve Act. They threatened confiscation.

Threats subsided somewhat when the Treasury officials were told the San Francisco Mint had given permission for Rooster's creation

Agents Grab Golden Cock

SPARKS, Nev. (AP)—U.S. marshals seized a gambler's golden rooster Thursday because, the government says, it isn't art.

The 9-inch high 15-pound solid gold rooster was carried off under a court order.

"If that rooster isn't art I don't know what is," said Dick Graves, owner of the Nugget Casino.

The complaint said the rooster contains 206 ounces of gold, 156 more than an individual can keep for more than a month without permission unless the gold is used for art work.

The government contends the rooster was displayed for advertising purposes.

Graves said the rooster contains $12,500 worth of gold but its value as an art object is $40,000.

Obviously, journalists had a lot of fun with the Golden Rooster case.

The jury trial, which was delayed until March 1962, was held in the old post office building in Carson City. It played to a packed house. Three hotshot lawyers from Washington represented the government. They were annoyed when the locals suggested that this was a waste of the taxpayers' money. Some even went so far as to suggest these lawyers had had nothing better to

The Golden Rooster being returned to its "rightful owner," Dick Graves (center), in 1962. *Special Collections, University of Nevada, Reno Library*

do since they'd sent Al Capone away.

The trial turned out to be a battle of "experts," who argued over whether the rooster was a "work of art." The Gold Reserve Act provided an exception for such items. If it was art, our guy was free. If it wasn't, as a headline at the time suggested, our rooster would be roasted.

Finally, on summation day, March 29, 1962, at a critical point, when I made reference to what a horrible thing it would be to melt down the rooster, the sun suddenly came through the window and settled on the rooster, giving him an almost divine aura. The jurors were riveted.

Needless to say, the jury found unanimously in our favor, and the rooster was returned to its "home" in the Nugget.

This gave rise to a celebration the likes of which western Nevada may never see again. A caravan of cars drove the rooster to Sparks, where hundreds of his devoted admirers cheered his arrival.

One golden rooster had escaped the tentacles of the federal government and would reign supreme in front of Dick's chicken house once again!

In the fall of 1960, Dick Graves sold the operating corporation of the Sparks Nugget to John Ascuaga, who had started as Dick's food manager for the Idaho operations in the early 1950s. Dick sold the Nugget building and the real estate to John in 1971. John Ascuaga has been immensely successful in running the Nugget over the years.

Harvey Gross

Harvey Gross and his wife, Llewellyn, were the founders of the Wagon Wheel Hotel & Casino at Lake Tahoe. He was originally a butcher in Sacramento, and his work had brought him frequently to the South Shore of Tahoe. Llewellyn, to whom Harvey was married in 1926, was from Fallon, Nevada. When they initially moved to Tahoe, they were broke, Harvey's meat company having gone bankrupt a few years earlier.

There was an old Episcopal church retreat just off the highway across the street from Sahati's, a gambling club (among the first at Tahoe). Harvey felt that putting in a gambling "joint" would result in a "higher and better" economic use of the church property, which totaled about seven acres. The deal was consummated in 1944, when Harvey swapped some land at Glenbrook, also at the South Shore of Tahoe, for the Episcopal Church land.

Before long, the Wagon Wheel expanded until it was so successful it invited the attention of the IRS in the late 1950s.

During their investigation, they discovered approximately $250,000 in a safe in Harvey's home. In those days, and probably now, if they can't prove specific violation, they take the "net worth" route.

Essentially, starting with a base line year, they added up all your assets (after deduction for taxes and expenses). Then they did the same for a later year. If you could not account for the increase in your net worth, then, as George Bush would put it, you were "in deep doo doo."

Unfortunately for Harvey, he didn't reconcile, particularly as to the money in his safe.

A criminal indictment was sought in Carson City. We immediately sought the services of Spurgeon "Sparky" Avakian, who years before had represented the Treasury Department but was now in a successful tax practice in Oakland, California. He was ably assisted by his partner, Dick Johnston. Without their guidance and support, only the good Lord knows what would have happened to Harvey.

Because we had what I thought was a good explanation, and because we knew that an indictment would be very harmful to Harvey Gross, we sought entrance before the grand jury. But no dice. Our request was summarily denied. No one — neither the prospective indictee nor his counsel — was permitted to appear before the grand jury unless invited. They didn't relent, and Harvey was indicted in June of 1957.

Between indictment and trial, we experienced the hard-assed

approach then used toward defendants by the IRS.

We sought information from them (to which we were entitled) to prepare for trial. They stonewalled. To make matters worse, we had relinquished documents to them which they refused to return.

So, we sued the IRS for recovery of the documents, plus damages. Eventually, they surrendered our documents. But I paid a price for taking on the IRS. For years, an audit of my records became almost routine.

Suing the IRS wasn't all negative, though. Later, when I ran for Governor, the legendary gambler Bill Harrah was one of my first contributors, saying, "Anyone with the balls to sue the IRS has my support."

In March 1959, the trial started in the federal court in Carson City. Jury selection went very well. "Sparky," Dick and I couldn't have been more pleased.

The government's case was an accountant's dream, which meant that most everyone, including the jury, was bored to death.

Harvey was unflappable. Here was a guy with everything on the line — his reputation, his business and his freedom — yet during the entire trial, all he did was suck on his pipe like a disinterested spectator.

"Sparky" and I agreed that the lack of concern on Harvey's part probably was a plus for the jury, particularly any jurors looking for what we called "guilty body language."

Following the presentation of the government's case — which we felt was less than solid — we started with our witnesses.

All was going well when suddenly, the roof fell in!

At a certain point, the court reporter was asked to repeat the testimony of a previous witness, but she couldn't locate her stenographic tapes!

We couldn't believe it. During the trial, we felt that the poor soul was past her prime, but no one realized, particularly the judge, how far past her prime she was.

The tapes weren't found, and a mistrial was declared on March 18th. After all that work and with the case going so well, a mistrial!

Harvey and Llewellyn Gross, who worked as a team to make Harvey's at Lake Tahoe a spectacular success. Along with Spurgeon Avakian, I successfully represented Harvey against income tax charges in the late 1950s.

The prosecutors realized, however, they had problems in the strength of their case against Harvey. A few months later, they finally agreed to a plea of nolo contendre. This took Harvey off the hook and preserved his gaming license, which he would have lost if convicted.

Thereafter, under Harvey's guidance and with Llewellyn's invaluable contributions, the Wagon Wheel grew and grew. It is now one of the finest resorts anywhere.

Unfortunately, in November of 1964, Llewellyn, while driving through Washoe Valley between Reno and Carson City, accidentally died from carbon monoxide poisoning in her car. We later learned that a 25 cent auto part would have avoided the problem, and her life would have been saved. She was a special lady and a great partner of Harvey's.

The Wagon Wheel at Tahoe, today known as Harvey's, is a tribute to their vision and hard work.

GEORGE WHITTELL

Many have taken false credit for preserving the Nevada side of Lake Tahoe. But no one, in my opinion, was more responsible for preserving this environmentally-precious land than George Whittell, who owned virtually all of the Lake Tahoe frontage on the Nevada side at one time.

He was a fabled and eccentric "Howard Hughes" type of character. Although he was an heir to the Whittell railroad, banking and real estate fortune, he was a restless young man who quickly tired of the social scene in the Bay Area.

In his early thirties, much to the consternation of his very conservative family, he decided to go to Italy to serve as a volunteer in the American ambulance unit during World War I. He was decorated for bravery by the French and Italian governments. He later transferred to the U.S. Army with the rank of Captain, a title which he bore with pride for the rest of his life.

After a few years, he returned home. In the late 1930s, Whittell astounded his trust officers when he decided to buy more than 14,000 acres of prime Lake Tahoe land between Crystal Bay and Zephyr Cove. Little did they realize how far-sighted (or lucky) the Captain was. By the time of his death in 1969, his purchase was worth many times the original investment.

After the purchase, he decided to build a magnificent house on the shores of Tahoe, just south of Sand Harbor Beach. Locally, it became known very quickly as "The Castle."

It gained the reputation of being "Whittell's play pen." The parties he held there were legendary. The word was that they would last days on end.

He would import the fairest damsels in the area which, to say the least, added an exciting dimension to the festivities.

To the complete shock of newcomers, he would also display some of his animals — lions, tigers and elephants, principally —

which he housed on the property. Although I never could quite accept it, some witnesses even stated that a lion or tiger would occasionally stroll among the partygoers. I guess there wasn't enough room for the elephants, who remained caged.

One of the many stories that circulated in those days was that one of his guests had died during a party, and he remained propped in a chair for hours before anyone noticed!

The castle also included a several-hundred-foot tunnel, which connected it to the boat house. The tunnel, which had several dungeon-like rooms along its sides, also connected the main house to a guest house in a rather peculiar fashion. One would have to enter one of the rooms along the tunnel, at the back of which was a doorway that opened to a spiral staircase. At the top of the staircase was another door, which opened into a bathtub in the guesthouse! Naturally, there was a lot of base speculation about the use of this unusual feature.

With this as background, imagine my reaction when a call from Captain Whittell came to my law office in the late 1950s. He asked that I visit with him at the Castle "to discuss some business." To say the least, I was excited, although slightly apprehensive, over the prospect of not only meeting the "Captain" but possibly even representing him as an attorney.

I was met at the gate by his caretaker, who escorted me down a winding road to the Castle. At the huge front door, a lady, whom I learned later was his long-time nurse, Ruth Casey, greeted me warmly. She led me into a huge, gloomy room with fireplaces at both ends. On a porch adjoining the room were some thirty or forty myna birds, with whom the Captain conversed regularly.

At one end of the room, seated in a wheel chair, was Captain Whittell himself. I had no idea that he was disabled and quite old.

He had a huge, distinguished, lion-sized head and piercing blue eyes. Warmly shaking my hand, with a twinkle in his eye, he said, "It's a pleasure to meet Dominique's kid."

My dad, for many years, had leased some of the Captain's property in the Tahoe area to graze the sheep. Over the years, they had become friends. Typical of Pop, I don't recall his ever mentioning his relationship with the Captain. He never was much impressed with pomp.

The Captain advised me that he had decided to sell a portion of his Incline property to an Oklahoma development group headed by a man named Art Wood.

Although the Captain "hated like hell selling," his bankers had long urged him to liquidate a portion of his Tahoe assets, and Incline was a natural. His investigation had revealed that the group were good developers, and the price was right.

Captain George Whittell with one of his "friends." Although highly eccentric, Whittell was a valued friend and client who helped protect a good portion of Lake Tahoe.
Special Collections, University of Nevada, Reno Library

When we signed the original agreement, the required "earnest money" amount was $1 million, which was delivered to me by certified check.

Upon delivery, I phoned the Captain and suggested that I drive to the Castle to hand it to him personally, whereupon he replied, "Hell, no. Drop it in the mail. Who is going to be able to cash a million dollar check, even if it is stolen?"

His logic was overwhelming, but I must confess to a sigh of relief when I learned that the check had been cashed.

The sale led to the development of Incline, which quickly became known as one of the finest anywhere. Today, it is fully matured and is still known as one of the prime areas of Tahoe.

In 1959, at my suggestion, the Captain donated the 3,500 acre "Little Valley," which was in the heart of the Sierra Nevada above Washoe Valley, to the University of Nevada and the Catholic Church.

The State of Nevada was able to purchase much of the Whittell land for state park land only because the conservation-minded Whittell selflessly kept the land together in pristine form.

My original visit to the Captain ripened into a close personal relationship. Not unlike many very wealthy people, he was rather lonely. Other than his faithful nurse, his birds (who were each given a name) and exotic animals, he had very few outside friends. He'd been hustled so much for money over the years that he became suspicious and wary of most. Not unlike Howard Hughes.

Like Hughes, he would call at all hours of the day and night simply to talk. Often, he was triggered by what "those political bastards" were doing in Sacramento, Carson City or Washington. He wasn't a political activist by any means, but he maintained a keen interest in politics. I learned a great deal from him.

Unfortunately, my later entry into public life caused a rupture in our relations.

When I was elected Lieutenant Governor in 1962, almost immediately a dispute arose between the State of Nevada and the Captain over the state's efforts to condemn major portions of his land. Finally, the dispute rose to a level where I had to make a choice between continuing as Lieutenant Governor or representing Captain Whittell. I came to the painful conclusion that I'd have to withdraw as the Captain's attorney to avoid a hopeless conflict of interest.

I just didn't have the courage to tell him personally, so I wrote him a letter instead. Quickly, he phoned. I told him how sorry I was, but I saw no other way to resolve the conflict, to which he tartly responded, "Well, there's one other way — you should have resigned as Lieutenant Governor. You'll have a lot better future with me than being in that shitty office."

When the story broke in the papers, my legal colleagues, almost to a person, thought that I'd taken leave of my senses. To give up one of the prime accounts in the state, to give up the possibility of representing his estate, where the fee would be millions of dollars, amounted, in their opinion, to sheer lunacy.

Beyond that, I'd lost a good and cherished friend.

I tried later to make contact, even when I was elected Governor, but to no avail.

He died during my Governorship, in April 1969, leaving most of his estate to various animal-rights groups. Sadly, he died having little faith in humans.

He was an unforgettable person, and I shall always cherish his memory.

CHAPTER 6

❖ *Plunging Into Party Politics* ❖

Growing up, we Laxalts lived in a "non-political world." Aside from the officials like Senator McCarran talking politics at the dinner table, politics simply wasn't part of our lives. In that respect, we were like most Americans.

After returning from the war and marrying Jackie, I became interested and involved through my father-in-law. He would take me to political meetings and once even took me to a state convention in Las Vegas.

Philosophically, he was quite conservative. So were almost all politicians, in either party, on the state level. Differences weren't so much philosophical as they were personal. Most were Republicans or Democrats because their parents were.

One day in 1958, a group of local Republican activists came to my law office. Their leaders were Ella Broderick, the owner of a popular local bar, "Broderick's," and Bill Dial, an insurance man. Both were good friends.

They asked me to consider running for Republican County Chairman. Ordinarily, one would be flattered, but this was no ordinary situation. They were asking me to oppose Ken and Kay Johnson, who operated the Senator Club in downtown Carson City.

More imposing was the fact that Ken, since 1943, had been the

State Senator for Ormsby County and was the powerful chairman of the Senate Finance Committee. In the view of many, he was the most powerful man in the state. His wife, Kay, was the Republican National Committeewoman for the state. She was tough and a very effective politician. They were the power brokers of Ormsby County.

The group set out to convince me that unless the Johnsons were taken down, the Republic would fall! Their arguments must have been convincing, because we declared war!

Their plan was simple. We would gain control of the county organization and then go to the state convention, campaigning to replace Kay as national committeewoman. That would effectively cripple Ken, and the Johnsons would come tumbling down.

They made it sound easy. Ella and Bill told me that with my leading the charge, there would be more than enough votes to capture control of the county delegation.

But they underestimated the intensity of the competition. Indeed, there is nothing more intense than a county convention fight. It's eyeball-to-eyeball, brass knuckles political warfare.

Naive young lawyer that I was, I had no idea what I was getting into when I answered the call. But the more I became involved, the sharper became my sense of competitiveness.

We learned very quickly that power can intimidate the average convention delegate, and the Johnsons were certainly not above scaring the hell out of delegates. As a result, they developed a solid base of committed supporters prior to the county convention.

We did our homework, too, and attracted our own bloc. When the convention started, no one knew just where some of the votes were. They were still "uncommitted."

The tumultuous convention had an inconclusive result. We ended up sending two delegations to the state convention. Once there, we were able to convince the credentials committee that ours was the duly authorized Ormsby County delegation, and we were seated.

When we went to the floor, State Senator Jim Slattery, a colorful character in Nevada political history and later a close friend and political ally, strode across the aisle and said, "Congratulations, Paul. I want you to know that I voted for you."

"Bullshit, Slats," I said, "I happen to know that you personally supported Kay before the credentials committee." Without missing a beat, he replied, "That's right, Paul, but when they voted to make it unanimous, I voted with you." At least he was an "honest rogue!"

After we were seated, the convention elected our candidate, a long-time activist from Reno, Amy Gulling. Her election was met with mixed reactions. Some in the Reno delegation were heard to say, "Now that Amy is national committeewoman, who's going to run our rummage sales?" Her political friends couldn't understand her meteoric political rise.

The Johnson dynasty came tumbling down in the elections of 1958, when Bill Dial won the state Senate seat held by Ken Johnson.

REX BELL

I met Rex Bell for the first time at the "Dump Johnson" state convention. He was Lieutenant Governor at the time, serving under Republican Governor Charles Russell.

Rex was one of the last of the old "cowboy actors" of the vintage of Tom Mix. He had also achieved a certain degree of added fame when he married the beautiful silent screen actress, Clara Bow. When their movie careers wound down, they moved to Las Vegas, where Rex went into business.

In 1954, he was elected to the office of Lieutenant Governor. He was as handsome as they come. Men and women alike adored him. In a later period, he would have been the prototype of the "Marlboro Man".

In 1962, the expiration year of his second term as Lieutenant Governor, he called and asked to have dinner at our house. Jackie

My first "photo-op" in 1962 with Nevada Lieutenant Governor Rex Bell at the Mapes Hotel in Reno. We had just announced we were running as a team — he for Governor and I for Lieutenant Governor.

and I were overwhelmed. We weren't accustomed to having celebrities in our social circle, much less to dinner in our house.

We assumed that he wanted help on a potential campaign against Sawyer.

At the conclusion of dinner, Rex asked if he could discuss an important matter with us. He started by confiding to us that he had decided to run for Governor. That wasn't a big surprise to us. Then, to our complete astonishment, he asked if I would consider being his running mate! He and his advisers, he said, felt that his being from Las Vegas and my being from Carson City would provide geographical balance to the ticket. He would look to me for "issues development" since I'd had a great deal of trial experience, and he would be responsible for raising the bulk of the campaign money.

After picking ourselves off the floor, we told him we'd let him know the next day.

The job of Lieutenant Governor made sense in many ways. It wouldn't require a move from our beloved Carson City. It was a part-time position with the principal responsibility being President of the Senate. Since the Legislature met only once every two years, and the Capitol was only five minutes from the law office, what could be more convenient? And with a popular figure such as Rex Bell heading the ticket, I just might get elected.

Our decision? "Let's go for it!"

After phoning Rex the next day and telling him of my decision, he asked me to meet him at his suite at the Mapes Hotel in Reno. I knocked on the door, and he called for me to come in. When I walked in, he was in the bathroom shaving. Here was Rex Bell, with his shirt collar turned down, shaving with a straight razor! I thought they had gone out with the Model T Ford!

After shaving, he told me that a photographer was coming in for pictures. Very soon, I was in my first "photo op" session. From the beginning, I was fascinated with how Rex, like turning a light switch on or off, could do the same with his smile.

Since the announcement of our candidacy was completely unexpected, it created a lot of excitement. The reaction statewide was favorable.

After our joint filing with the Secretary of State, we campaigned together in the northern part of Nevada.

This was a preliminary to a big Fourth of July rally scheduled for Las Vegas. We worked well together and quickly became fast friends.

July 4, 1962, was a wickedly hot day, even for Las Vegas. There was a big crowd at our afternoon outdoor rally. Most were there to see their old friend, Rex. Many came, too, for a first-hand look at his new political "bride."

The rally went well. Rex was gracious in his introduction of me, and the crowd seemed to receive me well, considering I was a "Northern Yankee." (Yes, sectionalism in Nevada very much existed in those days and still does!)

Later in the afternoon, after the rally, Rex dropped me and George Abbott, a friend and political adviser, at the Desert Inn. Rex said that he wanted to go home to freshen up, and later we'd get together for dinner. He looked great and was very pleased with our Las Vegas "debut."

I went to my room. Shortly, the phone rang. It was a friend of Rex's who tearfully told me that Rex had suffered a massive heart attack and was dead! I felt as though someone had kicked me in the pit of my stomach. My new friend was gone, taken in the prime of his life.

The next several hours were chaos. The press was everywhere. The switchboard was flooded with calls. I managed to call home to tell my family the terrible news.

I learned that night — first-hand — how quickly things and people change after the death of a political leader. Within hours, Rex seemed like a distant memory, and the entire focus was on a potential replacement.

Naturally, the press focused on me. So did many Republican political activists. This was a terrible period for me. As an obscure lawyer from Carson City, I wasn't accustomed to this kind of attention.

We decided to call a meeting in Las Vegas to try to develop a strategy. Republican leaders came from all over the state.

From the time of Rex's death, I focused on whether running for Governor made any sense for me. The more I thought about it, the less sense it made. Between my family obligations and my law practice, it simply wasn't timely for me to run for Governor, and I knew that if I didn't make the announcement at the beginning of the meeting, things might get out of hand.

When I announced my decision, the reaction, surprising to me, was one of shock and amazement. Being political animals, they couldn't understand how I could turn down an assured nomination for Governor, with a good shot at being elected.

But they sensed that my mind was made up, and trying to change it would be a waste of time. They were right.

The meeting resulted in a consensus being developed whereby the party would remain neutral in the primary process. Eventually, Mayor Oran Gragson of Las Vegas defeated Hank Greenspun, the fiery publisher of the Las Vegas Sun, in a spirited primary, but was thereafter defeated by the incumbent, Grant Sawyer, in the general election.

THE CAMPAIGN FOR LIEUTENANT GOVERNOR

The campaign for Lieutenant Governor was for me both exciting and fulfilling.

With Rex's passing, the Laxalt forces were on their own — without money, without experienced media people or campaign professionals. Even so, everything was refreshingly straightforward.

Rex, as I've noted, was to help raise my campaign money. Without him and without a fund-raising pro, I decided to go to the bank and borrow $25,000 for "seed money." My friendly banker in Carson City, Bob Butler, gave me an incredulous look when I told him why I needed the money. He was more accustomed to lending people money for cars and houses.

PAUL LAXALT

AT HOME WITH HIS FAMILY IN CARSON CITY
L. to R.: Kevin, Gail, Paul, John, Jackie, Michelle, Sheila, Kathleen.

REPUBLICAN FOR

LIEUTENANT GOVERNOR

My family at the time of the Lieutenant Governor's race in 1962 (L. to R.) Kevin, Gail, PL, John, Jackie, Michelle, Sheila and Kathleen. *Photo by Doc Kaminski*

That seed money launched us. Before the campaign was over, we were able to repay the original loan. The total campaign cost was about $50,000. This was 1962. Now, to run for Governor or U.S. Senator in Nevada costs several million dollars.

We were able to do what we did because we weren't deluged with costs for expensive campaign people, and our media campaign was very modest.

Volunteers — friends and family — pitched in without charge to do what's necessary in any political campaign.

Nowadays, regretfully, volunteers are few and far between in most campaigns. Almost everyone is paid, many of them very highly.

From the beginning, we decided we would wage a grassroots, shoe-leather campaign. Lots of coffee klatches, barbecues, lunches and dinners. All of it hard work, but effective.

We started the campaign in what was then known as the "Cow Counties."

Reno and Las Vegas were our only two urban areas. Working "the Cows" was easy for me. As the son of a Basque sheepherder, I had an easy entree into the fifteen agricultural counties in the state. We traveled by car and within several days had them covered.

The strategy was a simple one. Reno, where I was fairly well known, would offset Las Vegas, where I wasn't known at all. The election would then be settled eventually in "the Cows." The attention I paid to the folks in "the Cows" made them feel wanted and appreciated, and they were.

As the campaign developed, it was apparent that Paul Laxalt couldn't be elected dog-catcher without strong support from "the Cows." They supported me strongly in that first race and continued to do so throughout my political career.

We continued the same person-to-person approach in the Reno area, where I felt comfortable, too. Within several days, my name, though far from being a "household word," was far better known than before. As a result of the extensive media exposure from Rex's death and my subsequent decision not to run for Governor, I became known in media circles. This resulted in quite a bit of favorable news coverage.

Heartened by the positive response in the North, we flew to Las Vegas. In those days, flying from Reno to Las Vegas was a challenge. The plane was an old DC-3, a two-engine prop plane with an unpressurized cabin. When the plane tossed around in the Nevada winds, it was an adventure. The plane's detractors called it the "Vomit Comet."

After some three hours of tossing around, we finally landed in Las Vegas. On this occasion, no one in our party of six had become ill. After that flight, surrounded by dozens of "sick" passengers, we figured that campaigning in that foreign and intimidating place called Las Vegas might not be so bad in comparison.

Aside from my sister Sue, a Holy Family nun – in Las Vegas of all places – and a few attorney friends, I knew no one in town. Having only been there a couple of times before, I knew little about it. My brother John, a former Democratic county chairman in law practice at Lake Tahoe, volunteered to move to Las Vegas for the campaign.

In Sue and John, I had two stalwarts who "moved political mountains" in the months to come. Within a few weeks, as a result of their efforts, we developed a top-flight organization in nearly every precinct. With hundreds of supporters walking the streets, spreading the word and distributing my literature, the campaign ended up doing very well in Clark County, eventually losing in that Democrat stronghold by only a few thousand votes.

Media Campaign

After working for weeks in Las Vegas, I realized that I was facing a situation of "too many voters and too little time."

The answer was clear. I had to turn to media advertising – radio and television – to get my message out. We went to the three television stations in Las Vegas, Channels 3, 8 and 13.

Amazingly, we found that $50 could buy us 30 minutes on television in morning time.

So, for days on end, I sat on a stool telling the good people of Clark County who I was, family pictures and all. That was easy enough, but convincing them that the Lieutenant Governor's position was important to them and that I was the man to do the job was the real challenge.

This was all done live; no teleprompter; just cue cards which Brother John patiently held by the side of the camera.

We learned from this experience the power of television. Within days, I was being greeted warmly by strangers on the street.

By the time of the election, I was known as a guy from the North with a nice wife and six kids, who, by the way, wanted to be Lieutenant Governor, whatever that was.

We had some of the first political television spots in Nevada history – and homemade, too. We had fun coming up with ideas to fashion creative spots that were intended to do one thing: establish name identification for me. They were produced in the basement of Gordon Kent, a local television personality.

To give you a flavor, one depicted a small boy eyeing a cookie jar, then opening the lid. He cautiously extricated a big cookie with the name "Laxalt – Lt. Governor" on it. It was such a hit that we did others.

One showed a shapely Las Vegas showgirl putting a golf ball into the hole. She reached into the cup, pulled out the ball and yes, you guessed it, our political ad was on the ball.

One day, while walking through the Las Vegas airport, I saw a crowd around a shoeshine stand where a young black man was putting on a show by snapping the shoe rag to accompanying music. I talked to him and asked if he'd be willing to do a commercial showing my political logo on his rag. He agreed, and we brought Gordon and his camera in to film the spot.

It went beautifully. When it was finished, one of his buddies proclaimed, "A star is born!" The ad was hugely popular. Imagine trying to do this ad now in our period of political correctness. I can see all the militants in Vegas raising hell because we were "exploiting" the young man.

The campaign wasn't all glitz, of course. My friends and new-found supporters covered the state, distributing literature and spreading the word. We even had a busload of women travel from Northern Nevada to the South, campaigning as they went. They called themselves "Ladies for Laxalt" and proudly wore red berets. Years afterward, they still recall their experiences, particularly in the red-light districts of the various small towns.

So, with a balance of advertising and grassroots campaigning, we put together one hell of an effort.

My opponent was a former U.S. Senator and Representative from Las Vegas named Berkeley Bunker. He was respected, well known and a Mormon Bishop. The latter fact was a big asset in an area with a large Mormon vote.

Since we saw little activity from Berkeley on the campaign front, we concluded that his people, seasoned professionals, didn't take the candidacy of that-unknown-upstart-from-Carson City seriously. Thus, they slept through the campaign.

Election night, which became a ritual, was at Momma Laxalt's house in Carson City. It was overrun with family, supporters, and television sets. Since all of us were amateurs, the evening was spine-tingling. Returns started coming in around 8 p.m. Because the northern precincts came in first, we started with a healthy lead. Our initial excitement was tempered by the knowledge that when Las Vegas came in, we could get clobbered, and my early lead could be wiped out.

Wayne Pearson, my pollster and political associate, was the center of attention. He had sheets of papers before him. As each new report came in, he would analyze it and report to us what it meant.

As the evening went on, the tension mounted.

Finally, around 10 p.m., the Las Vegas returns started to trickle in. Then they poured in. Wayne worked feverishly to analyze the results. Finally, his customary worried look changed to a wide grin.

"We won," he proclaimed. Everyone cheered. Although we'd lost in Vegas, it was only by a few thousand votes, and our huge lead in the North held.

Berkeley called and conceded. He was a gentleman through and through. In later years, he consulted me often. He never admitted it, but some of his friends later told us that he may have even voted for me once or twice in other elections.

It was a particularly memorable victory because I was the only Republican elected statewide that year.

The Job

After the election, there really wasn't much of a transition for me since the position of Lieutenant Governor in Nevada is a part-time responsibility.

As President of the Senate, I would vote in the rare event of a tie. (I don't recall ever casting such a vote during my four-year term.)

Since my law office was only a few yards from the Capitol, where the Legislature met, it was easy for me to continue practicing law and preside over the Senate.

Governor Sawyer, although we had been friends before, was cordial but aloof. He sensed correctly that politically I was now the leader of the Republican Party, which in turn made me leader of the "loyal opposition." I don't recall his ever consulting me on any major policy decision. Our official relationship was much like the John Kennedy-Lyndon Johnson "shot-gun wedding" relationship nationally.

As the leader of the state GOP, I met frequently with the Republican legislators in an effort to present a united front on important issues. And, I became heavily involved in party affairs. For too long, Nevada had been a one-party state, and it was time to correct that.

Much of my time was spent prospecting for candidates to run in the future. The strength of any party, I believe, is directly related to its officeholders. In that area, we Republicans were woefully short.

Party-building also meant registration drives. Having just run in a statewide race where the registration was 2-to-1 against me, I had a personal interest in registering more Republicans. These efforts, I'm sure, contributed to the Nevada Republican Party's successes in future elections, including 1966, when I was elected Governor.

All this is not to suggest, however, that I was overly partisan in my approach.

During my term as Lieutenant Governor, I came to know and respect several Democrat leaders such as Senator Mahlon Brown of Las Vegas, the majority leader; Senator Floyd Lamb, from Lincoln County and the powerful Finance Committee chairman; and Warren "Snowy" Monroe of Elko, a journalist by trade, who was as partisan as they come, but fair-minded when it came to issues that weren't political in nature.

Later, when I became Governor, they were all invaluable in tackling such tough issues as corporate licensing in gaming, education, protecting Lake Tahoe and improving our relations with the FBI.

My role as leader of the loyal opposition proved to be an interesting one in many ways. Anyone with a beef against the Governor or the state seemed to find their way to my door. Although most, I learned, were merely venting, some had genuine complaints.

For example, I had to come to grips with the concerns being raised about how our state prison was being run. Security was so lax that inmates were routinely escaping. Meaningful educational programs did not exist at the prison. Also, historically, the job of warden had gone to political appointees, who were well-intentioned but woefully lacking in terms of having the necessary professional experience and technical background.

Many people, principally from Las Vegas, were concerned about the state's policy of more-or-less declaring war on the FBI, with the attendant barrage of negative publicity toward Nevada generally and Las Vegas in particular.

With Bobby Kennedy on the point, the "Easterners" were depicting us as the "sin state" and the center of organized crime. These citizens felt we had to mend our relations with FBI Director J. Edgar Hoover, who was alienated from Nevada and felt that we had "gone to bed with the bad guys."

I often heard, too, that we should change our gaming license structure so that corporations such as Hilton, Hyatt and Del Webb could qualify to come into Nevada. The "establishment" was opposed, not wanting to change a good thing. As a result, there was a good deal of talk about change, but no action.

Many educators came to me to say that our educational system badly needed strengthening. Too many of our high school graduates either couldn't qualify for or afford a university education.

Ranchers and miners complained bitterly about arbitrary regulation by the Bureau of Land Management and other federal agencies.

They wanted less federal intrusion and a stronger state voice in their behalf. These rumblings were the beginning of the "Sagebrush Rebellion" that broke wide open in the 1970s.

Environmentalists told me there was far too much development at Tahoe and that unless something was done, the lake might lose its clarity. They wanted a moratorium on development at Tahoe. Ironically, some of them had recently moved to Tahoe where they built large homes. "Now that they are safely in place, they want to lock everyone else out," one of the cynics said.

Also, a group from the highway department had gone to the local paper, The Nevada Appeal, and told the young editor, Ed

Allison (later my gubernatorial press secretary), that the procurement practices of the department were, if not fraudulent, extremely sloppy, thus costing the taxpayers millions of dollars. The paper ran a series devoted to the controversy, but Governor Sawyer and his people turned a deaf ear, feeling this was politically inspired.

In this instance, at the request of these concerned citizens, I decided to enter the fray. This resulted in my calling for a state grand jury to investigate the charges. Governor Sawyer didn't think this was a good idea, particularly coming from me.

As Lieutenant Governor, I had no authority to call the grand jury. Only the Governor did. But if the Governor left the state, the Lieutenant Governor became acting Governor. So I put the Governor on notice that if he left the state, I'd call the state grand jury.

For weeks, we had a standoff. Grant wouldn't leave. I couldn't call for a grand jury. All the while, the people observed with interest.

Finally, Grant, who loved to travel (one wag dubbed him "Gallivantin' Grant"), left the state. Within minutes, I called for the state grand jury. All hell broke lose.

The matter quickly went to court. The issue, of course, was whether, as acting Governor, I had the authority to call the grand jury.

Finally, the Supreme Court of Nevada, in one of the most convoluted decisions in its history, decided that I had no authority to do what I did as acting Governor.

Thereafter, some procurement reforms were put in place, and "The Great Highway Department Controversy" died.

I write the foregoing to point out that my four years as Lieutenant Governor were an invaluable learning experience. I got to know the players, learned the system, and became conversant with problems that, as a lawyer in Carson City, I hardly knew existed.

CHAPTER 7

❖ *A U.S. Senator — Almost* ❖

LAST-MINUTE ENTRY

Politics is an unpredictable business. When I was elected Lieutenant Governor, I assumed I would serve four uninterrupted, peaceful years, then run for reelection or return to private life.

Little did I realize that half-way through my term I would be in a tough race for the United States Senate. In my role as party leader, it was my job to make sure that Senator Howard Cannon, who was up for reelection in 1964, had strong opposition.

Early in the election year, I thought that we had an excellent candidate — Bill Raggio, an outstanding young District Attorney in Washoe County (Reno). First elected in 1958, Bill had a well-earned law-and-order reputation. He was involved in some highly-publicized run-ins with the notorious brothel operator, Joe Conforte. Eventually, he succeeded in putting Conforte in prison for extortion, and he took the further step of having Conforte's whorehouse burnt to the ground, declaring that it was a "public nuisance."

The U.S. Senate race looked like a natural for Bill.

Senator Cannon had been embroiled in a good deal of controversy in Washington. His name was frequently linked to Bobby Baker, the Lyndon Johnson crony who served as Secretary of the Senate until 1963, when he was convicted of using his office for personal gain.

When approached, Bill appeared interested, but he was also cautious. He would not commit to a public declaration of candidacy, much less a filing for office. As the weeks passed, we became increasingly nervous.

To beat an incumbent was tough enough, but to beat him with a last-minute candidacy was foolhardy. The filing deadline of July 15 was fast approaching. Finally, in late June, Bill decided that he wasn't going to run after all.

Here we were, approaching a Presidential campaign with our political hero, Arizona Senator Barry Goldwater, at the head of the ticket, and we had no credible candidate for the U.S. Senate in Nevada. All political eyes suddenly seemed to be directed at me.

Out of a sense of party loyalty – misguided or not – I decided to run.

So, on July 3, 1964, with the deadline for filing only days away, I announced to a rather surprised state (and I'm sure an even more surprised Senator Cannon), that I was a candidate for the U.S. Senate. I filed officially three days later.

Within the next several days, we had organized ourselves fairly well. Money would be a problem, but the Republican Senatorial Campaign Committee in Washington, headed by a friend, Senator John Tower of Texas, surely would help.

The money started to come in surprisingly well. I wasn't naive enough to believe that the contributions were due to my excellent chance to unseat Howard Cannon; hardly anyone gave me a chance. No, the money came in primarily because the Senate race would be "a good preliminary" for the Governor's race two years out. And that was what most interested the "money boys," particularly the gamblers.

Rather than using local resources for our media production, we went to Los Angeles. Instead of the warm pastel colors we used in the Lieutenant Governor's race, we signed off on a stark, black-and-white theme.

It was good media, but lacked the warmth we needed.

It had a funereal feeling, which turned out to be prophetic.

All in all, it was a good campaign. Its effectiveness was best measured by the fact that in the closing days, President Lyndon Johnson came into the state with Air Force One and all the trappings and told the people of Nevada that he couldn't possibly run the country without Howard Cannon in the U.S. Senate.

I don't know how many people he convinced, but what was reassuring from our standpoint was the fact that Washington must have been regarding the Laxalt/Cannon campaign as a real horse race. Otherwise, the President wouldn't have come.

The day after the Johnson visit, I had a call from former Vice President Dick Nixon, who was in New York. His opening line was, "I see where that big Texan came and kicked your ass real hard. Can I help?"

We quickly arranged a rally in Las Vegas where Nixon proceeded with great relish to "kick butt" himself. The attendant publicity was positive, and we all felt better having such an illustrious person going to bat for us.

It was thoughtful gestures like this that helped Nixon when he ran for President later. Not to help him would have been a case of ingratitude.

The 1964 Senate race went down to the wire.

Just before the election, we received word that Barry Goldwater, nearing the end of a grueling presidential campaign, wanted to drop by Las Vegas. My campaign people didn't want any part of a Goldwater visit. He was "toast" politically, and candidates across the country were ducking him. I couldn't. He was a good friend.

He appeared in Vegas the Friday before the election and, of course, opposition papers played the event to the hilt, featuring huge pictures of Barry and me. There was a great deal of post-election speculation that the Goldwater visit did us in. I'm not sure. In any case, I felt good not having ducked Barry.

Election Night

Election night, November 3, 1964, was at Momma Laxalt's again. Everyone had high hopes, even after Goldwater was counted out.

Greeting presidential candidate Barry Goldwater at the Las Vegas airport on the eve of my 1964 Senate race against Senator Howard Cannon. Some of my advisors wanted me to "duck" Barry, who was about to lose in a landslide. I didn't and ended up losing a highly controversial race by less than 50 votes.
Special Collections, University of Nevada, Reno Library

The voting was roughly in the same pattern as our Lieutenant Governor's race. I ran very well in the "Cow counties" and Reno. The unanswered question, again, was how badly we'd be beaten in Las Vegas. As the returns came in, Wayne Pearson, still our guru, brightened. We were doing better down south than expected.

Then in the wee hours, the unexpected announcement came on television. We had won! Everyone was near delirious. When the news came, I went to the bathroom and proceeded to heave my guts out. I had never come to grips with the fact that we might win!

Now, I was faced with the cold reality of leaving my beloved home in Carson City, and moving my wife and six young kids to a foreign country — Washington, D.C.

The day after the election, I traveled to Las Vegas for what was supposed to be a victory rally. During the three-hour trip, unbeknown to me, there had been an amazing development. A few paper ballot precincts in Las Vegas had not been counted the night before. That morning, they had been. As a result, when I deplaned in Las Vegas, instead of being a proud winner, I was now a loser by some 48 votes. As you can imagine, all hell broke lose. My people and some of the media were furious. There were cries of fraud.

What followed was probably the wildest post-election period in Nevada history. There was a recount, a Supreme Court proceeding. The County Clerk, who was in charge of the election in Las Vegas, suddenly felt an urge to leave town.

We toyed with the idea of appealing to the Rules Committee of the U.S. Senate, but decided that, with Democrat control of the Senate and Lyndon Johnson as President, it would be a wasted effort. In addition, none other than Howard Cannon was a member of the Rules Committee! Talk about a stacked deck!

After the recount, I was still 84 votes short. That hurt. We suspected the worst, but weren't able to prove it clearly. It became the subject of barroom debates for years. One consolation was the fact that at least I didn't have to move my family to that dreaded Washington.

RUN FOR GOVERNOR?
No sooner had the dust settled on the Senate race than the politicos speculated about the Governor's race two years off.

I was less than enthusiastic. After tough races in 1962 and 1964, I thought I had had enough of politics. Being constantly away from family and in the public eye had some unanticipated effects on the Laxalts.

We had been a close, very private family. Now, that seemed to be in jeopardy. I was tired of traveling on the "Vomit Comet," sleeping in strange hotel rooms, making speeches…all of it. Wisely, my people sensed all this and, for most of 1965, far fewer demands were made of me.

In the late summer, Wayne Pearson called the house and told me that he wanted to talk to me about a matter of great importance. As I suspected, he wanted to talk about the Governor's race.

When he raised the subject of my running, I told him, and it wasn't easy, for he was such a devoted friend, that I really was having a hard time with the thought of continuing in politics.

From his reaction, an unsympathetic stony face, I knew that I was wasting my time.

Drawing upon his extensive historical political background, he told me in no uncertain terms that I had no right to make this important decision purely on personal grounds.

My pollster and indispensable political advisor Wayne Pearson.

Painstakingly, he reviewed our past four political years, how thousands of Nevadans had worked their hearts out for me, not just to elect me Lieutenant Governor but one day to be Governor. I owed it to them, the party and yes, even my family, he contended. He concluded by forcefully pointing out that I had been given the rare opportunity, through circumstances, to occupy the highest office in the state, and I had no moral right to squander that chance.

Whew! What a load to have dropped on you on a beautiful summer day in Carson City, Nevada.

Not able to overcome his logic immediately, I did what any politician does when asked to do something he doesn't want to do: I stalled.

"What you say, Wayne, is persuasive, but you must understand that my family comes first, ahead of any responsibility to the people. Let me check with them and I'll get back to you."

"Okay", he said, "but this decision must be made quickly." He pointed out, correctly, that if I was going to beat Grant Sawyer, one of the most powerful and capable politicians in the history of Nevada, I'd have to start early — more than a year before the election, by Wayne's calculation.

Now I had a double problem. I not only didn't really want to run, but if I followed Wayne's timetable, I'd be on the campaign trail again within just a few days. Oh well, I figured, not to worry! The family won't go along anyhow. They've had enough of this "public life."

So, to the family I went to get a reading. "To go or not to go (apologies to Shakespeare), that is the question." The reaction I received confounded me. To a person, without exception, they felt I should run. They felt that as a family we had a duty to go, to pay back a little what Nevada had done for the Laxalts.

Momma, in her characteristically blunt fashion, said simply, "Paul, run. You should be Governor. It will be hard but worth it. Who would ever have thought that the son of a sheepherder could one day be Governor?"

After "sampling" my family, I told a very happy Wayne, "I don't know whether you brainwashed my family, but if it's okay with them, let's give it a shot!"

To the astonishment of every politico in the state, I announced my candidacy in late September 1965, fully 13 months before the election, the earliest announcement for any major political office in Nevada's history.

CHAPTER 8

❖ *Running for Governor* ❖

W e realized from the outset that if we were going to win the Governorship, we had to outwork and outorganize the incumbent, Grant Sawyer. Although Grant had indicated he might not run for an unprecedented third term, we assumed he would.

He liked the job and had a huge staff with a vested interest in staying on in the state house. Charlie Russell, whom Grant succeeded as Governor, really didn't want to run for a third term in 1958, but the pressure from family, supporters and staff was such that he finally ran. Sawyer, although he liked the job, wasn't sure he wanted to go for it again.

My previous runs for Lieutenant Governor and the U.S. Senate had taught me a lot about what was required to run an effective statewide campaign.

Basically, we needed many workers to "spread the word." In addition to organizing the precincts, we decided to organize businesses with 25 or more employees. Jerry Dondero, a former educator and close friend, undertook this huge task. By the time of the election, our people were covering almost every precinct and business throughout the state.

Part of the campaign plan was to have me personally visit every major business in the state. At each visit, instead of "bosses," we had workers take us through the companies. It proved to be one of the most satisfying aspects of the campaign. Some businesses were even decorated with our campaign materials, giving the visit a festive feeling.

From past campaigns, we had learned that many well-intentioned people wanted to help, but they simply didn't know what to do. So we established "schools" for workers. They were briefed on my campaign positions and told how best to approach voters at their houses. If, for example, it was apparent that our worker had knocked on the door at an inopportune time, the obvious response to the question, "Who the hell are you?" was to be, "I'm a volunteer for Grant Sawyer."

After the election, we analyzed the results. Invariably, we did better in precincts where we were organized effectively than in those where we were thin.

This confirms a basic rule of politics. To the extent that the candidate or his workers can meet voters in person, all the better. It's far more effective, when well executed, than expensive, glitzy media ads.

Unfortunately, the trend these days is away from precinct work — which is hard work — and toward the air-conditioned television studio, which is a lot easier.

DEVELOPING A MESSAGE

As to the issues we were going to stress, they were clear: corporate licensing for gaming; making peace with the FBI; establishing community colleges; protecting Lake Tahoe; reforming the state prison system; and creating a medical school. These were themes I emphasized repeatedly during the campaign.

And, we continually reminded voters that two terms were quite enough for any Governor, including Grant Sawyer, and we promised to pursue a constitutional amendment after the election which would limit Governors to two terms.

In the small counties, we reminded them that I was "one of them."

Nevada has never had an income tax, so frequent references to "no new income tax" were also made.

Media

While we were doing an effective job in communicating our message on a person-to-person basis, we needed to reinforce it through our media campaign. By media, I mean billboards, radio and television spots, yard signs and brochures.

Rather than go out of state, we decided to "go Nevada." Eventually, we settled on a small Las Vegas firm, Kelly and Reber, to do our work. They were imaginative, responsive and trustworthy.

So that our media would not go stale during such an extended campaign, we decided to change themes and designs every few weeks. This was commonly done with radio and television, but not with billboards. We would focus on education, for instance, but before long, the theme would be taxes.

We did the same with our billboards. In the summer, I wore a short-sleeve shirt without a tie. In early fall, I was seen in a coat and tie. In the final weeks, I was in a formal setting (dark suit, high backed chair). We called the latter the "Governor's shot."

With this constant change and movement, the media advertising created a sense of excitement, and thereby avoided boring the public, which can be fatal in a campaign. Las Vegas was a particular challenge. They'd seen almost everything.

The media ad campaign created so much interest that after the election, we showed it to several political groups around the country, where it was enthusiastically received.

"THE MOTHER'S MILK OF POLITICS"

If our campaign "engine" was to run, it, of course, had to have fuel. The fuel in any political campaign is money. As former House Speaker Tip O'Neill said, money is "the mother's milk of politics."

In those pre-Watergate days, there were scarcely any restraints when it came to raising money. It didn't have to be reported. Corporations were free to contribute. There was no limitation on amounts. Cash was welcome. Many of the Vegas operators preferred giving cash.

Often, they gave to both sides because they didn't want to "book a loser." There have been many times since, when I've observed the loose practices of modern "regulated" campaigns, that I've felt the old way worked better. There was a lot less hypocrisy and "loophole hunting."

Although we had a few fund-raising dinners at $1000 per head, most of the solicitations had to be done by the candidate, and I hated every moment of it.

Old friends such as Bill Harrah, Dick Graves and Harvey Gross knew how I felt, so shortly after I announced, they each delivered to me substantial contributions − in cash. This was my "seed money." Unlike the Lieutenant Governor's campaign, this time I didn't have to take out a loan to get started.

Then, as now, the bulk of the money for major races came from the gambling houses. This made sense, because gambling was the dominant industry in Nevada. As I often later pointed out throughout the country, gambling was to Nevada what the auto industry was to Michigan, if not more so.

Every major hotel was solicited. If they were licensed, they were presumably okay.

That brought me into contact for the first time with the heavies in the business. That was not the case in my past races because the majority didn't care who was the Lieutenant Governor or even U.S. Senator. Governor was another ball game. Whoever was Governor held the power of life and death over the industry, and they were very much aware of it.

Although most of them probably felt I didn't have a snowball's chance in hell of beating Sawyer, they wanted to hedge their bets. So, I was the beneficiary of several "insurance contributions." Since there was no reporting in those days, there was no way I could determine how well I did in contributions compared with Sawyer's, but if I did half as well as he did, it was alright.

Although it was hard for me, before the race was over, I met and solicited each and every one of them. That brought me into contact with such fabled characters as Harold Smith, Jr., of Harold's Club in Reno. When I sat down with him in his elegant office, I noticed that the lights kept going up and down. Finally, I asked him if there was a power problem. He said, "No, I just like my light to be at different levels. It's for my mood. I have a dimmer right here on my desk!" I was relieved to hear the news. For a while, I began to question whether the purpose of the visit was political or sexual!

Then there was Lincoln Fitzgerald, the owner of the Nevada Club in Reno, a "sawdust joint" which did very well. Fitz had attracted a lot of attention in 1949 when some assailants tried to wipe him out in a gangland-type shooting. He survived, but the incident caused most people to treat him very gingerly.

As a result, I was a bit apprehensive when I went to visit him. I expected a slick, George Raft-type character. Instead, to my delighted surprise, he met me in a small, simply furnished office dressed in what could have passed for carpenter's clothes — suspenders and all.

Instead of the stereotypical "cool Detroit cat," he was a quiet, mild-mannered person. He greeted me warmly, introduced me to his wife, who was much like him, thanked me for running and handed me an envelope containing several crisp one-hundred-dollar bills

"Working" Las Vegas was a different story in many ways. Coming from "the North" and not that well-known to them, I didn't know how I'd be received. Would I get a polite brush-off, or would they consider my candidacy a serious one?

I needn't have been concerned. They had done their home-work and concluded my candidacy was "real." Since the network on "The Strip" was a tight one, looking back, I've concluded that my reception wasn't accidental. When the word spread that the Desert Inn was openly supporting me, my stock rose overnight.

For a number of reasons, almost all related to regulatory de-cisions, the owners, "Moe" Dalitz and Allard Roen, were disap-pointed with Governor Sawyer.

One of my close friends, Paul McDermott, was in the insur-ance business with most of his policies coming from the Strip and the Desert Inn. When I declared for Governor, he arranged for me to meet Moe and Allard.

They, too, were warm, friendly and unlike their "images." Moe had operated illegally in the rum-running business in the Cleveland area and had been often described as being associated with the "Mayfield Road Gang."

When the Las Vegas Strip opened up, Dalitz's group built and later operated the elegant Desert Inn, which in the later Howard Hughes days, was to play a major role in my administration.

These allegedly "questionable characters," such as Moe, when they were allowed to operate legally in Nevada, were so grateful for the opportunity that they bent over backwards to be good Nevada citizens. In later years, I took a lot of heat for befriending and staying loyal to Moe Dalitz. If I had to do it over again, I'd do it exactly the same way. He was always straight and honorable with me and the state.

Our finance campaign was quite successful. Before it was over, we raised about $500,000, a lot for those days. As a result, we were able to fund an aggressive media campaign throughout the state and established several headquarters. And we were able to cover the costs of my travels throughout the state. Over the period of a year, gas, oil, hotel rooms and the like really added up.

When traveling by car became inefficient, we engaged Dick Canatsey, an experienced pilot and supporter, and his Beach Baron to fly me several times from one end of Nevada to the other and back. When it was over, we estimated that he and I had traveled more than 150,000 air miles during the campaign.

The costs would have been much higher had it not been for the hundreds of volunteers who put in thousands of hours, all without a nickel of compensation.

POLLSTERS

Also vital to our effort was reliable polling data. From the beginning, I relied heavily on my friend Wayne Pearson.

Rather than rely on telephone surveys and so-called "tracking" polls, he set out to duplicate actual voting conditions. That meant actually having the poll respondent cast a mock vote on an unwritten ballot.

Since those early days in Nevada, I've observed pollsters on the national level use their sophisticated methods in an attempt to detect voter trends. Some proved to be fairly accurate. Others were "off the wall." In recent years, methods have improved to the point where most major contests are predictable on election day. But, in my experience, none was more reliable than Wayne's.

At the outset of the Governor's campaign in 1965, he found that we were within five points of Governor Sawyer.

To my amazement, the results remained fairly constant throughout the year-long campaign. During the "FBI phase" of the campaign, when I defended Hoover and stated that we had to mend fences with the FBI if we were going to regulate gambling properly, we suffered a dip in Las Vegas, but as the voters reflected on the issue, we stabilized.

By election time, my position on the FBI may in fact have turned out to be a slight "plus."

High Noon With the John Birchers

At first, as we approached the Republican State Convention at the end of April 1966, we thought it would be smooth sailing. A consensus had developed on a statewide slate of Republican candidates, and the party was in agreement on a platform. The platform included a call for a review of state taxes, including gaming taxes, and financing additional support for education, while resisting undue federal intervention in Nevada affairs.

We decided also that we should be more responsive to minorities by achieving the goals of fair employment and educational opportunity.

Other planks called for repeal of the "early parole" law, and expansion of the state park system, including one at Lake Tahoe.

There were no highly-charged proposals dealing with abortion or gun control issues, which created a great deal of controversy among Republicans in later years. As we neared the opening of the convention in Las Vegas, however, storm clouds gathered.

During my Lieutenant Governor's campaign, I was asked regularly what my position was relative to the John Birch Society, an organization formed in 1958, supposedly as an educational tool to inform Americans as to the threat of communism to the American political system.

Gradually, the John Birch Society became more and more identified with the Republican Party. Having read much of their material, I concluded early on that the Society was extreme in its views with respect to unions and minorities, among other things. They were obsessed with conspiracy theories. In their view, many leaders of the minorities and the unions were simply tools of Moscow. When they took the position that President Eisenhower had been co-opted by the Communists, that was simply too much for most Republicans.

So, as the Gubernatorial campaign progressed, I was able to deflect the Birch issue by simply stating that I was not a member and did not agree with their extremist approach to politics.

That seemed to satisfy the press and the Democrats.

What made it awkward for me was that several of my strong Republican backers — all conservatives — also were John Birch Society supporters. Bill Wright, a prominent Elko County rancher and our candidate for the U.S. Senate in 1962, was, if not a member, sympathetic to the Society and its aims. Dr. John DeTar, a respected doctor in Reno, was its Nevada leader. He was a good friend. Jim Slattery, the colorful State Senator from Virginia City, was in the same category.

They all cautioned me, at one time or another, to be careful about denouncing the John Birch Society. Their message was that the Birchers all were "good Americans" and "loyal Republicans" who wouldn't hurt me or the party.

But as convention time approached, I was hearing a different story. Some of my key supporters were hearing troubling reports from around the state that the Birchers were considering trying to get some of their positions incorporated into our Republican platform. As far as I was concerned, we could not allow that to happen. That sort of activity had given Barry Goldwater fits during his 1964 presidential campaign.

I wasn't sure what to do. We could simply sit back and take our chances that the Birchers' actions would not be disruptive, or we could repudiate the Society and its goals without singling out its members.

Then came "the last straw." My brother Mick had previously joined the Board of Directors of The League of Women Voters. Several days before the convention, he was publicly chastised by the Birchers for doing so. That did it! If these people would attack my own brother in the midst of a Governor's race, they were capable of anything, and could do untold damage to the party and my candidacy.

Rather than wait, we decided to act. Almost all the party leaders agreed with me that a resolution denouncing the Society was necessary. I agreed to lead the charge. When word leaked out about this, the convention became a one-issue affair.

Opponents of the resolution, and there were many, contended we were too drastic. Assemblywoman Mary Frazzini of Reno, a good friend, said that anyone who will vote Republican should be allowed in the party. State Senator Slattery raised hell and said that he would oppose our efforts. Jim said, "If you are going to run people out of the party, why don't we start with a few left wingers and ADAers (members of the liberal Americans for Democratic Action)."

The fight wasn't easy. An original version of our resolution, which called for expelling the Birchers from the party, was modified to urge them to leave the party if they found themselves in a conflict. Even then, the resolution was approved in committee by only 20-17.

The floor fight was much easier. The committee loss took the steam out of the opposition. The resolution was overwhelmingly adopted on the floor.

To the Birch leaders' credit, they never held the convention action against me personally. They seemed to recognize that I had to act in the party's interest.

Afterwards, I did receive some critical letters to the effect that I had become a dupe of some Communist conspiracy.

Looking back, I don't know if what was done benefited me politically. Union and minority support for my candidacy was negligible. But there was one plus: I was never dogged thereafter by John Birch questions.

Down to the wire

As the election approached, Wayne Pearson's poll numbers indicated I had taken a comfortable lead. But to guarantee the result, as we had painfully learned in the 1964 Senate race, we had to have complete ballot security. Further, our organization had the responsibility of finding our voters to make darned sure that they voted.

On election day, I felt quite good about the fact that we had done all possible to maximize our chances for victory. The whole state — north to south, east to west — had been visited. We had thoroughly worked Reno and Las Vegas, but just as thoroughly, we had worked the small counties several times.

Our ballot security program, which was intended to avoid a repeat of 1964, would cover the state like a blanket. And, our organization was poised to do its work on Election Day to get out the vote.

Our closing rallies, replete with fireworks, had been exciting and drawn large crowds. The reception I received during the many closing parades was warm and enthusiastic.

During a Labor Day parade in Elko, all the candidates were present. The reaction to the office seekers from the onlookers was viewed as a barometer of voter support. We were heartened by the conclusion of a grizzled old miner who patiently watched the whole parade and then proclaimed to those present: "I don't know who's going to win the election, but Laxalt sure as hell won the parade!"

We had a memorable closing lunch in Las Vegas in the Stardust Hotel ballroom for 2000 women. It was the weekend before the election.

My message to them was plain: "You have husbands who are eligible to vote. Do what you have to do to make sure they vote for Paul Laxalt on Tuesday." They roared their approval. I have a hunch they exercised maximum leverage on their spouses!

I left the luncheon in high spirits. With this kind of turnout, it was a good sign that I wouldn't be clobbered in Las Vegas.

During the closing days, there were high school mock elections throughout the state. I did well, and the reported results helped. In any election, there is always a certain number of voters who don't make up their minds until the last moment. Their principal motivation is to vote for a winner. If a high school election might be persuasive, so be it!

ELECTION DAY — NOVEMBER 8, 1966

All these pre-election omens weren't nearly as significant as the exit polls on election day. For Wayne Pearson, this was part gut, part science. It involved interviewing voters after they'd voted. Discarded sample ballots were retrieved and worked into the mix.

In mid-afternoon on election day, Wayne came to our house. For one who was always cautiously pessimistic, and whom we referred to lovingly as "The Embalmer," Wayne was unusually upbeat. His latest exit poll indicated that I had a healthy lead in the sixteen northern counties and was doing surprisingly well in the seventeenth county, Clark County (Las Vegas), which had 73 percent Democrat registration.

One cloud over the Vegas scene, though, was the fact that the results were sparse from the west side, where most of the blacks in Las Vegas lived. This is an area in which I had been pounded in the Senate race. We thought that we might not have reliable data in this area until the actual ballots were counted.

That evening we gathered together, as we had before, at Momma Laxalt's house. Early in the evening, it was jammed with family, friends, and supporters. Wilson McGowan, the Republican candidate for State Controller, called me to say he wouldn't be coming. He said, "I think you're going to win, but I won't. I don't want to be a wet blanket." After some gentle urging, he did come.

The atmosphere in the house was electric.

None of us had been directly involved in a Governor's race before. For me, this was "the big leagues." Television sets were everywhere. And, as always, Wayne had set up his command center in the living room.

Returns started coming in around 8 p.m. Our poll watchers were calling in from all over the state. Wayne was far ahead of the television reports. As expected, the early returns established an early lead for me. That early bit of good news was tempered by the prospect of that huge Las Vegas vote coming in later.

Finally, the dam broke. One of our poll watchers in Henderson, which is just south of Las Vegas, reported in his precinct Wilson McGowan had won comfortably! That did it! If Wilson, with his meager campaign resources, could run well in southern Nevada, I was in great shape.

Then, like a tidal wave, the Las Vegas results poured in. By 10 p.m., Wayne announced, "Although we've lost Las Vegas by a few thousand votes, we have more than enough votes in the north to win comfortably!"

Bedlam ensued!

What had been a fond hope now was a reality.

Not only had I won, but in addition to Wilson, our Lieutenant Governor candidate, Ed Fike, had also won.

Mom, usually quiet and reserved, glowed when accepting everyone's congratulations.

Pop, as usual, ducked. He slipped off to his upstairs bedroom and didn't reappear until the next day. Small wonder. Gentle as he was, he didn't care at all for lawyers and politicians. Yet, even though he never mentioned it later, nor would I ask him, I like to believe that on that historic evening for the Laxalt family, he rose above his prejudices and was a bit proud of his eldest son, even if he hadn't become a sheepherder!

After greeting and thanking hundreds of supporters at a restaurant, Pagni's, in Washoe Valley, my son John and I flew to Las Vegas to meet our people there.

Landing at McCarran Airport, we drove to our headquarters near the Las Vegas Strip. Never in my life have I experienced such a reception!

All the pent-up effects of months of hard campaign work, combined with the strain of awaiting the results on election night, added to a healthy flow of spirits and the realization that we had finally won and pulled off a great upset in Las Vegas, created a sort of human equivalent of a volcanic eruption. John and I were absolutely man-handled. One overzealous female supporter even bit me on the arm — a vivid reminder of the intensity of the evening.

After surviving this, we made the rounds of the television stations. The level of respect was noticeably higher. That was most welcome, because during the next four years, they would be an important part of my public life.

Afterward, into the late hours of the night, John and I reminisced with our Las Vegas friends about the campaign and election.

We agreed that for me to run as well as this was due to the help of many people, most of whom had never been involved in a political campaign before. It was a case of genuine citizen involvement in the political process.

Early the next morning, John and I flew home. Only fourteen, John understandably slept all the way. I was dog-tired, but the adrenaline from our sweet victory regenerated me.

Wayne Pearson had been absolutely right about starting early. We were able to achieve early momentum and never lost it. Unlike many campaigns, we had avoided internal problems. Of course there were differences of opinion, but they never ruptured working relationships.

That was due to the fact that the team was "family." They were highly motivated and not in the campaign for a "fast buck" or personal gain.

Jackie and the children had been thoroughbreds.

They did whatever was asked of them, which included a lot of travel, strange hotels, public attention, interviews, handling the criticism of me – and endless parades. While they would have preferred to be at home in Carson City, they never complained. Long before "family values" became the vogue, the fact that our family was close and attractive was a huge campaign "plus."

My siblings were equally helpful. Brother Mick managed our law office during my year's absence. After the election, I happily concluded that the "shop" was stronger than when I'd left it.

Brother John suspended his law practice and based in Las Vegas where he'd performed so well in the Lieutenant Governor and Senate races. Over the years, he'd built a legion of close friends who were the core of our support there.

As before, Sister Sue was our secret weapon. People were fascinated by the fact that a Roman Catholic nun would be openly campaigning for her brother. Nuns just weren't supposed to do that! One of her principal projects was recruiting the Catholic priests in the area.

With Father Caesar Caviglia (left), Bishop Joseph Green at the 1968 Basque festival in Elko, Nevada. "Father C" was of great help to me throughout my political career.

Catholics and priests historically have tended to be Democrats. Jack Kennedy's candidacy for President reinforced that political fact. Alas, in my various campaigns, I never enjoyed the support of the Catholic clergy in Nevada. There were shining exceptions, of course, such as Father Caesar Caviglia, who had been an assistant in Carson City. As a result, he became "family" and remains so to this day. "Father C" was of enormous help.

And brother Robert, the writer, weighed in heavily on press matters. His classic book about our father, *Sweet Promised Land*, played an integral part in the success of our campaign.

My extended family went all out, too. Wayne Pearson, of course, was the "constant" – indispensable.

Jerry Dondero, a boyhood chum from Carson City, helped greatly on the organizational front. His steady, kindly style drew people to him. An educator, he was one of the prime movers behind our pledge to make Nevada a "Lighthouse for Education."

Alan Abner was my constant companion during the campaign. A decorated Army pilot in World War II, he was a television star in Reno conducting, among other things, "Meet-the-Press"-type public affairs programs. He gave our effort a great deal of credibility, particularly among the electronic press. In many ways, he was a psychologist for me. He presented an upbeat perspective of the "big picture," something sorely needed in tough campaigns.

"Big George" Abbott was a Gardnerville, Nevada, lawyer who came there with his beautiful Basque wife, Mary, a native of that area. They had met in Washington while Mary staffed for Senator McCarran and George had a senior position in the Department of the Interior under Secretary Fred Seaton, an Eisenhower appointee.

George, all 6'4" of him with the rich voice of an opera singer, was an astounding speaker who was one of the few designated speakers for President Eisenhower in his 1956 re-election campaign. He brought to the campaign a Washington perspective that was invaluable. He often spoke for me in the state, traveling everywhere. If there was ever a policy decision to be made, I made sure to vet it with George.

The Washoe County (Reno) campaign was skillfully run by Barbara Vucanovich and Hazel Gardella. Barbara later became the first Congresswoman from Nevada, retiring with distinction in 1996 after serving seven terms.

Hazel, who died while this book was being written and who will be greatly missed, was as steady as the Rock of Gibraltar. She related to men and women alike. She had been in party work for years, I never had to worry about organizational matters in Washoe County. Like in the "All State" commercials, I was "in good hands" with Barbie and Hazel.

My Carson High schoolmate, Bill Plummer, was the campaign treasurer. In addition to keeping the books, he watched our cash position carefully, saying "No" frequently to campaign requests. Due to Bill's good work, we ended up with all of our bills paid — a rarity in campaigns these days.

CHAPTER 9

❖ *Getting Ready to Govern* ❖

STAFFING

It didn't take long before the election glow dimmed, and I became immersed in making the many decisions associated with establishing a new administration.

Staffing wasn't difficult, mainly because the slots to be filled were few. Nevada in those days was very conservative in fiscal matters. Under a tight-fisted Finance Chairman, Senator Floyd Lamb, state agencies, including the Governor's office, had "barebones" budgets.

Bob Robertson of Carson City, former executive director of the Nevada Homebuilders Association, agreed to be my Chief of Staff. He had been very effective during the campaign.

Ed Allison, a Carsonite and a long-time friend, who had also been the editor of the local Carson City paper, The Nevada Appeal, became press secretary.

Bill Sinnott, the "old pro" and a former FBI official, became my special assistant in charge of protecting my "gaming flanks."

Carol Wilson, my longtime secretary, came over from the law firm to be my personal secretary, an important post. She was in charge of scheduling appointments and oversaw the various secretaries and clerks in the office.

Howard "Gene" Barrett, who had served with Governor

Sawyer, was kept as Budget Director. Some of my more partisan friends demanded Gene's "head," but the more I worked with him on the budget, the more I became convinced that he was an accomplished professional and basically apolitical. So I "bit the bullet" and selected him. Later, even his severest critics grudgingly admitted that he had been a good choice.

By far, the most challenging and controversial appointments were to the two gaming regulatory bodies — the Gaming Control Board and the Gaming Commission. The Board, consisting of three members, did the staff work. They conducted investigations of new gaming license applicants and monitored licensees for violations, such as cheating.

Obviously, this was a very important group. If they screwed up, there would be hell to pay for the Governor.

For the Board appointments, I decided to select three tough, street-smart individuals, who were completely loyal and who would give both the state and the licensees a fair shake. I chose Alan Abner to be Chairman, and I picked Wayne Pearson and Las Vegan Keith Campbell to be the other members.

The announcement resulted in criticism from some detractors who said I was rewarding "political cronies," particularly Abner and Pearson. But Alan's and Wayne's reputations were so solid that the storm quickly passed.

Frank Johnson, who served previously as the Public Information Officer for the Gaming Control Board, eventually became Chairman after Alan Abner stepped down, and in the fall of 1969, John Stratton of Carson City replaced Wayne Pearson.

For the Gaming Commission Chairman, I appointed George Dickerson, an old friend who was a former Clark County (Las Vegas) District Attorney. The son of former Governor Denver Dickerson and the brother of then-Attorney General Harvey Dickerson, George was a respected Democrat who had often declined serious efforts to get him to run for high political office. His wife, Dorie, had "crossed the line" to support me and had even chaired the fantastic "Stardust event" during the closing days of the campaign.

As I expected, George's appointment was well received throughout the state.

My other appointments to the Gaming Commission were Dr. Sam Davis, an optometrist from Las Vegas, George Von Tobel, a former state legislator whose father was one of the original land purchasers in Las Vegas, and Henry Berrum, a former legislator from Douglas County. Norman Brown, a rancher from Smith Valley who was originally appointed to the Commission in 1959, served as well. In the fall of 1968, I appointed a good friend, Jack Diehl of Fallon when George Dickerson decided to step down as Chairman. I later appointed to the Commission both Jim Robertson, former Mayor of Carson City, and Ken Turner of Las Vegas.

Also in the cabinet was Jerry Dondero, as Director of the Employment Security Commission. In 1968, Jerry became my Chief of Staff after Bob Robertson went to Vice President Spiro Agnew's staff.

In addition, Clark Russell became Director of the Department of Economic Development. Clark put together an aggressive business recruitment program, which proved to be successful in broadening Nevada's economic base so that we would not be as dependent on gaming as we had been.

Luther Mack, later one of the first McDonald's licensees, came into our administration as a special assistant to the Governor for labor/race relations. Over the years, he has continued to be very successful in business, and Luther has recently served with distinction on the Nevada Athletic Commission.

J. EDGAR HOOVER MEETING
During my Lieutenant Governor days, I became greatly concerned

with the fact that Nevada was constantly and publicly fighting the FBI. The situation was disquieting. How, I asked myself, could we properly keep track of the questionable figures "grandfathered" into Nevada gambling without the resources of the FBI to help us?

Over the years, Robert Kennedy had carped about the hoodlum influence in Las Vegas. His war with Jimmy Hoffa, whose Teamsters Union was a primary source of construction funding on the Strip, along with talk of "wire taps" and eavesdropping, all combined to create an unhealthy climate of distrust. Nevada felt the FBI was oppressive. The FBI felt Nevada was coddling hoodlums.

The gubernatorial campaign of 1966 produced a spirited debate on the issue. I took the position that we had to work with the FBI, and that our differences had to be resolved. At times on the Las Vegas Strip, I'd felt that riding the FBI horse was a political loser.

When the election was over, the FBI people felt that it was as much a victory for J. Edgar Hoover as for Paul Laxalt.

A few weeks after the election, I traveled to Washington to meet with the FBI director. Along with my brother Bob, accompanying me were two long-time friends of Hoover's, Art Smith, later President of First National Bank of Nevada, and Del Webb, a former professional baseball player and one-time owner of the New York Yankees baseball team, who was then a leading licensee on the Strip (the Del Webb Company). Art and Del felt they could act as intermediaries for this very important meeting.

At that time, Hoover was at the zenith of his power. Within the FBI building, he was either revered or totally feared. As we were led into an area adjoining his office, I felt we were about to meet someone akin to the Deity. Years later, when I met Pope John Paul II, the "preliminaries" were no more impressive than when meeting Hoover. Everyone spoke in hushed tones less they interfere with the "Great One."

When finally we were ushered into the meeting, I didn't know whether I should genuflect or kiss his ring. He was cordial to all of us. He warmly embraced Del, who addressed him as "Edgar" rather than "Mr. Director." Some of Hoover's people winced at that.

The Director opened the meeting by saying that he had followed the election closely, and that it was historic in that it was the first time the FBI had become a controversial issue in a major

Our meeting with FBI Director J. Edgar Hoover shortly after my election as Governor in 1966. (L. to R.) Brother Bob, Hoover, PL and Reno banker Art Smith.
Special Collections, University of Nevada, Reno Library

political campaign. He thanked me for "standing by" him and stated that he welcomed the opportunity to work with our people.

Sounding much like General George Patton addressing his

troops, Hoover instructed one of his aides to tell the FBI field people that henceforth there was to be complete cooperation with the Nevada authorities.

Thereafter, during our term and since, there has not been a major policy conflict between the state of Nevada and the FBI. Peace prevails.

INAUGURAL DECISIONS

Aside from the "affairs of state," other matters, such as preparation for the inauguration, had to be organized.

Historically, the inaugurals had been held in the warm confines of the Capitol. But, with the state growing rapidly, and inaugural crowds increasing, we had a problem: Was there a place with enough room to conduct the inaugural with some semblance of dignity? The old legislative chambers were just too small. A casino would hardly do. We came to the conclusion that there really wasn't a facility in Carson City big enough to handle the event.

What to do? Then a brainstorm hit me. Looking back, it was one of my worst. If they could hold outdoor inaugurals in Washington, D.C., I thought, why couldn't we do the same in Carson City? We did, and they have ever since.

At an inaugural for Governor Bob Miller in January of 1991, looking out at the freezing spectators on a very cold Nevada winter day, I thought to myself, "I hope no one here remembers that I started this!"

Inaugural balls were another challenge. During the campaign in Las Vegas, in a dreadful bit of pandering, I promised that if elected we'd have an inaugural ball in Las Vegas, in addition to the traditional ball in Northern Nevada.

At first blush, having a ball in Las Vegas sounds like a nice idea. But digging deeper, we became concerned that if it wasn't "done right" by Las Vegas standards it could be a disaster. After all, Las Vegas was the "entertainment capital of the world."

We solved the problem by constituting a group of Las Vegans to organize the ball. The results were spectacular. It was held on January 28th in the convention center, replete with chandeliers from "Gone With the Wind."

As "frosting on the inaugural cake," we had top entertainers like Bill Cosby, Red Skelton, Frank Sinatra and Jimmy Durante.

Preceding the Las Vegas ball was one in Reno's Centennial Coliseum on January 7th, also well-produced and well-attended.

So socially, at least, our administration was off to a good start.

The Mansion

One of the downsides of being elected Governor, at least for our family, was that we had to move from our comfortable home on the outskirts of the city to the Governor's Mansion. They were not thrilled about leaving our ranch-style house and the recreational activities it afforded.

When I pointed out that it was traditional for the first family to live in the Mansion, they quickly noted that my friends, the Reagans, had refused to live in California's antiquated Mansion.

Far more serious than the prospect of the Governor rattling around in the Mansion all by himself was the question of whether there would even be a Mansion — at least as we'd known it.

Built in the early 1900s, it had gradually fallen into disrepair. The Legislatures over the years had been downright cheap in doling out funds to maintain it. After assuming office, I found there was a serious effort underway to tear down "the old dump" and build a "contemporary" Mansion. That, to us, was unacceptable.

We finally worked out an arrangement whereby the Legislature would increase its appropriation to replace the basics such as plumbing and wiring, if I would agree to go to the people for private funds to remodel the Mansion.

With a pledge that the work would be faithful to the history of the Mansion, we went to work. We had a positive response and within a few weeks had raised enough to do the job right.

We engaged Scott Mitchell of San Francisco, who had done much of the work at Williamsburg, Virginia, to handle furnishing and decor.

Within a few months, the Mansion was completely refurbished. Working closely with Jackie, Scott did a fine job. In addition, Ralph Eissmann, the state architect, deserves a lot of credit for a job well done.

The formal reopening of the Mansion in 1968 turned out to be a major event. Over the years, the people had taken great pride in "their Mansion" — as they should. And each "first family" has enjoyed living in it.

In 1998, Governor Bob Miller, whose term expired in January 1999, embarked on a $5 million renovation of the Mansion, the first since our renovation project in 1967-1968.

In front of the newly renovated Governor's Mansion.
Special Collections, University of Nevada, Reno Library

The current Governor, Kenny Guinn, and his wife, Dema, completed the project. The Millers and the Guinns deserve a lot of credit for making sure that the "People's Mansion" continues to be a source of pride for Nevadans.

CHAPTER 10

❖ *The Governorship, 1967–1971* ❖

OUR MAJOR PROBLEMS

During my term as Lieutenant Governor and during the campaign, several major problems came to light.

Lake Tahoe was in trouble. Virtually uncontrolled development had already affected its clarity. Something had to be done.

The Las Vegas economy, particularly gaming, was sick. Although the major clubs were doing well, several smaller ones were on the verge of bankruptcy. Several financial institutions were in trouble. At the heart of the problem was the fact that the financing of the clubs was almost completely limited to the Teamsters Union's Central States Pension Fund.

Many major hotel chains, such as Hilton and Hyatt, wanted to come to Nevada, but our licensing requirements were too stringent.

We became convinced that corporate licensing (licensing corporations instead of each participant) would open the doors to the "chains" and bring significant public financing for the first time to Nevada.

I had pledged during the campaign to make Nevada the "Lighthouse of Education." In addition to raising teachers' salaries and lowering classroom size, I had said it was time for Nevada to create a community college system and a medical school

In addition, we were woefully short of state park land. If we didn't acquire thousands of choice acres, particularly in the Tahoe area, they would be lost to development. There was already enough of that at Tahoe.

For years, our state prison had been a joke. The wardens, ever since Nevada became a state, had been appointed on a political basis. It was time for professionalism.

Although it might seem a minor matter on the surface, the taxicab situation in Las Vegas was a serious problem that had to be addressed. Customers were being cheated, and competing interests were resorting to violence. We needed to establish a taxicab authority and give it the resources to regulate this important business effectively.

TAXES

Even though we knew the aforementioned would be among our major problems, our budget hearings before I took office revealed a huge and unpleasant problem. It was clear, unless drastic measures were taken, that we would not be able to fulfill our constitutional responsibility to balance the state budget.

State revenue was down due to the "Vegas recession." With the promised new programs, expenditures would be up.

Of course, as conservatives, we looked first at the spending side for relief. We made quite a few cuts, but they didn't begin to close the gap.

We came to the painful conclusion that we needed more revenue. How could a conservative new Governor justify a tax increase in his first year in office? There was no way out.

My political pain was eased somewhat when I called Ronald Reagan, who was newly inaugurated as Governor of California. He said, "I have the same problem, and I'm going to ask for a tax increase. It's the responsible thing to do."

We finally decided we could safely increase the tax on the

major clubs without there being an adverse economic result. When I made the decision, I knew I'd be subjected to sharp criticism from gaming owners, many of whom had supported me. Before going "public," I contacted every major owner to explain this difficult decision and expressed my hope they would understand it had to be done in the public interest.

I'm sure none of them believed me, but they at least did not raise hell with me. Tommy Callahan, one of the owners and a good friend, captured their true feelings when he said, "Paul, why did you do this to us? We thought you were our friend."

In order to make the tax hike "fair," I tried to spread the burden as broadly as possible. As a result, I proposed increasing the gross gaming-revenue tax and the state sales tax. Eventually, with the help of such people as State Senators Carl Dodge and Jim Gibson, we put together a bi-partisan coalition in the Legislature which produced a package that increased the gaming tax by 20 percent and the sales tax by 50 percent (from two to three cents).

Guess what? We balanced the budget, and the economy survived nicely. In fact, the Las Vegas economy picked up spectacularly in 1967.

ENTER HOWARD HUGHES

In late 1966, after my election, I was told that the famous, eccentric and wildly-rich Howard Hughes had decided to settle in Nevada. He had moved to the top floor of Las Vegas' Desert Inn.

I reacted to the news almost casually. I knew that Hughes was a fabled Hollywood type who had frequented Vegas in playboy style, who had dated one Hollywood beauty after another, who had made a fortune in business, most recently from the sale of his TWA stock, and who had had a much-publicized run-in with a Congressional committee over his famous plane, the Spruce Goose.

But little did I realize then the impact Mr. Hughes was to have on Nevada and my administration!

Hughes' entry into the state caught the attention of the national news media. His occupancy of an entire floor of the Desert Inn gave rise to the question of what Moe Dalitz and the hotel's management would do with their new guest, particularly with all the high-rollers on their way to Vegas for the Christmas holidays. Hughes became a titillating media subject.

Would Moe evict Howard to honor long-standing, high-roller reservations? Would Howard honor an eviction?

After all, he was known at that time as "one of the richest men in the United States."

Finally, the problem was solved in classic Howard Hughes fashion. He decided to buy the Desert Inn for $13 million ($6 million in cash and the assumption of $7 million of liabilities). In those days, that was an impressive amount of money.

Thus, early in 1967, our gaming licensing people were in a quandary. On the one hand, it was welcome news that Hughes would buy the Desert Inn. The Feds had suspicions about its ties to organized crime. On the other hand, what would we do about having Hughes adhere to our strict licensing requirements – such as fingerprinting, "mug shots" and the like?

He let us know, through his right-hand man, Bob Maheu, that he would prefer that the requirements concerning personal appearances be waived in view of his failing health. We decided to grant the waiver.

After all, having Howard Hughes invest in Las Vegas in a casino was a huge plus for Nevada. His eccentricities aside, Hughes gave Las Vegas gambling a sort of "seal of approval." If Hughes, one of the world's shrewdest businessmen, didn't feel that he could conduct business in a legitimate manner in Las Vegas, he wouldn't touch it with a ten-foot-pole.

Thereafter, he bought the Castaways, Sands, Frontier, Silver Slipper and Landmark in Las Vegas and Harold's Club in Reno.

We welcomed all the acquisitions – to a point. We eventually became concerned about "too much Hughes." Our concerns were reinforced when we were advised by the U.S. Justice Department that they were concerned about the anti-trust implications of Hughes' "buying spree," especially after he tried to buy the Stardust Hotel.

We advised him to back off, and he did.

With each new buy, the pressure grew from the news media to insist that Hughes be treated like everyone else. The press suggested that personal appearances, photographs and finger prints should be required of him like everybody else.

It came to a head when Hughes indicated an interest in Harrah's, a major northern Nevada casino.

In January 1968, at a dinner at the Holiday Hotel in Reno, Bill Sinnott and I told Bob Maheu that the time had come to establish personal contact with Hughes.

Bob said that he would try to arrange it. We adjourned to Bob's suite, where he called the Desert Inn and dictated a memo to one of Hughes' male "nurses." Bob relayed our concerns about the need for personal contact, and the problems associated with further gaming acquisitions. In view of the situation, Bob said, Hughes should talk personally with me.

Apparently, the message was hand-delivered to Hughes. A few minutes later, Bob handed me the phone saying that Mr. Hughes was on the line.

Hughes was very cordial, articulate and spoke in a distinct Midwestern accent. He apologized for not having contacted me previously, calling it "poor politics."

I stated that although I was personally comfortable with the waivers, the pressure was building to the point that a personal meeting between the two of us might be necessary.

Normally, this would not have seemed like a "big deal," but it was in Howard Hughes' case. For years, he had carefully guarded his privacy, and no one but his doctors and personal staff were permitted to visit him. I had learned that day that his chief of staff, Bob Maheu, had never personally met with him! They communicated by phone or couriered memo.

Howard Hughes had an enormous impact on my gubernatorial administration and the state of Nevada.
Photo courtesy The Howard Hughes Corporation, Las Vegas, Nevada.

During our conversation, Hughes said, "I'd like to meet with you personally, but I look like hell." He said that he was quite ill upon his arrival in Las Vegas and was still not feeling well.

Knowing how obsessed he was with privacy, I told him that I respected his position and had no desire to invade his privacy to satisfy my curiosity or ego. Nonetheless, I had a public responsibility to fulfill, which overrode my personal feelings.

"I hope that doesn't happen, Governor. I look like a goddamn cadaver," Hughes emphasized.

He then said that he hoped to be feeling better in a few months, and would like to meet personally sometime thereafter.

He claimed to have checked out my background immediately after he arrived in the state. He also said that in observing me the last several months, he was convinced that in four or eight years I could be elected President. He said "the time to start planning is now," and he assured me that he would give me any assistance that I needed.

In response, I remained silent. I figured that he was either trying to flatter me or, like many rich people, he had an irresistible "kingmaker impulse."

He then proceeded to analyze the 1968 presidential campaign that was already underway. He mentioned Ronald Reagan ("started well, but he's fouled up") and George Romney ("running out of steam"). He also said that he hoped "the present administration (Johnson) will leave office."

During the entire conversation, we had some difficulty communicating. He apologized repeatedly, stating that he was "deaf as a post."

At the end of the conversation, he was assured that the request for a public meeting wouldn't be made unless it was absolutely necessary.

Fortunately, I never had to press him and never met him. People find that hard to believe, but Howard Hughes was a special man as far as I was concerned, and he did an enormous amount of good for Nevada.

After our initial conversation, he phoned me day or night. Constantly alone, in bed, and in semi-darkness, he clearly didn't know the difference between day and night.

After several post-midnight calls, I finally told him that I'd appreciate it if he would call in the daytime, unless there was an emergency, because I had a hectic, exhausting schedule and badly needed my sleep. He apologized profusely and never called me late at night again.

What else did we talk about? Strangely, he rarely made any reference to his gaming acquisition frenzy. Those matters were "all up to Maheu," he told me. He loved to talk politics. Being very intelligent and curious, he was always current on Washington matters. I learned later that he was equally conversant on state matters.

Because of his experience testifying in Washington before a hostile Congressional committee, he had a deep distrust of the federal government institutionally, but nonetheless liked certain "national" politicians such as Hubert Humphrey ("great man") and Barry Goldwater ("should've been President").

His pet subject in talking with me was the nuclear testing that was being carried out at the Nevada Test Site, which is about 100 miles north of Las Vegas. Hughes had a "germ phobia," and stories abounded regarding his attempts to create a germ-free environment around him.

Imagine, with that underlying phobia, how he reacted when he found that underground nuclear tests were being conducted a few miles from where he lived, and that there was a possibility of an accident that could result in exposure to radiation.

I tried to assure him that all precautions were being taken so there would be no "radiation leaks."

He was aghast when I told him that in the early 1950s these tests were conducted above ground, and thousands of people had come to witness the spectacle. "The Best Show in Town," they used to call the tests.

Now the tests were being conducted "safely" underground. He politely scoffed at what he must have considered my naivete, stating that the underground tests would endanger the safety and health of Nevadans "for generations to come," and that for certain, our underground water was being contaminated.

He had scientific reports to back him up, which he delivered to me. I'd ship them to Washington to be examined by experts at the Atomic Energy Commission. AEC would report back that "Hughes' science has no basis." In addition, long-time test site workers like Troy Wade assured me the tests were being conducted safely.

And so the tests continued for several years until a self-imposed U.S. moratorium in 1992.

The Hughes influence in matters nuclear, though, is still felt in the Las Vegas area. His early warnings frightened many influential people.

In 1987, Congress decided that a site near Las Vegas, Yucca Mountain, should be the sole site in the U.S. to be examined to determine if it would be an appropriate site for permanent high-level nuclear waste storage. Nevada, through its elected representatives, has fiercely fought the project.

And what is one of the underlying concerns? That storage of nuclear waste might contaminate Nevada's underground water! I suspect that Howard Hughes is looking down on the situation and "cheering on" the anti-nuclear waste forces.

BOB MAHEU

If one went to central casting to find someone to play the role of Howard Hughes' alter ego, it would be difficult to fill the role with someone more qualified than Bob Maheu.

Bob was a New Englander through and through. He spoke in a clipped Boston accent, was very Catholic and a family man.

After graduating from Holy Cross, he went to the FBI, where he worked closely for many years with J. Edgar Hoover.

Thereafter, he went to the CIA — "The Agency" or "The Outfit," they called it. There, he became involved in highly-sensitive covert activity and gained great respect in intelligence circles as a shrewd, tough but fair and discreet operative.

It was widely speculated that he had been the link between organized crime and the government to "take care of" the Castro problem. His recounting of the events of that period are found in his autobiography, "Next to Hughes," published in 1992.

After Bob left the CIA, it was almost inevitable that he would end up with Hughes, which he did after successfully handling some "sensitive matters" for Hughes.

Shortly after Hughes' arrival in Las Vegas in November 1966, Maheu contacted Bill Sinnott of my Gubernatorial staff. As

former FBI colleagues, they had known each other for years. Bill agreed to a proposed meeting with me, telling me that Maheu was "a good man" and "completely trustworthy."

At our meeting, Bob indicated that Hughes had decided to make Nevada his home and wanted to be a "good citizen." According to Bob, Hughes hadn't decided what he wanted to do businesswise, but he had "a bundle of cash" (in excess of $546 million) from the sale of his

Howard Hughes' right-hand man, Bob Maheu, a good man who eventually ran afoul of Hughes' "Mormon Mafia."

TWA stock, which was "dying to be put to work."

From the beginning, I was relieved that Hughes had selected a solid man such as Bob to serve as his link to Nevada. In the years that followed, we became close friends and even played tennis together frequently. He and my brother John became "buddies" and continue so to this day.

Through all the "Hughes years," Bob kept us advised as to Hughes' plans. When he exhibited any interest relating to Nevada gambling, we knew about it first. There were no "street rumors" or press leaks.

When Hughes decided to invest in mining, Bob called me to express his surprise and disapproval. When the community college and the medical school programs were in peril, it was Bob Maheu who called to say that Hughes wanted to help. He could have easily played the "hot shot" role, but he never did.

Whenever I could, I commended Bob to Mr. Hughes, who always agreed with me — until 1970, Hughes' last year in Nevada.

I've long believed that one learns more from what leaders don't say, as opposed to what they do say. In spring 1970, I noticed in talking to Hughes that he rarely mentioned Bob, and when I complimented Bob, there was no response — a sure sign of trouble.

Finally, I asked Bob if he was having trouble with Hughes. He confided to me that they hadn't talked together on the phone for weeks, and that he was being "frozen out by the Mormon Mafia," led by one Bill Gay, a Hughes Tool Company executive.

Not wanting to intervene in what was obviously a serious "family" fight, I stayed out. I figured, wrongly as it turned out, that Bob would strategize a plan to end-run Bill Gay.

In November, however, my worst fears were realized. Bill Sinnott advised me that there was "all-out war" in Las Vegas among the Hughes people. On November 14th, Bill Gay and Chester Davis, a Hughes lawyer allied with Gay, had secured from Hughes written authority to fire Maheu.

To make matters worse, Hughes vanished on Thanksgiving Eve, November 25, 1970. For several days, Maheu and his people had no idea where he'd gone. Concerns about kidnapping were rampant. Finally, some Maheu-hired private detectives found that Hughes was staying on the top floor of the Britannia Beach Hotel on Paradise Island in the Bahamas.

Despite every effort by the Hughes people to put a lid on this incredible development, Hank Greenspun of the Las Vegas Sun broke the story on December 2 with a banner headline that read, "Howard Hughes Vanishes! Mystery Baffles Close Associates." The story made headlines around the world.

On December 4, Ed Morgan, a respected Washington, D.C., lawyer representing Maheu, was advised by Gay and Davis that they had fired Bob. That caused Bob the following day to obtain a temporary restraining order that sought to maintain the status quo.

Bill Sinnott advised me to "get your tail to Vegas pronto." If the "firing order" was carried out and Maheu resisted, there could be "all hell to pay," and thousands of jobs would be jeopardized. I asked Bill to contact the warring parties for an emergency meeting.

I met first with Bob Maheu and then with Bill Gay and Chester Davis to try to learn in person the full story. The issue was quickly defined. Gay and Davis indicated that Hughes had designated them, along with Raymond Holliday, another top official with the Hughes Tool Company, as his "true and lawful attorneys" and authorized them "to vote and to otherwise exercise all rights" with respect to Hughes' Nevada holdings.

That being the case, they had decided to fire Maheu "forthwith." Maheu questioned the validity of what he considered to be a ruthless power grab, stating that on several occasions Hughes had told him he could "barely tolerate" Gay, Davis and Holliday.

It was clear to me there was little, if any, room for compromise. The "Big Three" wanted Maheu's head. Maheu detested all of them. I doubted if there was any chance they could set aside their deep feelings against one another in favor of the "greater good" of

Hughes' Nevada operations and thousands of employees.

Recognizing that these issues would be litigated, I obtained assurances from them that the status quo would be maintained until the conflict could be resolved by a court. If they didn't go along, I had no choice but to request that our gaming people take appropriate action to protect the properties.

On December 6, I was requested to join George Franklin, the District Attorney of Clark County, and Frank Johnson, our Gaming Control Board Chairman, to talk to Hughes personally on the phone. We gathered at the Sands Hotel for the conference call.

The timing was classic Howard Hughes: One o'clock in the morning of December 7, Pearl Harbor Day. After a long day at the office, I needed a 1:00 a.m. phone conference like the proverbial "hole in the head."

This personal inconvenience paled in light of the chance to talk personally to Hughes to learn what his plans were. Sadly for Bob Maheu, his wishes were clear: Hughes had signed a proxy in favor of Gray, Davis and Holliday, and he wanted Maheu fired. He said he was on vacation and would be back in Nevada soon; however, he never returned. That was the last time I talked with Howard Hughes.

Afterward, I went to Bob Maheu's house and delivered the bad news. It was one of the most difficult things I've had to do. The blood drained out of Bob's face upon hearing the news. I have never seen a more crestfallen man.

Thereafter, Bob Maheu spent years with lawyers in courtrooms. He sued Hughes for breach of contract, and later sued him for slander when Hughes, during an audio-taped interview, accused Bob of stealing from him. All the while, the IRS was on Bob's back for some $3 million, which they asserted was due. He contested the claim. To cap it off, he suffered a heart attack.

A lesser person would have given up. Not Bob. He finally

prevailed in a settlement with Hughes. The proceeds were distributed to his lawyers and the IRS.

For the last several years, he has resided quietly in Las Vegas with his wife, Yve. He consults from time-to-time and enjoys the trust and respect of those who have dealt with him. He's had it all, power-wise and financially, but now is content with being a very private person with modest means. In my view, Howard Hughes was well served by Bob Maheu in connection with his Nevada interests.

Bob's downfall actually started when he built a spectacular house on the Desert Inn golf course. It was quickly referred to as "Little Caesar's Palace." Events held there were by far the most tasteful and spectacular anywhere in the state. Unfortunately for Bob, it became a symbol to his enemies in the Hughes camp that he had "overplayed his hand."

As to Howard Hughes, he will always have my gratitude and appreciation for the contributions he made to Nevada at a critical time in our history.

From a personal standpoint, he was always courteous and fair in his dealings with me.

His investing in Nevada gambling in the 1960s was enormously helpful, not only in terms of his capital contributions but also the positive message his involvement conveyed to the business community worldwide.

Without Howard Hughes, Las Vegas gambling, fickle animal that it is, could have easily suffered a severe recession, which would have jeopardized thousands of jobs.

And without Howard Hughes, Nevada might not have created a community college system or a medical school.

Unfortunately, his contributions to our national security through Hughes Tool Company have largely been overlooked.

It's truly a tragedy that in April 1976 this man should die as he did, virtually alone, on an airplane, weighing only 93 pounds on a 6'4" frame. He deserved a better fate.

After I announced that I wasn't going to seek re-election in 1970, Bob Maheu informed me that Hughes would like to have me join his organization. I wrote a letter to Hughes in August 1970 explaining to him the many reasons why this was not possible. Not only did I want more personal freedom after four exhausting years in the "fishbowl" that is the Governorship, but I also did not want it to appear that the cooperation my administration provided to Hughes was on a "quid pro quo" basis.

CORPORATE LICENSING

During my years as Lieutenant Governor and in the campaign for Governor, people whose judgment I respected expressed deep concern about the future of Nevada gambling. There was a continuing federal threat to tax it out of existence. As previously noted, financing for hotel and casino expansion was extremely limited, principally being provided by Teamster Union sources.

Nevada first authorized casino gambling in 1931. It was a reaction to a depressed economy, including the collapse of the mining and agricultural industries in Nevada.

Following Senator John Tower's dictum to the Senate when confronting a tough vote — "If you're going to be a bear, be a grizzly" — Nevada went all the way. Coupled with the gambling measure was a law permitting "quickie" divorces. If one established residence for a period of six weeks, it was sufficient to be granted a divorce. There was nothing comparable anywhere else in the U.S.

The reaction from throughout the country was immediate and negative. Nevada became known as the "Sin State," a label that unfortunately has stuck.

Within the state, the few thousand voters then living in

Nevada closed ranks, flying the banner of "states' rights." If Nevada, for reasons of its own, wanted to approve casino gambling and quickie divorces, it was no one else's business, so the reasoning went.

Regulation of Nevada gambling, such as it was, was left to the cities and counties. Licenses were granted to small places with two or three tables. Patrons were almost entirely locals. Las Vegas was still a small railroad town of a few thousand people with very little gambling activity.

Then two events, one in Vegas and one in Reno, dramatically changed everything.

In Reno, a former carnival barker by the name of Raymond "Pappy" Smith opened a "hole in the wall joint" in 1935 on Virginia Street. He named it "Harold's Club" (after his second son) and used a unique advertising program. Billboards throughout the country simply said, "Harold's Club or Bust." An accompanying signpost indicated the number of miles to Harold's Club. It was an overnight sensation.

Thousands flocked to Reno. Other clubs flourished. Casinos were placed in hotels such as the Riverside in Reno.

The Commercial Hotel in Elko followed. Newt Crumley, the owner, added famous entertainers such as Lawrence Welk. The mix was complete. Casino and hotel entertainment added up to success, unless bad management fouled it up.

In Las Vegas, the construction of Hoover Dam, which began in 1930, added thousands of potential customers, all well paid. The local casinos did well for awhile, but when the dam construction concluded, gambling in southern Nevada started to slide until World War II.

By the 1940s, the "big boys" from such places as Cleveland, Los Angeles, Baltimore and Miami decided that the Las Vegas Strip was fruit "ripe for pickin'."

Among the pioneers was one Benjamin "Bugsy" Siegel, a ruthless gangster from Chicago and Los Angeles, who oversaw the construction of the first mega-resort, the Flamingo Hotel, which
opened to great fanfare in 1946. His assassination in June 1947 in
Beverly Hills by gangland enemies brought forth a spate of bad
publicity for the Flamingo, the Las Vegas Strip and the state.

On the heels of Bugsy's untimely demise, publication of sensational books such as "Green Felt Jungle," a purported insider
story of the workings of the Strip, didn't help Nevada's image.

One would think that gangland killings and a Mafia presence
would greatly damage the Strip. After all, what decent, law-abid-
ing tourist would risk coming to the seat of sin and corruption?

To almost everyone's surprise (except the shrewd operators),
the public, instead of being repulsed, became enthralled. By the
millions, they traveled from all over the world to "do Las Vegas."

Resort after resort was built, each with a spectacular opening.
People loved the glitter of the hotels, their glamorous casinos and
beautiful showgirls.

Even with tourism booming in Nevada and even though tax
revenues were rising dramatically, Nevada officialdom became
concerned. They feared that they had "a tiger by the tail" and felt
steps to better regulate this creature had to be taken. Otherwise,
Nevada gambling stood a real chance of being taken over by the
mob, or the "Feds" would move in.

Their concerns were justified. On the heels of Bugsy's assassination, "Russian Louie," one of the top figures in organized
crime, shot and killed Harry Sherwood, another gambler, at Lake
Tahoe. Northern Nevadans were shocked.

Many northerners felt that Las Vegas was a haven for the
mob, but a mob killing at pristine Lake Tahoe, right in their
own backyard, was stunning. Then came the "hit" on Lincoln
Fitzgerald at his house in Reno. Even though "Fitz" survived,

the cold realization that the Mafia virus had spread north was frightening to many.

The political broadsides started, too. Tennessee Senator Estes Kefauver's "Special Committee to Investigate Organized Crime in Interstate Commerce," otherwise known as the Kefauver Committee, commenced hearings in 1950. Kefauver sensed that this would be a hot political issue and, not surprisingly, there was plenty of national press coverage.

On November 15, 1950, Kefauver held a dramatic hearing in Las Vegas, which was followed up with a series of hearings in California. One of Kefauver's main objectives was to make the case that organized crime was firmly entrenched in Las Vegas.

Federal legislative action followed the Kefauver hearings. A bill was introduced in Congress levying a 10 percent tax on gross gambling profits. This was so confiscatory it would have put Nevada's casinos out of business – precisely the result the proponents wanted.

Were it not for the fact that Nevada was represented by a very powerful U.S. Senator, Pat McCarran, Nevada gambling could have come to an early death some 50 years ago.

Even McCarran had mixed feelings about gambling. On the one hand, he respected the right of Nevadans to do what they wanted to do. He was a fierce believer in "states' rights." On the other hand, he could see that Nevada was becoming unhealthily dependent upon gambling. He expressed his concerns in a private letter to a friend, journalist Joseph McDonald of Reno, in 1951:

"It isn't a very laudable position for one to have to defend gambling. One doesn't feel very lofty when his feet are resting on the argument that gambling must prevail in the state that he represents. The rest of the world looks upon him with disdain even though every other state in the union is harboring gambling in one form or another, illegally, of course, and even though the state that he defends and represents has legalized gambling, it doesn't take from the actuality in defending the thing in open forum, where men in all walks of life and all particular phase and religious bents are listening and laughing, condemning or ridiculing." But "when the gambling business is involved in the economic structure of one's state, one must lay away pride and put on the hide of a rhinoceros and go to it."

The Senator's statements often came back to me in my years in public life when I tried to defend gambling, particularly in the "Bible Belt."

Senator McCarran successfully killed the gaming tax bill, and Nevada was granted a reprieve. The next serious move by the federal government to tax Nevada gambling came in 1996 when the Clinton Administration tried to levy a four percent gross tax. It also died.

REGULATION

Because of the early problems associated with legalized gambling, Nevada's Governors quickly became involved. In the mid-1940s, Governor Vail Pittman moved the regulatory and licensing authority from the cities and counties to the state. In addition, a state Tax Commission was established to help regulate gambling and was given the authority to issue and deny licenses.

Then, in 1955, Governor Charles Russell courageously decided to create a Gaming Control Board, vested with powers to investigate applicants for licenses and regulate them thereafter. In addition, the state Tax Commission was beefed up.

The industry strongly opposed these moves.

Legislation was introduced in Carson City, which would have effectively stripped the board of its powers. It passed the Legislature. However, Governor Russell vetoed the bill and his veto was sustained — barely. This was a watershed event insofar as regulation of Nevada gambling is concerned. Had Governor Russell been overridden, Nevada's gambling credibility would have been severely undercut.

During Governor Grant Sawyer's administration, the Nevada Gaming Commission was established. It supplanted the Tax Commission and has acted in a quasi-judicial capacity as the ultimate authority on licensing matters. It also has functioned well over the years.

Under Bill Sinnott, later a key member of my gubernatorial staff, procedures were established by the Control Board which are followed to this day.

Today, Nevada's regulation of gambling is the model for other states. In my view, it has functioned effectively and honestly. As I later pointed out to audiences throughout the country, it is the ultimate testament to Nevada's integrity that it has regulated gambling since 1931 free of any major scandal.

It was against this historical backdrop that my Administration came into office in 1967.

Although much had been done and a foundation for effective, credible gambling control had been laid, there were improvements to be made. We had "mended fences" with the FBI through Hoover. We hoped that this would ease tensions and help us regulate the industry.

While gaming had done well economically, cracks were starting to appear by the time I became Governor. Financing sources for new construction and expansion, as noted earlier, were very few. Conventional banking sources were leery of getting involved with questionable sources such as the Teamsters. Further, Bobby Kennedy and others had been after Jimmy Hoffa and the Teamsters, and Nevada was squarely in their sights.

We concluded that the time for corporate licensing had come. From the inception of gambling in Nevada, any individual with any ownership interest in gambling had to be licensed. This required extensive investigation and background checks. Many who might otherwise invest were not inclined to undergo such intensive investigation. Further, there was no way that a major company such as Hilton could be induced to come to Nevada under those circumstances.

We had to devise a method where stockholders in major corporations could invest in Nevada gaming through the corporation, and yet Nevada had to retain effective control over the operation.

The answer turned out to be the 1969 corporate gaming law.

In 1967, the state Legislature passed legislation that was intended to open the door to gambling for publicly-owned corporations, but due to technical errors in the drafting of the bill, it proved unworkable.

The 1969 law permitted indirect investment by large numbers of persons in one or more holding companies, but centered responsibility for operation of the licensed corporation in a small group who would be thoroughly investigated and strictly controlled, whether they be officers and directors of the licensed corporation or of the holding company.

The primary purposes of the 1969 corporate gaming act were to broaden the opportunity for investment in gaming through the pooling of capital in corporate form, to maintain effective control over the conduct of gaming by corporate licensees and to restrain any speculative promotion of the stock or other securities of gaming enterprises.

This, we assumed, was "motherhood" legislation.

Who could object?

I found out quickly that "fear of the unknown" can pose formidable problems for any substantial reform. Many of the operators were comfortable doing business as they were. They didn't need, nor want, "Wall Street types" coming into the industry.

Visionaries such as Kirk Kerkorian, though, pointed out that corporate gaming would ease federal tensions and quickly open the door to major hotel chains. He was right. He was one of the first to take advantage of the new law.

Ironically, one staunch supporter and good friend was solidly opposed. He was of the "If-it-ain't-broke-don't-fix-it" school. Still, not too long after the bill was passed, he was one of the first to "go public" and make a financial killing. His name was Bill Harrah.

The Legislators who herded this through the State Senate and Assembly deserve a great deal of credit. The leaders, such as Senators Floyd Lamb and Mahlon Brown, did the right thing, knowing they would pay a political price, since the Las Vegas gamblers, most of whom opposed the legislation, were among their strongest supporters. Senator "Snowy" Monroe, as chairman of the Senate Judiciary Committee, was invaluable as well. The same can be said for Carl Dodge of Fallon, one of the most thoughtful legislators of that or any other session.

Most observers of the Nevada gambling scene believe that corporate gaming opened the doors to the new industry we find in Nevada today. It has served its purpose well and exceeded our expectations. In 1998, total gaming revenue in Nevada exceeded $8 billion!

The U.S. Congress established The National Gambling Impact Study Commission in 1997 to study the impact of gambling in America – pro and con.

The Commission's final report, issued in June 1999, included the following statement: "All of the evidence presented to the Commission indicates that effective state regulation, coupled with the takeover of much of the industry by public corporations, has eliminated organized crime from the direct ownership and operation of casinos." Need I say more?

Tahoe Turning Gray?

Lake Tahoe is the "crown jewel" of the Sierra Nevada, nestled more than 6,000 feet above sea level along the California-Nevada border. As youngsters, it was our playground in the summertime. It was a half-hour drive up the old two-lane road from our home in Carson City to Zephyr Cove beach. The lake was a vital part of our lives. In those days, we gave no thought to things such as nutrients, algae and clarity. All we knew was that the water was so clear and pure and oh-so cold!

When the gambling clubs started to sprout on the south end of Tahoe at the state line between Nevada and California, we thought it was great. We were now "big time." One of my proudest days was when Harvey Gross, whom I had represented as a lawyer, opened the new Wagon Wheel tower in 1963.

As these developments came along, the concerns of the environmentalists and preservationists rose to a fever pitch. When I was Lieutenant Governor, I met with their representatives from time to time. Such groups as the Sierra Club and the League to Save Lake Tahoe gradually became prominent "on my screen."

Most of the people in my circles, both politically and socially, dismissed these folks as "deep breathers" and "well-intentioned nuisances" who had nothing better to do. They were also described as "rich people" who now had their slices of heaven at Tahoe and wanted to "lock everyone else out."

The more I discussed the subject with knowledgeable people, however, the more I came to share the environmentalists' concerns. Rollie Westergard, State Engineer, Division of Water Resources, and Elmo DeRicco, Director of the Department of Conservation and Natural Resources, both told me there was justified cause for concern.

They contended that development at Tahoe was out of control, and that if it continued unabated, "Lord only knows what might happen." They pointed out that lakes in other parts of the world had been lost due to overdevelopment and neglect.

By the time I took office in 1967, my level of consciousness toward the "fragility" of Tahoe had been raised considerably.

With Ron Reagan at Heavenly Valley (Lake Tahoe) ski resort shortly after being elected Governors of our respective states. Ron looks great! *Special Collections, Univ. of Nevada, Reno Library*

Shortly after taking office, I talked to Ron Reagan, who had just been elected Governor of California. I mentioned to him my increasing concern about overdevelopment at Tahoe, and the fact that some people had told me that unless something was done, Tahoe could "turn gray" on our watch. We both decided that this was not the kind of legacy we wanted to leave.

Recognizing that there might be a problem, perhaps a serious one, we looked for a solution.

Ron advised me in early 1967 that some legislators in California were looking at the problem, and he had assigned some of his people to work with them.

The more we explored solutions, the more it was apparent that Tahoe suffered from a "serious governmental overload." Believe it or not, there were several dozen agencies in both states with some form of policy jurisdiction over Tahoe.

The conclusion was inescapable: The structure had to be drastically simplified. That meant substituting all the locals with a regional agency with representatives from both states. Ron and I both gasped! It was "metro government," the abomination of any good conservative!

It was finally decided that California would take the lead. We would monitor and offer suggestions for improvement. Before putting him out on some political limb, I told Ron that if California passed a bill, I couldn't assure him of passage in Nevada.

We had a lot of conservatives in the legislature who would abhor any form of regional government. Further, most didn't believe there was a serious problem. The environmentalists were, as usual, greatly exaggerating the seriousness of the problem, they contended.

Ron advised me that the California vehicle would be a bill sponsored by Assemblyman Edwin Z'Berg of Sacramento, and that he and his people would keep us posted. Meanwhile, we agreed to start quietly the marshalling of support in our respective Legislatures.

We both agreed, too, that the agency should be for planning purposes only. Implementation of any plan should be left to the locals. This seemed to be a tidy philosophical compromise, although we wondered about how compatible regional planning would be with local implementation.

In the months that followed, the Z'Berg bill made its way

through the California legislative minefields. In June 1967, Governor Reagan called and said the legislation was generally acceptable, but several California legislators had indicated they wouldn't go along unless they knew what Nevada would do with the legislation when it was forwarded. He asked if I would convene a meeting of legislators and county commissioners to brief them and get a reading.

In July 1967, I met a representative group of interested legislators and county commissioners. As I expected, there was strong opposition from some of those present, particularly the commissioners and Assemblyman from Douglas County, which encompassed part of the lake. Assemblyman Lawrence "Jake" Jacobsen, later to become a state Senator for several terms, was the most vocal — and the most convincing.

Jake stated that he was unconvinced there was a Tahoe pollution problem, that it was dangerous to enter into any regional arrangement with California, and that Douglas County was fully capable of handling its own planning problems.

Lastly, he warned that if this came to pass, thousands of small land owners in the Tahoe Basin would eventually suffer by being restricted in their use of their own land.

How prophetic he was!

Nonetheless, we did the deal. The regional agency, through its master plan, effectively precluded thousands of small lot owners from building their "dream houses" at Tahoe. I still feel badly that they weren't "grandfathered" into the original legislation.

After the briefing regarding the status of the "Z'Berg bill," Senator Coe Swobe of Reno was asked to deliver a set of suggested Nevada amendments to Governor Reagan and the California legislative leadership. The amendments were incorporated into the bill and it passed the California Legislature.

For the next several months, Senator Swobe worked feverishly with public and private interests to fashion the Nevada version, which eventually became known as the "Swobe bill."

Mark Twain once described Lake Tahoe as "the fairest picture the whole earth affords." Ron Reagan and I helped form a regional government – called the Tahoe Regional Planning Agency – in order to protect this gem. *Photo by Peggy Lear Bowen*

Since Nevada's Legislature meets only every two years, my office was deluged with requests to call a special session to consider establishment of the Lake Tahoe Regional Planning Agency. I was wary. Although the agendas are supposed to be as prescribed by the Governor, legislatures often were known to create mischief for Governors during these special sessions.

Despite my reservations, I decided to "bite the bullet" and call the special session. I was fearful that delaying the process for a year might arrest the momentum created by the California bill and thus imperil the legislation.

On February 5, 1968, the special session convened. After an unusual joint hearing before four Assembly and Senate committees, Senate Bill 9, otherwise known as the Swobe bill, was approved in the Senate by a vote of 19-0 and in the Assembly by a margin of 37-2. Guess how "Jake" voted?

After the compact legislation passed the Nevada Legislature, I said, "This legislation may well prove to be one of the most significant conservation measures in the history of the nation," and was "designed to protect a priceless treasure."

Because this was a bi-state compact, California had to adopt Nevada's amendments and pass an identical bill, which they eventually did in July 1968.

The compact also required ratification by Congress, which happened in December 1969, when President Nixon signed the compact legislation, which had been introduced by, among others, Nevada Senators Alan Bible and Howard Cannon and Congressman Walter Baring.

Senator Swobe, a 39-year-old State Senator at the time, was enormously helpful. To this day, I owe him a debt of gratitude for a job well done.

The Tahoe Regional Planning Agency has been the subject of intense controversy since its inception; however, many conscientious citizens from both states have contributed greatly to its basic goal, the preservation of Lake Tahoe.

I guess our reward for these efforts is being able to view beautiful Lake Tahoe — still blue, still clear — and say, "We had a little bit to do with saving it."

COMMUNITY COLLEGE

During my campaign for Governor, I pledged to do my best to make Nevada "The Lighthouse of Education."

In educational matters, I relied heavily on Jerry Dondero, a good friend who had taught in high school in Sparks for years, and Dr. Tom Tucker, a top administrator at the University of Nevada.

Dr. Tom was originally from Tennessee and a "political junkie." His sage advice was helpful during my entire political career.

Together, Jerry and Tom were a stimulating duo. Aside from the usual educational needs such as increased teacher pay and student-teacher ratios, Jerry and Tom contended during my years as Lieutenant Governor that while Nevada's schools were adequate, we had a fundamental void in our system.

For a student who had completed high school and who didn't want to go to a technical school and couldn't afford college, his education was at a dead end.

Additionally, many adults who wanted to pursue their education, particularly in rural areas, were effectively restricted to "adult education classes," which were wholly unsatisfactory.

To meet this need, many states were turning to community colleges.

The more we studied the concept of community colleges and its acceptance throughout the country, the more appealing it became to me. More and more, the subject of community colleges became a significant part of my proposed program. Whenever I raised the subject, it was well received.

What was more heartening than anything else was an exercise in self-help going on in Elko, a northeastern Nevada community with a population of less than 10,000, but with enough pride and energy in its people to serve a community several times that size.

Since Elko is so isolated, several of its leading citizens felt that a community college was needed. Ironically, the people of Elko had founded the first university in Nevada – in 1874 – but it was moved to Reno in 1886.

Because there were no community colleges in Nevada, a group from Elko went to Oregon to check out the thriving five-year-old Treasure Valley Community College in Ontario.

After visiting with faculty and students, the group returned to

Elko convinced they could do the same, but with one huge unanswered question: How much would it cost to launch? They finally concluded that it would cost about $40,000 to start the college. That "optimistic" figure assumed there would be a great deal of volunteer work.

They also decided that to go to the state for help would be a waste of time. The university was already strapped for funds. If appropriations were to be made available, the funds would probably go to Las Vegas, which wanted a university of its own. There was also a growing demand for a medical school in Nevada.

With the negligible political power it could assert, particularly in competition with populous Las Vegas, Elko's conclusion was clear: If they wanted a community college, they would have to go it alone. And go it alone they did!

Headed by a respected and energetic Chevrolet dealer, Paul Sawyer, they formed a committee called the "Yo Yo Club," which earned its name because of the ups and downs of the project. The committee included such "doers" as Bill Wunderlich, Fred Harris, Mark Chilton, Carl Shuck, Mel Steninger, Mike Marfisi, Dr. Lee Moren, Dorothy Gallagher, Bob Burns, Jr., Al Huber and others. They went to work raising money. Eventually, thanks to the tenacity of Paul Sawyer and the others, they raised some $44,000.

They combined the fund-raising with a statewide public relations program, which included talking to groups and newspaper people throughout the state. They helped lay the groundwork with the people, which proved to be very helpful later.

On September 25, 1967, the first community college – called Nevada Community College – opened in Elko. More than 300 people enrolled and some 25 courses were offered.

The dissenters surfaced as soon as the doors opened. Some felt that Elko was too small to support a local college. Much like the university, the public school teachers, already strapped for funds, felt threatened. The dissenters argued that even though Elko was now private, soon it would be asking for public funding, putting them in competition for scarce money.

County Superintendents, though, were solidly in favor. Kenny Guinn, Superintendent of Clark County, and Marv Picollo, Superintendent of Washoe County, were leaders of this group. Because they worked at the grassroots level, they recognized the enormous need for community colleges. Tom Tucker and Jerry Dondero worked closely with them.

But the dissenters had a negative impact. Although the $40,000 seed money target had been met, there was little likelihood that much more could be raised to finance the college beyond May 1968.

If the college were to survive, it would eventually require public support. With the enthusiasm that the students and faculty displayed, I concluded that the state government needed to help.

This school was created and opened by the work of the citizens of Elko County, but to look to them to continue operation was simply not practical. A visit to Elko and later to Ontario convinced me that Nevada had to embrace and fund a statewide community college system, with initial funding going to Elko.

The next regular session of the Legislature wasn't until January 1969. By then, the community college in Elko could be history.

When I decided to call a special session for February 1968 to consider the Tahoe legislation, I decided to add to the agenda funding for the Elko community college "pilot project."

Norm Glaser and Roy Young, Elko's representatives in the State Assembly, introduced legislation calling for a $79,000 appropriation to Elko for the pilot program. After a great effort by the Elko supporters, the Governor's office included, the bill passed in the Assembly.

We were cautiously optimistic about the prospect of passage in the Senate, although that body had the reputation for being the "gas house" for assembly bills. Our opponents, mainly defending the university's turf and protecting its funding for the future, were ready for us.

After much emotional debate and rancor, the "gas house" lived up to its name. The measure was defeated in the Senate.

Perennial optimists contended that we had managed to put a "foot in the door," and that the Legislature's "level of knowledge" about community colleges had been "raised substantially."

But those who were more realistic realized that the Senate vote effectively spelled doom for the Elko Community College and that in May, at the conclusion of the school year, its doors would have to be closed.

A meeting was scheduled in late May by Mike Marfisi to consider the future of the school. Signs for continuation were dismal. The President of the Community College had even left Elko for greener pastures.

Mike invited me to attend the meeting. I did not want to go; a root canal would have been more appealing. Not being Irish, attending a "wake" was something I'd prefer to duck, but there was no way out. I told Mike I'd attend. The least I could do was console these fine people who had worked so hard for so long.

Then, the darndest thing happened. Shortly before my trip to Elko on the state plane, I received an unexpected call from one Howard Hughes. He told me that he had followed the Elko Community College story, and it was a "damned shame" that it was going to die.

"I don't want that to happen, Governor," he said. "Will you please tell them that I'd like to contribute some money to keep the school going."

Hughes contributed $250,000, half of which went to the Elko

Community College and half of which went to spawn other community college pilot projects in the state.

At first, I was speechless. Then, on behalf of the people of Elko, I thanked him. I also asked him not to reveal the news to anyone else until I broke the story at the Elko meeting.

When I arrived in Elko, my greeters were glum. At the Commercial Hotel where the lunch was held, the mood was depressing. Normally a happy go-lucky typical western hotel, the place was eerily quiet.

After lunch, the program began. Various speakers spoke of the history of the project and how close they had come to making Nevada history by privately starting a community college. It all had the flavor of — "Hell, we gave it a good shot, but it didn't quite work, though we all ought to be proud that we at least tried."

After the various speakers had finished, I was called. Last place was reserved for the Governor.

The setting couldn't have been more perfect. Not a soul had any idea that salvation was on the way.

When I stood up and told them of my earlier conversation with Hughes, you could have heard a pin drop. Then, when I told them of the unexpected $125,000 gift there was the strangest reaction. For seconds, there were looks of disbelief, as if they were thinking, "That damned Governor is putting us on!"

Then, when they were convinced the message was real, the room, full of hardened ranchers, miners and businessmen, dissolved. Everywhere I looked, people wept openly. Snowy Monroe, Elko's state senator, sobbed as if he'd lost his best friend. Then, the audience cheered lustily.

Never in all my years of public life have I ever seen such an outpouring of appreciation. For me, it will always be one of my most cherished memories.

Judge Ted Lunsford closed the meeting by saying simply:

"Thank you, Howard, wherever you are."

When I later told Hughes of the reaction, his response was simply, "They deserved it."

The rest, of course, is history. Elko, thanks to the $125,000 "infusion," revived and went on to develop a fine community college.

I had suggested to Hughes that the other half of the $250,000 gift be used to help start similar pilot projects in other parts of the state, which is exactly what happened.

Other community colleges quickly sprouted up throughout the state. The Board of Regents, at its February 1969 meeting, accepted my request that the community colleges be made a division of the University of Nevada. Later, the legislature passed a bill that gave the Board of Regents responsibility for developing and administering community colleges in Nevada.

People such as Jack Davis, Jim Eardley and Charles Donnelly quickly established themselves as leaders in the Community College movement and gave it the boost it needed to maintain momentum.

In the last 30 years or so, hundreds of thousands of Nevadans have had the benefit of a community college education. It has raised the quality of life in Nevada. Today, its numbers are the highest in the entire university system. In the fall of 1998, there were almost 50,000 students enrolled in the four community colleges in Nevada.

And, in 1998, my daughter, Kevin, with a doctorate in education, was engaged by the Community College of Southern Nevada.

What goes around does come around, doesn't it?

A MEDICAL SCHOOL FOR NEVADA

When I was growing up in Carson City, as I recall it, we had two doctors: Dr. James Thom and Dr. Edward Hamer. In the adjoining valley, Dr. Mary Fulstone, one of the legends of Nevada medicine, tenderly cared for the sick of Lyon County. They were dedicated professionals.

Time and time again, at all times of the day or night, in all kinds of weather, they made house calls caring for the sick and comforting families. What a relief it was to the Laxalt family to see Dr. Thom coming to the house when someone was ill.

One wintry night, he candidly told us that we'd better get brother Bob to St. Mary's Hospital in Reno "in a hurry." He said that Bob may have had a heart attack, and that Dr. George Cann, the Reno heart specialist, should see him.

Since ambulances were unknown in those days in the rural areas, we drove Bob to Reno late at night in a snowstorm, frightened every inch of the way that our brother might die at any moment.

What a relief it was to reach St. Mary's, my birthplace, and have Dr. Cann tell us that Bob hadn't had a heart attack at all.

Thus, my early experiences with these selfless doctors were all very positive. They performed a vital role in society, yet received little compensation. In those days, in small towns, there were very few rich doctors.

Thereafter, during my years in the Army's Medical Corps, I came to know doctors on a personal basis. To a person, they were intelligent, hard working and conscientious. My commanding officer was the former dean of the St. Louis Medical School. When I was discharged from the Army, I seriously considered going to medical school, but finally opted for law school.

Later, after my election as Lieutenant Governor, in traveling the state, in almost every small town when I asked what their most serious community problem was, the answer almost always was, "We desperately need doctors."

In a few instances, I talked with "doctor prospects" to try to persuade them to go to a particular small town. In two or three instances, I thought I was successful, but each time I was vetoed by a spouse who felt that Reno or Las Vegas was preferable to a town out in "the Cows."

After my election as Governor, we decided to make the establishment of a medical school for Nevada a priority. I felt that "selling" a medical school was going to be difficult, at best. I believed we should attempt to "depoliticize it." For me to be the "point person" might cost us valuable support on a purely partisan basis.

Forming a political action group composed of medical professionals seemed the way to go. Such respected doctors as Fred Anderson, Ernie Mack, Bill O'Brien and Wes Hall had been pushing hard for a school for years.

They had witnessed the great change in health care in Nevada since World War II. Nevada's population was rapidly increasing, with every prospect for even more dramatic growth in the future.

In 1964, several small western states such as Idaho, Montana and Wyoming were experiencing the same problems as Nevada. Too many people, too few doctors. But there were not formal studies to buttress the case for a medical school.

Just then, the Western Interstate Commission on Higher Education (WICHE) came to the rescue. In 1964, they examined in depth the feasibility of opening medical schools in small western states such as Nevada. Dr. James Faulkner was engaged to conduct the study.

The study proved to be an invaluable catalyst. Dr. Anderson, who at the time was Chairman of the Board of Regents of the University of Nevada, was deeply involved in formulating the guidelines for the study.

The report, which was widely circulated, found – not surprisingly – that Nevada was in desperate need of a medical school. If possible, the report concluded, it should be created immediately and its doors opened for medical students by 1972.

Seemingly, the climate and timing was right for the creation of a medical school in Nevada.

The state was growing rapidly, and there seemed to be no valid reason for not going forward. The rural counties were in great need of additional health care. Lastly, our students were having a difficult time gaining admission to out-of-state medical schools, which gave priority to their own students.

One would think that securing approval would be relatively simple. Yet, as was the case with the community college program, the naysayers weighed in at the outset and easily prevailed. Legislators, already caught in the crossfire between the North and the South on funding generally, were gun-shy. The university system, always fearful of intrusions into its limited funding, was opposed.

Of all the objections, the North-South rivalry was the most difficult politically. Historically, Northern Nevada had received the bulk of state funding. Now, the Las Vegas area was "feeling its oats." The Las Vegans believed the time had come to level out the imbalances of the past. The North contended that the university in Reno already had in place many of the programs necessary for "pre-med" training. The fact that the North assured the South that all students would have equal access didn't seem to help.

Finally, then-President Charles Armstrong of UNR appointed a select committee to do a feasibility study for the Board of Regents. Respected doctors such as Dr. Fred Andersen, who in time became known as the "Father of the Medical School," along with Drs. Mack, O'Brien and Dave Roberts, agreed to serve. They inquired throughout the country in an effort to find the most feasible way to fund a two-year medical school.

Even the proposed study was controversial. The Senate voted to kill it. Shortly thereafter the assembly killed the Senate bill and provided for a study.

Dr. Wes Hall traveled the state soliciting support. Dr. George

Smith, later to become dean of the medical school, effectively lobbied individual legislators.

This all amounted to a great deal of well-intentioned activity but with few measurable results. Then came a "triggering event." A group of Southern Nevada physicians purchased a "full-page ad" in the Las Vegas Sun supporting the medical school in Reno.

Fortunately, it caught the eye of Howard Hughes. He called me and said he'd been following the medical school fight and wanted to help, but was concerned lest his intervention would "screw things up." I assured him that in my judgment his offer would help greatly.

The next day, I received his telegram in which he pledged to give between $200,000 and $300,000 a year for twenty years.

The logjam was broken.

On March 25, 1969, I signed legislation establishing the two-year medical school. In 1977, a four-year school was authorized. Since that time, the medical school has established facilities and programs throughout the state. By any measure, thanks to many dedicated people – and especially to Howard Hughes – it has been an outstanding success.

PRISON REFORM

Growing up in Carson City made us all familiar with the Nevada State Prison, situated on the eastern outskirts of town. Constructed from the granite that was also used at the State Capitol, it was a foreboding presence in the community. Over the years, parents have driven errant offspring by the prison to tell them that if they didn't shape up, they would be taking up residence behind the high prison walls. Powerful medicine!

On Sundays, during baseball season, we kids used to go there to see the prison team perform. The ballplayers became local favorites. Inmates in those days, once they became "trustees," were often used in town to clean streets, sidewalks and so forth. We even had trustees who were assigned to the Governor's Mansion. It was a sort of "perk" for Governors and their families.

As a young lawyer working for Jack Ross, I visited the prison frequently to consult two death row inmates, Ted Gregory and Owen Butner, who had murdered their wives.

Being young and impressionable, I bought their protestations of innocence "hook, line and sinker." I learned later that most inmates in prison "have their story," which leads to a conclusion for the gullible that they've been framed and shouldn't be incarcerated at all. Despite many moves we made in their behalf, both Ted and Owen eventually went to the gas chamber, much to my chagrin.

Later, as a prosecutor, I learned that even though some who are arrested may be innocent, most are guilty.

Having grown up so close to it, I found it ironic when the prison and its operation became a major issue in the 1966 Governor's campaign.

I contended that the time had come for professionalism in the operation of the prison. Historically, the warden had been a political appointee, and too often a crony of the Governor. Nonetheless, some such as Art Bernard, who had been appointed by Governor Charles Russell, did a superb job.

I further contended that after he left, security had deteriorated rapidly. My campaign commercial on the subject suggested that so many prisoners were escaping that they were causing traffic jams on the streets adjoining the prison!

After the election, we conducted an extensive search for a prison professional. It produced Carl Hocker, who had been at San Quentin State Prison in Northern California. Carl had a well-deserved reputation as a tough corrections officer. He was just what we needed in Nevada.

He quickly instituted procedures which conveyed to the guards and inmates that "business as usual" would no longer be tolerated.

The results were dramatic. The morale of the guards shot up, and the escapes stopped. It appeared the "prison problem" had been solved.

Then one day, in 1968, my contentment with prison affairs was shattered. The warden called and asked to see me immediately. He informed me that he had an inmate strike on his hands. It had been fermenting for weeks and finally flared up, prison-wide.

There were serious charges being made by the inmates, including complaints of abuse by certain guards. The warden had just met with the inmates and was unable to pacify them. He felt the place could "blow sky high" at any time.

The inmate leaders had insisted on meeting with me. Apparently, they believed my campaign statements that things weren't right at the prison and that reforms were needed.

My staff was unanimously opposed to my meeting with the inmates, contending that it would establish a bad precedent, and that there was no way my security could be assured.

Despite their concerns, I decided to go to the prison. Instead of just meeting with the leaders, however, I stipulated that the meeting should be in the yard with all inmates present – except those on death row.

I went to the yard accompanied only by the warden. It was chancy, I felt, but the fact that I was willing personally to hear their grievances should neutralize any trouble-makers.

The meeting was uneventful. The inmates were respectful and told me there were some guards who were "downright cruel" and abused the inmates. After hearing them out, I assured them I'd personally look into it, and if their claims were true, corrective action would be taken.

Afterwards, in meeting with the press, I was asked why I felt the inmates had been so friendly toward me. I told them there was a simple explanation: As they knew, after my prosecutor days, I had done a great deal of criminal defense work and hadn't been too successful. "Hell," I said, "I was perfectly comfortable out there. Many of them were my former clients!"

The checkout revealed that a couple of the guards had grossly mistreated the inmates. They were promptly dismissed, and the Nevada State Prison became a relatively peaceful place again.

POMP AND CIRCUMSTANCE

Being asked to speak at graduations and school functions was a particularly satisfying part of my public life.

As a young lawyer and alumnus of Carson High, I gained experience as a graduation speaker there. I remembered how other speakers had orated endlessly at various ceremonies over the years, so I tried to keep them short, with congratulations well spread among teachers, parents and students alike.

This approach apparently worked because for a time there were very few years when "Paul D. Laxalt, Esq., Attorney at Law," was not the commencement speaker at Carson High.

After my election as Lieutenant Governor, my constituency expanded. Soon, I was speaking at high schools throughout the state. The demand became even greater after my election as Governor.

I was even invited to my alma mater, Santa Clara University, to deliver the commencement address in June of 1967. The ceremony was held in the garden area near the mission chapel. The graduates, which included a future Governor of Nevada, Bob Miller, seemed to enjoy thoroughly the story about my being "hand-delivered" to Father President by Momma Laxalt in 1940. The reception accorded me, and the event itself, were among my most unforgettable experiences. To have my family there, including Momma Laxalt, etched the day in my memory.

Not everything went as smoothly as the Santa Clara commencement. There seemed almost always to be some unexpected event to spice up the evening.

Shortly after I was elected, I was on the usual "head trip" of a newly-elected Governor. Surely everyone in Nevada, I thought, must be aware of the election and my triumphant victory. Reality crashed in on me while attending a high school gathering in Fallon, Nevada. The young man introducing me was the student body President.

Obviously, he had spent a great deal of time on the introduction. He was very complimentary. The longer he went, the more I glowed…until he concluded with these words: "And now, my fellow students, I have the great honor and pleasure to introduce to you, Governor Grant Sawyer!"

Last I heard, the poor fellow still hadn't lived down his famous introduction.

Austin, Nevada, is a historic mining town in central Nevada. Like most mining towns, its growth ebbed and flowed with the condition of the mining economy. I loved the little town and its people and happily accepted the graduating class's invitation to deliver a commencement address.

The ceremony took place in the school's small auditorium. It was a hot, steamy June night, and the room was filled with proud Austinites.

After I was seated on the platform, we awaited the arrival of the 10 graduates. We waited…and waited. Still no graduates. Finally, the principal rushed off the stage. His flushed face showed his patience was exhausted. In a short while, in came the graduates. They weren't marching to the processional, they were stumbling.

It was soon apparent that the Austin graduating class had detoured to a local bar and was showing the effects of the visit. Almost without exception, they were drunk. Nonetheless, they finally made it to their seats, much to the relief of the audience.

The hall was stifling. It was doubtful if these seniors would survive their graduation. Finally, one good-looking lad, totally pickled, stood up uncertainly to introduce me. He had a sheaf of notes in his hand to which he clung.

He started reading the introduction reasonably well, even though his knees shook. Finally, after getting through a few sentences, he exhaled. (Probably a sigh of relief for having survived to that point.) Then, his life preserver, his notes, flew off the podium and slowly drifted into the audience. Panic ensued. I've never seen such terror in anyone's eyes — even in combat during the war.

Then suddenly it happened. My introducer proceeded to vomit all over the platform. We all ran for cover lest we be covered with used red wine.

The young man, though, was gutsy. This descendant of Austin pioneers was not going to abandon ship. He gallantly turned to me and said, "Oh, hell, Governor. You take over."

After a badly-needed clean-up period, the ceremony resumed, and I delivered what must have been the shortest graduation speech in Austin history.

The "Most Difficult" Decision

During my various campaigns, I had taken a strong position in favor of the death penalty.

I found out in February 1969 that it's easy to talk about an issue like capital punishment in the abstract, but it's another ball game when you're confronted by an actual case in which you must decide whether a convicted murderer should live or die.

The case involved a man by the name of Lester Morford, who pled guilty to one of the most heinous crimes in Nevada's history. An itinerant 18-year-old ranch hand from Santa Rosa, California,

Morford, in August 1962, accosted Jack and Patricia Foster, a newly-married couple, by brandishing a pistol as the Fosters were preparing to leave their motel south of Reno.

Morford compelled the Fosters to drive him in their car to the Mount Rose Highway, above Lake Tahoe. There, Morford ordered Mr. Foster to stop the car, and then proceeded in cold blood to shoot the young man twice in the head. Foster later died from the shots. As if that wasn't enough, Morford then raped Mrs. Foster twice. While driving through Carson City, Mrs. Foster managed to escape in front of a gas station.

The Foster's honeymoon had lasted exactly one day.

Morford was captured shortly thereafter. In 1963, he pled guilty before a three-judge panel and was sentenced to death in Nevada's gas chamber.

The next few years were spent in the usual legal maneuvers, with Morford's lawyers trying to change the result. Finally, in 1969, his execution date was set for April 1st.

On February 24, 1969, the Nevada Board of Pardons held a hearing to consider clemency for Morford. By that time, his case had caused various anti-death penalty advocates to become involved.

They contended that there hadn't been an execution in Nevada since 1961 and none in the entire country since 1967. Their position was that the U.S. Supreme Court would in the near future rule on the constitutionality of the death penalty, and that to go forward with Morford's execution would be wrong.

During the debate, even one of the Justices of the Nevada Supreme Court contended that Nevada should not be portrayed as "an ogre anxious to kill."

The hearing room where the Board of Pardons met was packed. Morford was present, of course, as were his parents, who appeared to be decent folks, obviously crushed by what had tran-

Poppa Laxalt's ancestral home near Tardets in the Basque province of
Soule, France. *Photo by Joyce Laxalt. Nevada Historical Society.*

Poppa "in the saddle."

Dinner at the Indart Hotel in Reno after Poppa and
Momma's wedding — October 8, 1921. *Nevada Historical Society.*

Main ranch house of the Allied Land and Livestock Company.
Nevada Historical Society.

In my "birthday suit" — 1922.

With brother Bob (left) at our First Communion,
St. Theresa's Catholic Church in Carson City.
Special Collections, University of Nevada, Reno Library

My fifth grade class in 1932. I'm seated in the middle row, fourth student from the left.

At Marlette Lake in the 1940s.

The Laxalt family "all grown up." Clockwise from top left:
PL, Dominique, Theresa, Robert, John, Sue, Marie and
Peter. *Special Collections, University of Nevada, Reno Library*

Campaigning for Lieutenant Governor in 1962 with my political
Godfather, Barry Goldwater. *Special Collections, University of Nevada, Reno Library*

One of our billboards from the 1966 campaign for
Governor. *Special Collections, University of Nevada, Reno Library*

Poppa (left) with State
Controller Wilson McGowan at
my swearing-in as Governor.
Poppa wouldn't come to the
public swearing-in, so we
arranged a private ceremony.

At the Governor's Mansion with my basketball heroes from Carson High. (l. to r.) Geno Lencioni, PL, Coach George McElroy and Caesar Congdon. *Special Collections, University of Nevada, Reno Library*

Playing games at the Elko Basque festival while Governor. *Special Collections, University of Nevada, Reno Library*

Having fun with some of the cast of Bonanza. (l. to r.) Michael Landon, daughter Sheila, PL and Lorne Greene. *Special Collections, University of Nevada, Reno Library*

Willie Wynn, whom I had the privilege of appointing to my cabinet – the first African-American appointed to a cabinet-level position in Nevada's history. *Special Collections, University of Nevada, Reno Library*

My gubernatorial cabinet posing in front of the State Capitol in 1970. (Front row, l. to r.) Willie Wynn, Hugo Quilici, Elmo DeRicco, Jerry Dondero, PL, Bill Sinnott, Wilson McGowan, Floyd Edsall, Burnell Larson. (Middle row) Lee Burnham, Bill Hancock, Gene Barrett, Clark Russell, John Bawden, Frank Johnson, Roy Nixon, Stan Jones. (Back row) "Speed" Hutchins, Gene Milliken, Lee Birge, Carl Hocker, Jim Bailey, Tom Carter and Karl Harris. *Special Collections, University of Nevada, Reno Library*

Taking a ride with Governor Ron near Santa Barbara. He's on a Tennessee Walker. I have a quarter horse. Any message here?

Taking a hike with my beloved dog, Barbo.

With former Vice President Nelson Rockefeller at a convention of Governors in the late 1960s. *Special Collections, University of Nevada, Reno Library*

Playing golf in Reno in the late 1960s with Joe DiMaggio. Who has the better batting stance? *Special Collections, University of Nevada, Reno Library*

One of my camping buddies at Marlette, Billy Budd.

September 22, 1969

Dear Paul:

I want you to know how much I enjoyed our very candid
discussion today with regard to your political plans.

I just want to re-emphasize what I believe is the most
important consideration you should have in mind in making
your decision. You are blessed with the rare gift of
communicating your ideas which few of your colleagues in
politics can equal. In this critical period of the nation's
history, there is a desperate need for men of your views
but particularly for men with your gift of communication
in the United States Senate.

As an old friend, having your personal interests in mind
as well as the admittedly selfish interests I have for the
Administration and the nation, I strongly urge that you
make an affirmative decision when you return home.

Whatever you do, of course, I shall understand although
I will naturally be deeply disappointed because of the considerations I have mentioned if you decide against making
the race.

With warmest personal regards,

Sincerely,

Honorable Paul Laxalt
Governor of Nevada
Carson City

Richard Nixon's letter encouraging me to run for the
U.S. Senate, September 1969.

In the Oval Office with President
Nixon — September 1969. *White House
photo. Special Collections, University of Nevada,
Reno Library*

George Abbott, PL and Senator Howard Cannon greeting Momma Laxalt at my swearing in as U.S. Senator – January 1975. *Special Collections, University of Nevada, Reno Library*

Meeting China's Deng Xiaoping in the early 1980s. *Special Collections, University of Nevada, Reno Library*

Talking with two of the giants of the U.S. Senate, Strom Thurmond (center) and Bob Dole.

With my good friend and esteemed colleague, Utah Senator Orrin Hatch.

With Sen. Dewey Bartlett of Oklahoma (left) and Sen.
Cliff Hansen of Wyoming. Cowboy boots came in handy
on the floor of the Senate.

A grilling before a tough panel of journalists on Meet the Press in 1981 – a
frequent occurrence after Reagan was elected President.

Special Collections, University of Nevada, Reno Library

Dear Paul – Thanks To Your Loyalty & Hard Work, (and I could add – courage) You & I Finally Live In The Same Town, After Many Years of Friendship With Warmest Regard
Ron

A favorite picture, sent to me shortly after Ron was elected President. *White House photo*

The President during a visit to my Senate office in 1983. *Special Collections, University of Nevada, Reno Library*

Lunch in the U.S. Senate dining room. Clockwise from top left: Senator Chic Hecht, Congressman Harry Reid, PL, Republican National Committee Chairman Frank Fahrenkopf, Carol, entertainer Wayne Newton and Congresswoman Barbara Vucanovich. *Special Collections, University of Nevada, Reno Library*

Dear Paul – I Don't Know What I Was Saying But It Should Have Been "Thanks" To a Best Friend.

Ron

With Ron in the East Room of the White House on his birthday, February 6, 1981. (Dick Schweiker is dancing at the left.) *White House photo*

Who says that it's all business in the Oval Office? Sharing a laugh with Attorney General William French Smith and the President. *White House photo*

There is no limit to what a man can do or where he can go if he doesn't mind who gets the credit.

Ron sent this to me shortly after my election as Governor. How true!

In an and of Politics you are a man Paul whom I respect & admire
Barry.

With Senator Barry Goldwater at Ronald Reagan's second Inauguration, held inside the Capitol rotunda due to the cold weather, January 21, 1985. *White House photo*

Introducing Ron at a political event on the campus of the University of Nevada-Reno in 1982. *White House photo*

With my long-time aide, Tom Loranger, on his wedding day in Lexington, Kentucky, May 1991.

Watching a performance by the Oak Ridge Boys on the South Lawn
of the White House. (l. to r.) Bob Michel, Nancy, PL, Carol, Ron and
Corinne Michel. *White House photo*

Meeting with French President Francois Mitterand in Suston, France in 1981.

President Reagan signing the papers to form a re-election committee in 1983. In the background are (l. to r.) Ed Rollins, Bay Buchanan, Drew Lewis and Frank Fahrenkopf. *White House photo*

The "Irisher" swapping stories with his favorite listener, Carol. *White House photo*

Marlette Lake – August 1985. (l. to r.) Peter, Sue, PL, Robert and John.

A gathering of former Nevada State Legislators in 1986. (l. to r.) Jake Jacobsen, Henry Berrum, Archie Pozzi, Wilson McGowan, John Fransway, Floyd Lamb, PL, Coe Swobe, Snowy Monroe, Jim Slattery, Charley Joerg, Bill Dial (seated).

President Reagan surrounded by my Senate staff in 1984. Standing (l-r), Beverly McKittrick, Rick Spees, Bill Miller, Barbara Burgess, Cary Evans, Santal Manos, Linda Carter, Eileen Brennan, Alexandra Wheeler, Vicki Higgins, Janet Ewing, Kevin Berry, unidentified, Kay Fundis, Ruby Eaves, Kelton Abbott, Debbie Murdock, Fred Nelson, Melody Wright, Sam Ballenger, Jock Nash, Ollie Kinney and Harry Schlegelmilch. Sitting (l-r), PL, Tom Loranger, Michelle Price, Angela Sessions, Cecelia Hines, Karen Pobega and President Reagan. Kneeling (l-r) John Shank, Janene Assuras, Kathy Farrell, Eileen deLatour, Kathleen Rosenauer, Pat Dondero and Ed Allison.

Dedication of the Paul Laxalt State Building, Carson City, May 15, 1999. (l.to.r.) PL, Judge Howard McKibben, Gov. Kenny Guinn, Sen. Harry Reid, Rep. Jim Gibbons, Sen. Richard Bryan, Fmr. Rep. Barbara Vucanovich and Father Caesar Caviglia.

With Carol at our McLean, Virginia home, Christmas 1997.

My Grandkids...

Clockwise: PL, Kevin Laxalt, Adam Laxalt, David Laxalt, Danielle Laxalt, Mackenzie Lokan, Sean Bernard, Jackalyn Laxalt, Kelly Rose Laxalt-Olsen.

Christopher Johnson

Jamie Lokan

Therese and Victoria Laxalt-McDonald

Photo by Patricia Hansen, Alexandria, Virginia

spired and loyally doing all possible to save their son from the gas chamber. They even assumed some of the responsibility for their son's behavior by stating that they had over-disciplined him during his childhood.

The lawyers contended that Morford was an admitted "glue sniffer" and was not competent at the time of the crimes. They also raised the point that we should wait for the U.S. Supreme Court determination. These were points that had been raised in various legal forums and had been rejected. Morford himself had testified as to his lack of recollection due to his glue sniffing and asked the Board for mercy.

At the hearing, he was well-dressed and groomed and appeared sincere, a far cry from how he appeared to the Fosters on the dreaded day of the murder and rapes.

By the time the hearing was winding down, it became clear that the Board was divided on the issue, and mine would be the deciding vote.

Under Nevada law, the Board of Pardons consisted of seven members (five Supreme Court Justices, the Attorney General and the Governor, who acted as the chairman, and therefore voted last).

Of all the decisions I've had to make, the Morford vote was probably the most difficult emotionally. On the one hand, I realized that the Board's function was to act mercifully in a proper case. The courts had to decide purely on a cold, legal basis. But the Board had to consider whether to temper justice with mercy.

In my past experiences in criminal work, even as a prosecutor, very often my heart would go out to the defendant. And to some extent, it did in this case as well. What harm would there really be in waiting for the U.S. Supreme Court? Would society really be harmed?

Finally, I decided that there had been a cold-blooded killing to which Morford pled guilty. The "glue sniffing" and "hard love" by the parents as defenses were not compelling at all. To wait for the U.S. Supreme Court, which might never rule on the death penalty, would be a miscarriage of justice.

So, when the roll was called, I cast the deciding vote in voting "No," thereby denying Morford relief.

I shall never forget the looks I received not only from Morford but his parents as well. I'm sure they felt that I was some hard-hearted S.O.B. with no compassion.

All the anguish I felt, however, turned out to be for naught. Just before the April 1 execution date, Federal Judge Bruce Thompson granted a stay of execution on the ground that we should wait for the U.S. Supreme Court decision.

In 1972, the Supreme Court did act, ruling that the death penalty processes in the various states constituted cruel and unusual punishment and were therefore unconstitutional.

Gradually, over the years, the states have enacted corrective legislation to meet the constitutional standard set by the Court. Today, executions are almost commonplace, with the vast majority of Americans in support of the death penalty.

As it finally developed, Lester Morford saved the state the trouble of executing him. He committed suicide in prison in June 1987.

EXPANDING THE PARKS

We decided to make state park acquisition a high priority. Since 87 percent of Nevada was in federal ownership, there hadn't been much pressure for the state to spend money for parks. After all, between the Bureau of Land Management and U.S. Forest Service, they owned all the park land a small state would ever want or need.

With the development of Tahoe and other areas, though, it

became clear additional areas needed to be protected. The federal agencies expressed little interest in expanding their inventories for lack of funds.

One of the prime targets for the state park people was Lake Tahoe. Huge tracts of land were privately owned, and if not put into public ownership, the park advocates contended, would probably be developed, thereby impairing the ecological balance of a very sensitive area.

Given the green light, the park people began acquiring huge parcels of private property. Between 1967 and 1970, more than 12,000 acres at Lake Tahoe were acquired for the Nevada State Park System.

The park program proved to be so popular that in 1970 a $5 million bond issue was passed, which led to additional purchases.

THE UNION PEOPLE

Although I numbered several union leaders as personal friends, I never enjoyed actual union support during any of my races. In large part, that was due to the fact that to a typical union person, a Republican was enemy.

Over the years, Republican opposition to the labor movements, such as embracing the Right-to-Work laws and passage of the infamous (in their eyes) Taft-Hartley Act, caused labor to view Republicans as the opposition.

This made it difficult for any Republican, including me, to gain support from the unions. The fact that I later led the fight in the U.S. Senate against common situs picketing didn't help. To some, that was a litmus test to determine whether one was pro or anti-union.

In Nevada, during my Governorship, the strongest unions were the Teamsters and the Culinary. The Teamsters had been involved in the Vegas area since the late 40s. Most of the early hotels had been financed by Teamster loans.

Working closely with the Teamsters, the Culinary Union quickly organized the hotels. Vegas, therefore, was "a union town."

During my campaign for Lieutenant Governor, I became acquainted with Al Bramlet, who handled Culinary Union matters in Vegas. He was politically skilled and had an affable personality toward those he considered to be on the same peer level. Otherwise, he could be "hard as nails" if he had to be.

After my election as Governor, he, like many others, advised me that he had "quietly" helped me (even though he was a strong Democrat supporter). During my term as Governor, Al stayed in constant touch with my staff, usually Robbie McBride. I can't recall any instance where he made any unreasonable demands of my office.

Unfortunately, he met an untimely end after disappearing in February 1977. He was found shortly thereafter in the nearby desert. Obviously, he had incurred the wrath of the wrong people.

I recall meeting Jimmy Hoffa in Las Vegas in the early days of my Lieutenant Governorship. It was at a reception on the Strip. What struck me more than anything else was how short he was. In manner, he was cordial and correct, but not the least bit affable.

People handled Hoffa very carefully. He was a person you didn't "fool with." His encounters with Bobby Kennedy, who was hated in Las Vegas, had made him a hero on the Strip. Later, he was convicted of jury tampering and defrauding the Teamsters' Central States Pension Fund, and was sent to prison in 1967, much to the chagrin of his many supporters in Vegas.

In 1971, after I left office — at the behest of several mutual friends — I foolishly wrote President Nixon a letter asking for clemency for Hoffa on the basis that he had been a victim of a political prosecution. I received no reply. I doubt if my letter ever came to the President's attention. If it did, he never mentioned it to me.

After Hoffa went to prison, Frank Fitzsimmons replaced him, but as executive vice president. Hoffa had, of course, blessed Fitzsimmons. The word was that he would be a "caretaker" only. When Hoffa was "sprung," he would take over once again. But, as often happens, Fitz liked the job – a lot.

At the 1971 Teamsters Convention, Fitzsimmons was elected President. Hoffa was released at about that time, but with the understanding that he would not seek office with the Teamsters. Nonetheless, he planned on challenging Fitzsimmons at the 1976 Teamsters Convention.

But, as everyone knows, Jimmy Hoffa disappeared in the Detroit area in July 1975, and was never heard from again. There's little doubt that certain elements feared that he would "tell all" and was thus expendable.

The same fate befell Al Dorfman from Chicago. His father had long been a power in Teamster circles, and Al succeeded him. Urbane and sophisticated, with movie-star good-looks, he was regularly in Las Vegas on Teamster business. I saw him from time to time.

He, too, was murdered in cold blood in January 1983, shortly after being convicted of fraud.

In Las Vegas and nationally, there has been no group in this country which has come under more fire politically than the Teamsters. At times, the federal government has even taken control of its operations.

As Las Vegas grew, and after passage of the corporate gaming legislation, financing for construction and operation came more and more from conventional sources, thus dramatically reducing the influence of the Teamsters.

Nationally, in recent times, we've seen Ron Carey removed as Teamster President as a result of questionable campaign tactics. Teamster money even surfaced in the Clinton campaign finance controversy in recent years. Ironically, Jimmy Hoffa's son is now President of the Teamsters.

For whatever reason, Teamster leadership too often has been questionable. All Americans should continue to hope that the Teamsters Union members themselves clean up the situation. The millions of hard-working, honest Teamster members deserve as much.

CHAPTER II

❖ *Run or Not Run Again?* ❖

Run for Re-election?

Looking toward the 1970 election, I decided I would make a decision on my political future by the end of September 1969. The date was arbitrarily set, but was similar to the same time frame in which I'd announced my candidacy for Governor in 1965.

There were three options: First, of course, I could run for re-election as Governor. The poll numbers were good. It appeared that there would not be any serious opposition.

My wife had grown fairly used to the spotlight, and while my family still resented the intrusion upon their private lives, four more years in the Governor's Mansion would have been acceptable to them if that's what I decided to do. Professionally, there were still a lot of challenges out there for a Nevada Governor.

Another possibility would be to run for the U.S. Senate against Howard Cannon — a re-run of the 1964 race.

Any incumbent U.S. Senator, if he's done his homework, is very difficult to topple. Our polls indicated that if I took Cannon on, it would be a tough race. And there was always the downside of moving the family from Carson City to Washington, D.C. The youngsters did not find that appealing at all. They were happy and content in Nevada. And for that matter, Jackie and I weren't enthused about the prospect of a huge, transcontinental move.

The third option was to get out of politics altogether and return to private life. In many ways, I'd had a stomach full of politics. I had found it to be a tough, invasive experience. At times, it could be downright cruel, particularly when attacks were made against family and friends.

Another factor in the equation was Momma Laxalt, who badly wanted me to build a new Ormsby House, thus replacing the famous old hotel, which had been torn down. Although she was proud of my becoming Governor, she wasn't happy at all about the prospect of her son becoming a career politician. I didn't even consult Poppa Laxalt, feeling that his disdain for politicians and lawyers was a constant.

The September deadline would add a certain amount of excitement to the announcement, and also deter my family, supporters and me from delaying a decision.

Deciding was difficult, but shortly after setting a September 30 deadline, I was contacted by none other than the President of the United States, Richard M. Nixon. He felt that I had essentially completed my work as Governor and another four years would be "caretaker duty," which would "bore the hell" out of me.

He strongly wanted me to "do the Senate race" against Cannon. He thought that securing a Republican majority in the U.S. Senate was possible, even though the Democrats enjoyed a 57-43 advantage at the time. His "political people" had advised him that Nevada was prime for a Republican Senate turnover, and that I was "the man."

Because of the aura of the office, any President is persuasive, but Nixon was more than persuasive: He was overwhelming. To his credit, however, he never gave me the "you owe me" argument.

Indeed, he had been helpful to me in the past. He had come to Las Vegas after President Johnson had pounded me in the 1964 Cannon race. He spoke at my rally to announce for Governor in

Reno, in 1965. Later, as a Presidential candidate in 1968, he and his entourage had spent hours at the mansion in Carson City.

When we first talked about my plans for 1970, I explained to him the reason for the announcement deadline, the options as I saw them, and, in particular, the personal considerations. I'm not sure he related to any of them. President Nixon was a consummate political animal.

He finally decided that the matter was important enough to

With Dick Nixon in front of the Governor's Mansion. He was of great assistance to me on several occasions. It was these types of gestures that endeared him to so many Republicans. *Photo by Bob Davis. Special Collections, University of Nevada, Reno Library*

warrant an Oval Office meeting. When the President suggested such a meeting, my level of apprehension rose considerably. I had been to the White House a few times during my Governorship for meetings, but never had I set foot in the Oval Office.

The realization that the meeting would be a full-court press to convince me to run for the Senate made me even more apprehensive.

Ed Allison, my press secretary, accompanied me on the trip. He'd never been in the White House and eagerly looked forward to the experience, although we both knew that the presidential meeting would be "one on one."

When I was being escorted to the Oval Office, I said to myself: "You'll be completely intimidated by the meeting, but don't commit one way or the other."

I confess that when I entered the Oval Office the sense of history was overwhelming. To think that in this very room most of the important events in our nation's history had occurred!

The President greeted me warmly. After the usual Presidential "photo op," he asked me to sit down in one of the chairs at the Presidential desk. He asked whether or not I'd made up my mind. I told him I had not, that I had decided to defer the decision until after our meeting.

He then proceeded to give me his analysis of my situation. He felt I was suited for public service, and that the highest calling for persons who had the ability and were so inclined was public office. He asked if I felt fulfilled by what we had accomplished during my Governorship. I told him I was.

"If you come here as a Senator, you'll have the chance not only to help Nevadans, but people throughout the country," he stated. In fact, he said, the whole world would be my new constituency, since Senators, if they so choose, deal with worldwide problems. With his emphasis on foreign policy, he said that he would involve me in such issues.

He wasn't persuaded at all by family considerations. In fairness, how could he relate? As a young Congressman, he had moved his young family from California to Washington, and it had worked out well for him.

He closed by giving me his views on the political situation in the Senate. He was within several seats of gaining a Republican majority. A majority, obviously, would help him greatly in advancing his administration's programs.

I thanked him for his time and courtesy and told him that I'd advise him shortly of my decision.

I left the White House relieved that I hadn't been stampeded into a quick decision. To Nixon's credit, he sensed that this was a tough decision, personally and politically, and that I needed more time.

As "announcement day" approached, the pressure built. Those close to me leaned heavily toward my staying in public life.

I made my decision on the weekend before "announcement day." What tipped me more than anything were the personal considerations. Bottom line: I'd served eight years in state office – four as Lieutenant Governor and four as Governor. They were great years, but each succeeding year, our family seemed to pay a higher price.

Just as the youngsters were in their formative years, my duties more and more seemed to prevent my helping Jackie do the parental job that was required. And over the years, Jackie and I were growing dangerously apart. In addition, when our youngest, Neena, started calling me "Governor," I figured something was amiss. It was time for me to reorder my family priorities. Politics and public service had to be secondary.

ANNOUNCEMENT DAY

September 30, 1969, was one of the most unforgettable days of my life. We decided that the most appropriate place for the event would be the Senate chamber in the State Capitol. It was the place where I'd served for four years in the role of President of the Senate as Lieutenant Governor.

In order to protect against leaks, I kept my decision to myself. Hardly anyone expected me to bow out of office at the price of my political life. Most felt that I would run for re-election. After all, only one former Governor, Richard Kirman, had stepped aside after only one term.

Announcing my decision to retire after one term as Governor on September 30, 1969 in the old Nevada State Senate chambers.

Many others felt it was "time to move on" and run for the Senate. Prospects for winning this time were good, they felt. And with the President having a personal interest in me, a career in the Senate had great potential, which would inure to the benefit of Nevada.

To announce under these circumstances that I was getting out of politics altogether would be a shocker – one of the great surprises in Nevada political history – but that is precisely what I did.

I decided to use as the vehicle for the announcement a handwritten letter to President Nixon advising him I would not run for *any* office.

Looking back, it was the theatrical thing to do, but it wasn't right. Those close to me – my family, my loyal supporters – should have been told first.

One in particular, Wayne Pearson, who had been of such help in my political career, deserved to know in advance. He was very dismayed by my decision and abruptly resigned the next day from his post on the Gaming Control Board. I shall always feel badly about the pain I caused him unnecessarily.

Much later, I saw the same mistake made by George Bush when he announced in New Orleans that Dan Quayle was his choice for Vice President. Wholly unprepared or conditioned, Dan was so "hyped" at his first appearances that the country's first impression of him was that of an overexcited schoolboy rather than a serious politician.

Dan never really recovered from that disastrous start. Had he received ample notice so that he could prepare for his debut, politically and psychologically, he would have come across as a young, appealing and serious candidate.

The reaction to my announcement was generally positive. Family and friends understood. The press was magnanimously understanding. The state didn't fall apart at the seams. In short, "school kept."

President Nixon promptly acknowledged my decision with a gracious and understanding letter.

The Last 15 Months

One would think that after a retirement announcement, things would slow down a bit. They certainly didn't.

My staff and cabinet, almost without exception, stayed on until the very end. I didn't have to exhort them to do so. They recognized that the people had elected us to a four-year term, and we were going to do our work faithfully to the end.

Time passed very quickly.

Politically, we were deeply involved with Ed Fike, our Lieutenant Governor, who decided to run for Governor. He was eventually pitted against Mike O'Callaghan, a popular Irishman from Henderson, Nevada. Mike was a Korean War vet who had lost a leg in that conflict. Ed found that campaigning against Mike's wooden leg, which Mike would regularly place on the bars he visited during the race, was tough indeed! Mike won the election.

Remembering how shabbily we'd been treated when I was elected (being locked out of the Mansion until the last moment), we offered the Mansion to the O'Callaghans for the Christmas period, which they've always greatly appreciated.

During the close of the last year, the Hughes family fight broke out and ended in total war. My last several weeks were spent trying to resolve that dispute, which was unpleasant duty.

There were many other important things to do so that the transition to the new administration would be a smooth one.

Of personal interest, I wanted to make certain that my people would be placed in the private sector when I left office. Fortunately, that took care of itself when, at the behest of Momma Laxalt, we decided as a family to rebuild the fabled Ormsby House.

Post-Gubernatorial Reflections

I've had the honor of being elected to various public offices at the local, state and federal levels. Each, for different reasons, was challenging and a valuable learning experience.

In looking back, being Governor of my state was by far the most difficult and demanding. And serving in my hometown of Carson City made it even more stressful. I so wanted not to let my family and hometown friends down.

Having the press constantly at hand wasn't always pleasant, either. In my Senate years, the Washington press had one hundred Senators in their sights. If you were careful, you usually only dealt with the "stringers" of your state's major newspapers. At times, there might be as few as two or three.

As Governor, though, you're "it" as far as the press is concerned. Each day you know they are watching your every move.

To have a press conference in the Capitol with a half dozen reporters seemed to me like heavy duty at the time.

Compared to the press conferences I had in the Senate years, with banks of cameras and a host of reporters, my Gubernatorial press conferences should have been a cakewalk. But in those early days, I had no basis of comparison.

Also, during my years as Governor, I gave the situation far more importance than I should have. From the time I took office until I left, I had the erroneous view that every Nevadan was intensely interested in everything I did as their Governor.

Actually, most people had concerns of their own which far outweighed what was going on in the Governor's office. That point was strongly underscored when we built the Ormsby House.

What an eye-opener it was for me to go for days on end, mixing with hundreds of employees and customers, and never hearing a single reference to the Governor down the street!

But the exaggeration – in my mind – of the "downside" of the job was far exceeded by the benefits.

A Governor, assuming the economy is good, has almost

unlimited potential for helping the people in his or her state. The beauty of the position is that executive power can be utilized effectively and quickly, unlike the legislative branch, which moves so slowly it drove me up the wall when I was in the U.S. Senate.

Nearly everything in the Congress is "long-term." If you have an important initiative, it usually takes years before you can complete the job. As Governor, something can happen in days and weeks rather than years.

Overall, being Governor was a fulfilling experience. The ability to "spread the light" makes it so. Looking back, it helped that the people in those days were far less cynical than now as far as public officials were concerned.

Whenever I went throughout the state, regardless of political affiliations, people would simply "light up." That wasn't because of Paul Laxalt — I knew that. It was because they had entrusted to me the power to handle the reins of government as their Governor.

Would I do it again with the advantage of hindsight? Yes! It was a high honor and privilege to serve the people of Nevada as their Governor, and I think my team was able to do a lot of good for the people.

Not bad for a Basque sheepherder's kid!

CHAPTER 12

❖ *U.S. Senate Campaign, 1974* ❖

Back to Private Life

In leaving politics and returning to private life, I had three goals:

First, I wanted to put the pieces back together in a damaged marriage. I felt that by returning to our King Street home — spending more time with the family — that we could once again be a happy, tightly-knit family.

I was dead wrong. The older kids had gone off to college and were concerned about doing well there. And, unfortunately, the marriage was beyond repair and was eventually dissolved in February 1972.

With the children as constant links, Jackie and I over the years have maintained communications on a very amicable basis.

Returning to the law firm was a confusing experience. Since I had left, it had grown and moved into a new Spanish-style building directly across Minnesota Street from the family home where we were all raised.

I found trying cases, as I had done before, to be frustrating. During the time of my Governorship, many new judges were authorized on the district court level, and I'd appointed several throughout the state. Although there wasn't a legal conflict, the perception wasn't good, so I avoided those courtrooms.

My legal work was limited, too, by the fact that I became totally committed to fulfilling Momma Laxalt's dream of building a new Ormsby House. I naively thought that the acquisition of land for the project, securing financing, dealing with architects and contractors, and finally staffing the hotel for operation could be delegated. How wrong I was!

The original Ormsby House property was too small for a modern hotel, so a great deal of time had to be devoted to acquiring sufficient land for the hotel proper and for adequate parking. This required personally contacting the owners – mostly old friends – telling them of the project, leasing their land and at the same time agreeing to subordinate their leases to the ultimate long-term financing.

Once all this was in place, a package was prepared to take to First National Bank of Nevada, which we hoped would be our primary lender. That required the submission of volumes of documents – copies of the leases, pro-forma projections, appraisals and the like. We, as a family, would have preferred to have had a hotel without gambling, but the bankers indicated that unless we had gambling to help pay the loan, the loan would not be approved.

Then, to obtain funds for furnishing and equipping the hotel, we secured secondary financing from other banks such as First Chicago and Valley Bank.

Fortunately, I was able to induce Clark Russell, former Governor Russell's son, to be the general manager. Although he had no previous experience, Clark was an excellent manager because he was a "quick study," straight as an arrow and tough as he needed to be. Without him, the hotel project would have been an intolerable burden.

Clark faithfully stayed on board until we sold the hotel in 1975, after I was elected to the Senate (in 1974). Since then, he has continued to be in the hotel and casino business and now owns several businesses. His is an outstanding and well-deserved success story.

Building and operating the Ormsby House was an experience I would not look forward to repeating. We found first-hand how difficult the hotel business is. Add gambling and food, and you have a first-class hassle on your hands.

Ormsby House had an exciting and successful start, but then the energy crisis hit. While our locals would constitute the base

A rendering of the Ormsby House, which our family built and operated after I stepped down as Governor. *Special Collections, University of Nevada, Reno Library*

of our income, what would make us profitable, like all Nevada hotels, were the tourists.

Since there was no air service to Carson City, we relied almost entirely on those who could reach us by car. When the gasoline crunch hit, our business, like millions of others throughout the country, was seriously hurt.

While the "patient" was in "intensive care," we applied "artificial respiration" through promotions and "bus business" (transportation of seniors from northern California in the hope that they would leave a few dollars).

When proceeds from the bus customers were disappointing,

we rationalized by saying that the costs were justified since the program was filling the place with "bodies." After all, who wants to patronize an empty casino?

On the expense side, we cut costs to the bone.

The banks, too, were patient. They realized that most new hotels struggle for awhile and the energy crisis aggravated the struggle.

Finally, in 1975, after I was elected to the U.S. Senate, we sold Ormsby House to an old-time Nevada gambler, Woody Lofton. He turned our elegant hotel into a "sawdust joint," and it became quite successful.

It continued to do well until Woody died a few years later, whereupon his son assumed control. It finally hit upon hard times and even went into bankruptcy.

But as this was being written, the Ormsby House is attempting a comeback under the leadership of Bob Cashell, a good friend and former Lieutenant Governor.

Back Into Public Life?

After leaving the Governorship, my political activity was practically nil. This was due to the fact that I was tired of politics and was totally involved in family repair, building and opening the hotel and trying to be useful to the law firm.

I didn't attend the 1972 state party convention, and I didn't even try to become a delegate to the national Republican convention when Nixon was nominated by acclamation to be the GOP standard-bearer for President once again.

My political "contacts" were almost nil, other than occasional phone calls with Barry Goldwater, Dick Nixon and Ron Reagan. I even lost contact with my fellow Governors.

Not being involved in politics proved to be easier than I expected. After we started the Ormsby House, I found that even though the Capitol was only a few hundred feet away, days would go by without any mention of politics.

My lone political link those days was daughter Michelle, who lived with me at the hotel after it opened.

Even then, as a teenager, she was a political junkie. She constantly told me what was happening in the world of politics. And, at times, without badgering me, she would indicate that my real calling was public service – not running a hotel.

She wasn't alone in that view. One day a group of Governors' wives came to the hotel. The Governors were in a nearby conference. Washington Governor Dan Evans' wife, Nancy, came up to me and said, "Paul, what in the world are you doing in a place like this?" I almost responded defensively, but didn't. I smiled and simply "dummied up." When I told Michelle, she responded, "Well, Dad, you know she's right!"

Despite my conscience whispering in my ear, I felt no urge to get back into politics. Life in Carson City was good, and I didn't want to give it up.

Then suddenly, things started to change. Senator Alan Bible, who had served Nevada since 1954 in the U.S. Senate, unexpectedly announced in August 1973 that he was going to retire!

It was a surprise to almost everyone, particularly me. I had thought Senator Bible would be a "Senator for life" – just like Pat McCarran.

Immediately, there was much speculation about who would follow Alan Bible in the U.S. Senate. Some of it was to the effect that Paul Laxalt might once again be a candidate; that he had fulfilled his pledge to his mother to rebuild Ormsby House; his family situation had stabilized; and that he could win.

Senator Bible tried to recruit former Governor Sawyer and Governor O'Callaghan to run, but both "passed." The stated reason for both was that they didn't want to move to Washington. Eventually, 33-year-old Harry Reid, who had been elected Lieutenant Governor in 1970, announced that he was running.

Despite these developments, I still had no appetite to run.

Nonetheless, in late 1973, as speculation increased that I would run, my law partners wondered what the future held for us. We finally decided to discuss the matter fully.

I thought going into the meeting that my partners – brother Mick, Bob Berry, George Allison, Reese Taylor, Mel Brunetti and Andy MacKenzie – knowing how content I was in private life, would concur with my wish not to go back to the political wars. I was wrong.

They were approaching the matter on a far higher level than I. They felt it was my duty to consider seriously my responsibility to my state and country. They felt strongly that my place was in public office, not in private life.

Mel Brunetti, whom I later had the pleasure of nominating to the 9th Circuit Court of Appeals, put it succinctly: "Paul, we'd like nothing better than to have you with us, but it won't be long before you'll get sick and tired of counting pine cones at Marlette." His message wasn't lost on me.

Still, when pressed for an answer by the Republican Senatorial Committee, I advised them that it was a "no go" as far as running was concerned. I told them that they had better recruit someone else.

Shortly thereafter, I received a fateful phone call from Senator Barry Goldwater, who was in Washington. His opening line – in characteristically blunt Goldwater fashion – was, "What's this crap I hear about your not running?"

I respectfully pointed out to him that I had spent 12 years of my life in public service and that was quite long enough. Besides, I was enjoying private life a lot.

My response didn't sell. He tartly observed: "That's bullshit! First of all, you should view public service as a high honor, not a burden. Besides, if people like you and I check out of this business, what in the hell is going to happen to this country?"

I had to admit that I had no right to place my personal pleasure ahead of my public responsibility.

In 1974, in the wake of Watergate, the Republican Party was severely hurt. Although running in that year was a disadvantage in terms of timing, the Senate seat was open, and I did have a good chance to win.

After the Goldwater call, I conferred with my closest political supporters. They agreed with Barry.

So, in February 1974, I publicly announced my candidacy. Barry was delighted, but not more than daughter Michelle!

1974 Senate Campaign

My first challenge in the 1974 race was to shore up my political base. I'd been out of politics for four years, and I sensed that there were a lot of bruised feelings out there on the part of the party activists who blamed me for the Governorship now being in Democrat hands in the person of Mike O'Callaghan.

It was like starting all over again. I went to coffee klatches, small lunches and the like. Much handholding was required. Jerry Dondero and Dick Horton, a Reno attorney, did yeoman work for me through their embarrassingly glowing introductions of me.

Little by little, we were able to revitalize the political organization we'd put together in my days as Governor. And at the same time, we were successful in raising enough money to run a credible campaign.

All of it was time-consuming work. I had learned early on that in running for any office you are only as strong as your base of supporters.

While it was generally known I was in the race, we made it "official" with a kickoff rally in Elko.

As a result of all this effort, I won the Republican primary in September handily. It was good to know that my party was still solidly in my corner.

The Democrats nominated Lieutenant Governor Harry Reid. I first met Harry when, in 1968, he was elected to the Assembly from Southern Nevada. He and Richard Bryan, who was elected the same year, were known as the "Gold Dust Twins" because, even as freshmen in the state Legislature, they were highly visible and aggressive. They had the same drive then that eventually propelled the two of them to the U.S. Senate.

Although I didn't know Harry well in my days as Governor, the few contacts I had with him were positive. He is a low-key, dedicated politician with a Mormon base, who is willing to work his tail off — a tough combination in any league.

He came from the small town of Searchlight, Nevada, and with his wife, Landra, was raising a large family.

Political Bombshell: The Nixon Pardon

After the primaries, our polls showed me ahead. The Republicans were solid, and we were also attracting a respectable share of Democrats, many of them holdover supporters from the Governorship days.

When the poll results leaked out, as they usually do, the crowds on the campaign trail became larger and more enthusiastic. We began to be somewhat optimistic that I would win, despite the problems of Watergate.

But when things look good in politics, that's the time to be extra vigilant — or nervous. Too often the unforeseen event over which you have no control can do you in.

If you don't believe me, ask George Bush, who after the Gulf War had approval ratings of 90 percent, and yet several months later was toppled by a little-known Governor from Arkansas. In his case, the unforeseen event was a deep recession, which he didn't handle well, at least politically.

In my case, the unforeseen event was the pardon of Richard Nixon by President Gerald Ford. Whether it was the right thing to do is for historians to judge. Politically, it was a disaster.

Without any conditioning of the people as to why a pardon was in the public interest, the news of the pardon came like an unexpected cold shower. President Ford's poll numbers plummeted overnight. So did the polls for Republican candidates throughout the country, including my Senate campaign in Nevada. Talk about a "trickle down" effect!

Dick Wirthlin, who was Barry Goldwater's pollster and later became Ronald Reagan's, and who was doing my polling in 1974, told me afterward that in all his years of polling, he had never seen such a disastrous political event.

Jake Garn, who was running for the Senate in neighboring Utah, was in the same boat. Very quickly, he dropped from being a near-certain winner to a probable loser.

The day the news of the pardon broke from Washington, I had an event scheduled before a business group in Sparks. The devout coward in me surfaced quickly. I tried to figure a way to skip the event but couldn't. I knew that if I escaped from being "tarred and feathered," I'd be one lucky Basque.

The event was worse — much worse — than I had expected.

The group, composed of conservative businessmen, many of them friends, couldn't kick Gerald Ford in the ass, so mine would have to do!

They were outraged. They had concluded that some sort of deal had been made — Nixon resigning and Ford made President in exchange for a pardon. They thought it was rotten and could ruin the Republican Party.

This could translate into a huge "turnoff" of Republican

voters. It meant that I would be in the political fight of my life. Fortunately, I was free of all things Watergate, including the pardon. I had been in the private sector the whole time.

Finally, a line which popped into my head during a question-and-answer session, provided an answer to my getting blamed for Watergate.

"I had as much to do with Watergate as Harry Reid had to do with Chappaquiddick." That one line put out the Watergate fire as well as all the rhetoric in the world!

Even though we did as well as could be expected, I never would have won the race had we not received help from an unexpected quarter, the Reid campaign team.

I said after the election, and I believe it to be true now, that if Harry Reid had left Nevada on the day of the pardon and spent the rest of the campaign on the beaches of Waikiki in Hawaii, we never would have won. As happens so often in politics, the Reid campaign instead blew this one by indulging in overkill.

Harry had some campaign operatives who weren't content to beat an opponent "fair and square." They couldn't resist going for the jugular. And they did!

They conducted a negative campaign that attempted to question the integrity and reputation of the entire Laxalt family. We Laxalts had been around Nevada a long time, and no one had ever tried to sully our reputations before.

The low point of the effort came when they demanded financial disclosures from each of my brothers and sisters. When I pointed out that Sister Sue was a Catholic nun with a vow of poverty, the requests for disclosures — except from shrill partisans — died.

Aiding in the negative campaign against me, unfortunately, was Hank Greenspun, publisher of the Las Vegas Sun, who was unhappy with me since my days as Governor because I wouldn't accede to the many favors he asked of the Governor's office.

He ran front-page editorials raising questions about how the Ormsby House had been financed and generally making the case that, in his humble opinion, I was unqualified to serve as a U.S. Senator. As I said at the time, each time he ran a vicious editorial, he enraged my supporters, who worked all the harder on my behalf.

Shaking hands with U.S. Senator Alan Bible, whom I succeeded as Senator in 1974. He graciously stepped down early to give me a leg up on seniority.
Special Collections, University of Nevada, Reno Library

Thus, without the help of the Reid campaign team and Hank Greenspun, I doubt if I would have overcome the Nixon pardon. Their tactics backfired and provided me with the political "life preserver" I needed after the pardon.

To this day, I still cannot figure out why the decision to pardon couldn't have been delayed until after the election.

Nonetheless, in November, I was elected to the Senate by 624 votes. Harry Reid called for a recount, but it didn't change the result.

Greenspun, however, didn't accept the election results. He took his vendetta to Washington and contacted Senator Henry "Scoop" Jackson, Democrat of Washington state, with whom

Greenspun had been in contact previously on matters pertaining to Israel. He later told me that Hank had tried to disqualify me from taking the oath. Scoop, who became a good friend, also told me that no one in Washington took Greenspun seriously.

Alan Bible, God bless his soul, in order to give me an advantage in seniority, resigned early – on December 17, 1974 – and I was sworn in as a U.S. Senator the next day.

A few days later, Jake Garn was sworn in as the new Senator from Utah. His predecessor, Wallace Bennett, also resigned early but after Senator Bible, thus giving me a slight seniority edge over Jake, which I constantly reminded him of over the years.

I was the only Republican elected to a "Democrat" Senate seat in that "Watergate year," and Jake and I were the only two new Republicans elected to the Senate. We ended up being seatmates for 12 years and fast friends for life.

❖ *Starting Out in Washington, D.C.* ❖

Opening Day — Senate

Within moments of taking my oath of office, I was placed on the floor next to Barry Goldwater. Just before, in the Senate gallery, Momma Laxalt had cautioned him: "Take care of my boy," to which Barry meekly responded, "Don't worry, Momma, I will."

Later, on the floor, Barry said, "Well, you're now one of us. How do you feel?"

"Senator," I said, "I can scarcely believe I'm here."

"Well, Paul," he responded, "don't worry a hell of a lot about it. In a few months, you'll wonder how in the hell the rest of us got here."

It was appropriate that I be seated next to Barry Goldwater. I had admired and respected him since his ill-fated Presidential race in 1964. He was western, he was gutsy and he was conservative. That was good enough for me.

In 1964, as Lieutenant Governor, I had been the first high-ranking state official to commit publicly for him. Then, in mid-summer of that election year, I had filed for the Senate when our consensus candidate, Bill Raggio, decided at the last moment not to run.

After the bitter 1964 San Francisco convention, where Senator Goldwater was nominated for President, he became a prominent issue in my senatorial campaign. In October that year, when it was apparent that Lyndon Johnson was going to win in a landslide, the "Goldwater problem" became a burdensome political issue for many Republican candidates.

In the closing hours of the campaign, as Barry made his last campaign swing through the country, candidate after candidate "ducked" him. As he proceeded West to close out his campaign in Arizona, I came under increasing pressure from my campaign team to do the same.

I was locked in a tough head-to-head battle with Senator Howard Cannon, and although President Lyndon Johnson had come into Nevada to deliver his "I need Howard Cannon with me in Washington" pitch, it still looked as if I could win.

My politicos, with every good intention, pleaded, "Don't show when Goldwater comes to Vegas." He was due within hours of the election. "He'll understand," they said. "Just tell him you have to campaign up north in Reno."

I decided that I couldn't do that. So, on a bright sunny Las Vegas day – October 30, 1964 – the Friday before the election, I warmly greeted Barry at an airport rally.

And I was so glad that I did! His eyes showed such understanding and appreciation that I shall never forget it.

I lost the Senate race by less than 100 votes after a recount. The pundits attributed my loss to the meeting with Barry. Who knows? Some of the newspapers splashed huge pictures of the two of us on their front pages the day after the meeting.

Maybe enough voters responded negatively and voted against me. Or maybe many voted for me because I hadn't resorted to ducking a friend going through difficult days.

Whether it made the difference, we'll never know. But I do know that I was able to look Barry Goldwater in the eye ever after.

There's a saying in politics that there are many bends in the road, and that if you turn someone around, it will one day come back to haunt you.

So, what happened? In 1974, I ran for the Senate. (You can see that I have a great sense of political timing: 1964 with Goldwater and 1974 with Watergate.)

If I had turned my back on Barry Goldwater in 1964, do you think that he would have called me 10 years later to implore me to run for the U.S. Senate? I doubt it.

A FRESHMAN VIEW OF THE SENATE

Today, as I write this, almost 25 years after I was sworn into the Senate, I can still vividly recall the excitement that I experienced with each new day.

I was in awe of the whole scene.

The Senate chamber, with its traditions and history; each desk initialed by every Senator who had used it; the galleries, full of interested people. All this combined to give me a feeling of unreality.

Yes, Barry, I could hardly believe I was there!

In later years, I had occasion to see many legislative chambers throughout the world but none began to equal ours.

The cloakrooms, however, about which so much has been written over the years, didn't meet my expectations. They are long, narrow rooms adjoining the Senate floor — one each for the Democrats and Republicans. In many ways, though, the cloakroom had an operational utility. Fully staffed, they were convenient for quick party caucuses (and a great place to watch Monday Night Football!).

When I first arrived, the entire Capitol area was quite accessible. You could come and go as you pleased. But when a bomb exploded near the Republican cloakroom in 1983, the informality quickly changed. In fact, a number of Nevadans, including me, had attended a reception near the cloakroom a short time before the explosion.

In addition, the truck bombing of the Marine barracks in Beirut in October 1983 caused a quick realization that the entire Capitol complex was just as vulnerable. Soon thereafter, new procedures were established to monitor every vehicle's contents before being admitted to the parking areas of the Capitol.

I still can't get used to all the metal detectors and armed security people on Capitol Hill. It's an unfortunate sign of the times.

Hugh Scott of Pennsylvania, the Republican leader in those days, was very helpful in getting me settled. Most of the other Senators were also quite gracious in welcoming me to the Senate. Although I was a total stranger to most of them, you'd have never known it.

The conservatives quickly took me under their wing, rightly assuming that any political godson of Barry Goldwater must be "acceptable." Their admonition to me was to not become too tightly associated with "those eastern Republican moderates," who had their own "Wednesday Club."

The conservative group was known then, and still is today, as the "Republican Steering Committee." Although I certainly never joined the "Wednesday Club," in time I became close to many of them. I learned that they did not have horns. They probably felt the same about me.

I quickly learned that it was easier to be a committed conservative in a small western state such as Nevada than representing large eastern states, where constituents were mainly big-city, minority and union-dominated.

Moreover, I did not believe that political differences need become personal. After all, whether we are liberal, conservative or somewhere in between, we were all trying to do the public good, recognizing that we travel different political roads to get there.

What I didn't expect, although I should have, was how warmly the Democrats welcomed me.

MIKE MANSFIELD

Mike Mansfield of Montana was the Senate Majority Leader when I arrived in the Senate. He was a classic westerner, although he had taught Chinese history at the University of Montana before being elected to the Senate.

That experience served him well when he retired from the Senate. He served as Ambassador to Japan for many years. I had the pleasure of visiting him there, and still recall the absolute reverence in which the Japanese held "Big Mike" – almost like Douglas MacArthur.

And as this is being written, Senator Mansfield is still busily engaged in Washington consulting on Far Eastern matters. He's well into his nineties but just as lively and alert as always.

When I first went to Mike for advice, he told me he "wasn't into counseling," but he said, and I've never forgotten, "Don't take yourself too seriously in this town, because no one else will."

One other recollection: Within a few weeks of my coming to the Senate, Mansfield invited me to join his delegation in going to a legislative conference in Mexico. We were to meet with our Mexican counterparts to exchange ideas, mainly on legislative process.

After the first day's meeting, the Mexicans had a reception for us. I decided to wear my "Las Vegas best" – a bright red plaid jacket, with matching red trousers.

As soon as I arrived at the reception, I knew all wasn't well. Mike took me aside with the terse message: "Paul, when you're in Las Vegas, dress as you like. But at meetings like this, goddamnit, dress like a United States Senator."

Thereafter, at foreign receptions, I was probably the most

conservative dresser in the whole delegation!

HUBERT HUMPHREY

Hubert Humphrey was the very liberal and colorful senator from Minnesota, Vice President to Lyndon Johnson and thereafter, in 1968, the Democrat nominee running for President against Richard Nixon.

Hubert was "larger than life," as far as I was concerned. Shortly

after my arrival, he invited me to lunch with him in the Senate dining room, a rare honor. His grandson, about 10-years-old, joined us. Although I helped raise six youngsters myself, I was amazed to see how well the Senator related to this lad, who obviously adored his granddad.

On another occasion, I remember returning from the White House after a meeting with President Ford, who had just advised a group of us Republican conservatives

U. S. Senator Hubert H. Humphrey. Although we were on opposite ends of the political spectrum, I considered him to be a close friend and a giant in the U.S. Senate.

that although he had tried to balance the budget for the oncoming year, he couldn't, and would therefore present a budget with a $23 billion deficit.

For one who had submitted balanced budgets during his Governorship and who had campaigned on a platform of "fiscal responsibility," the news from President Ford was depressing.

I ran into Senator Humphrey shortly after and must have looked downcast. He inquired why, and I told him of the Ford meeting, whereupon he replied, "Don't worry about the damned deficits! After all, we only owe the money to ourselves."

And thereafter, when we had one huge deficit after another, and the political sky didn't come falling down, I couldn't help but think, "Maybe Hubert was right." Still, I never really believed it, for the burden would fall to future generations.

The most poignant moment of all my years in the Senate occurred after Hubert contracted terminal cancer and returned to the Senate floor for a farewell. He spoke from the well, beautifully recounting his days in the Senate.

When he concluded, there was the most resounding applause from his colleagues and the galleries that I've ever heard in that historic chamber.

And who was the first to leave his seat on the floor, rush to the well and embrace Hubert? None other than that other old war-horse, Barry Goldwater. For those of us who knew them both, there was hardly a dry eye in the chamber.

The Southerners

I guess Watergate, and the so-called reforms it precipitated, did some good. However, at times when I was in the Senate and thereafter, I often have wondered whether they were worth it.

Since the founding of the Republic, the Senate has been a stable, generally respected institution. It has survived a Civil War, assassinations and the resignation of a sitting President, and has plodded forward, doing its job in a deliberate manner.

In my opinion, one of the principal reasons the Senate has been so stable is because of the seniority system.

When I came to the Senate, the chairmanships of many important committees were held by long-serving southerners: John

Stennis of Mississippi was Chairman of the Armed Services Committee; John McClellan of Arkansas was Chairman of the Appropriations Committee; James Eastland of Mississippi was Chairman of the Judiciary Committee (He ran the committee with an iron hand so, as he put it, "those damn liberals don't steal the store."); Herman Talmadge of Georgia was Chairman of the Agriculture and Forestry Committee; and Russell Long of Louisiana was Chairman of the Finance Committee.

Each was held in high regard, in and out of the institution. They constituted a core of "wise men" who kept the Senate on an even keel.

In recent years, we've heard more and more discord among Senators, with even the loss of basic civility. What a shame!

In the early days of my Senate career, politics reared its head at election time, but rarely carried over. The Senate was a "comfort zone" for all its members. You might be catching hell on the outside, but as soon as you hit the floor, you knew, regardless of party, that you were among friends.

JUDGING YOUR OWN

There were exceptions to the foregoing description of the Senate. I'm referring to the treatment of two Democrats, Herman Talmadge of Georgia and Harrison "Pete" Williams of New Jersey, two Senators who had befriended me early in my Senate career. After Herman and Pete became involved in separate scandals, their colleagues did turn on them. Some years later, the same thing happened to Oregon's Bob Packwood.

Talmadge, in the wake of a nasty divorce, was accused of secreting large amounts of "campaign cash" and not reporting it. He was also accused of falsely claiming reimbursement of expense money.

Some of the more sensational evidence against him involved his wife (before the divorce), and an overcoat full of $100 bills.

Talmadge, in my view, was caught in the transition from the "old politics" to the new. From the beginning of the Republic, cash contributions were perfectly legal. As a result, many Senators had "cash reserves."

Some "tin canned" the money. Some had safes for the purpose. Herman's safe was his overcoat. Until the reforms were instituted after Watergate, unreported overcoat money raised no eyebrows. Since the cash didn't need to be reported, all was well.

Talmadge never made the transition. It was a sad day when he was "denounced" by the Senate in 1979. I voted against the resolution. Eventually, he was defeated in the 1980 election. Everyone liked him and many were depressed that his career had to end in such a tawdry manner.

Pete Williams was caught in an FBI sting operation known as Abscam, which targeted several members of the House and Senate in 1980. The FBI agents posed as wealthy Arabs, who in turn tried to bribe various public officials. The FBI recorded the meetings on video or audio tape.

Pete was eventually convicted for his participation in a phony business venture, even though he had turned down a cash bribe. When the Senate considered his fate, Pete defended himself on the basis that he'd been set up and the purported Williams voice on the tape was not his. To back this claim, he brought in voice experts who supported his view. They concluded that a new voice, duplicating Pete's and incriminating him, had been "dubbed in."

Unfortunately for him, the Senate didn't believe him. Before a vote was taken to expel him, Pete wisely decided to resign. Many of us felt that the entire Abscam investigation had been misguided. It had all the earmarks of entrapment.

I stayed in touch with both Herman and Pete after their respective downfalls. They survived the humiliation that goes hand-in-hand with leaving office under these circumstances. To their great credit, they continue to play constructive roles in their respective states.

Organizing the Office

I'm told that nowadays new Senators have orientation sessions to familiarize them with what the Senate is all about.

When Jake Garn and I came to the Senate, there was nothing of the sort. They pushed you into the deep water, and you were on your own. I guess they assumed that since we had each held elected executive offices before, we already were "pros." That was far from the truth.

While we knew our way around a state capitol or city hall, Washington and the Senate were brand new to us. Jake and I eventually learned the "ins and outs" of the Senate, including the power centers, but it took awhile.

As to organizing the office, my long-time friend Jerry Dondero, who became my administrative assistant, the top staff position in most Senate and House offices, and George Abbott, a Minden, Nevada, lawyer and an old Washington hand, were most helpful.

Carol Wilson, my future wife, had come from Carson City to Washington. Since she had run the Governor's office, she knew the basics of setting up the office and trying to make the new personalities compatible. She was enormously helpful.

Carol and I were married January 2, 1976. We both felt that her staying on as office manager, which would have been perfectly legal, nonetheless would have created problems. So while I gained a wife, I lost a very gifted staff member.

Fortunately, Carol had groomed a very capable "backstop" in Eileen deLatour, who was in our Senate office from the very beginning. She had, from time-to-time, filled in for Carol in assisting me. Eileen, who came to our office from the Republican Senatorial Campaign Committee, was a bright, beautiful "Irisher" with great political instincts. She quickly became my "right arm."

Even though she later married Dr. Frank deLatour and started raising a family, Eileen loyally stayed on board for the remainder of my Senate term. Her coming to me when I desperately needed someone with her Washington experience was truly a Godsend.

As to office space, Senator Bible, after garnering valuable seniority through 20 years in the Senate, had secured prime offices on the first floor of the Russell Senate Office Building. I had hoped to inherit the offices.

The suite faced Delaware Avenue and a beautiful park. All in all, it was one of the most spacious and convenient offices in the entire Senate. I was, as the southerners say, "in high cotton," and feeling mighty important.

One day, a request for an appointment came from Senator Ed Muskie of Maine. A veteran of many years in the Senate, he was also a leading national figure in the Democratic party. When informed of the request, I felt proud that such a distinguished man was coming to pay his respects to this lowly freshman.

At the appointed time, he and several aides marched into the office. Rather than visiting me, I thought, this guy is coveting our suite! He and his people were doing a reconnaissance of our offices.

And surely they were. In January, Muskie moved in, and we all moved to the basement. I found out quickly what Senate seniority was all about.

A few years later, since I was senior in the class of 1974, I succeeded to a beautiful suite in the Russell Building across from the famous caucus room, with a private balcony overlooking the Capitol dome. Ted Kennedy took over the suite after I retired and has been there since.

In January 1975, the committee assignments were made, again based on seniority.

I was given the Aeronautical and Space Sciences Committee, chaired by Frank Moss of Utah, and the Labor and Public Welfare Committee, chaired by Harrison "Pete" Williams of New Jersey.

My heart sank when I learned that I was going to the Labor Committee. All my conservative friends had advised me that Labor was a "purgatory" for conservatives.

Every liberal worth his salt was on the committee: such Republicans as Jacob Javits and Democrats Walter Mondale and Ted Kennedy. I was sure that they'd eat me up.

Some of the conservatives knew what they were talking about from personal experience, for they had served in "purgatory" themselves for two years, and then had gotten the hell out at the first opportunity.

Little did I realize at the time that being the only conservative on that committee would quickly provide a rookie freshman with a legislative challenge much earlier than anyone expected, including me.

CHAPTER 14

❖ *Legislative Battles* ❖

CUTTING MY TEETH ON COMMON SITUS PICKETING

Ironically, the Labor and Public Welfare Committee to which I'd been assigned in January 1975, would become the focal point of one of the most controversial pieces of legislation in history.

It involved what became known as "common situs picketing."

This form of picketing, if allowed, would have permitted unions to picket an entire construction site over a dispute with one contractor working at the site. The union-backed bill would have overturned a 1951 Supreme Court decision that such picketing constituted an illegal secondary boycott.

Labor tried for years to pass this legislation, but contractors and other employer organizations had successfully prevented legislation from reaching the floor.

But after the Watergate election in 1974, Labor saw 1975 as the ideal year to try again. The new Congress was overwhelmingly Democratic, with many of those Democrats beholden to Labor as a result of campaign contributions. Passage in the House was considered a "slam dunk," but the Senate would be more difficult.

The key Senate committee was Labor and Public Welfare, which was solidly committed to Labor, with the exception of a rookie from Nevada by the name of Laxalt.

In addition to the rosy Congressional picture, the White

House, even though occupied by a Republican President, appeared to be in Labor's pocket. President Ford, both publicly and privately, had promised to sign a common situs picketing bill if it incorporated certain "safeguards" he wanted, and if he also received legislation creating a collective bargaining committee.

As predicted, the House, in late July 1975, easily passed H.R. 5900, which included President Ford's "safeguards," and in September, the House also passed the collective bargaining bill sought by the Administration.

The debate in the House, such as it was, centered on Labor's contention that the Supreme Court decision effectively neutralized a strike as a bargaining tool.

What really rankled them the most, though, was that the court ruling prohibited unions from striking against contractors who employed non-union labor. That was the real play. The unions were seeking to undermine seriously the right-to-work laws, which existed in some 19 states, including Nevada. That brought into play the lobbying resources of the potent National Right-to-Work Committee, headed by Reed Larson.

With House passage of the legislation, the spotlight quickly turned to the Senate and the Labor Committee, which had jurisdiction over the bill. Under Senate tradition, I would take the lead in opposing the bill both within the committee and on the floor.

The committee hearings went about as expected. Various cosmetic amendments were offered and rejected. I offered an amendment that would have continued to prohibit common site picketing in the right-to-work states and gained a "moral" victory of sorts. Instead of my usual one vote in favor, the amendment received three votes. I had tripled my strength in the committee!

But the die was cast. On October 29, common situs and construction industry collective bargaining bills were voted out of the committee by votes of 13-1, with yours truly being the lone dissenting vote.

According to a news report, the committee, in its majority report, "strongly endorsed the principle that a union with a legitimate grievance against one contractor or subcontractor should be able to bring economic pressure to bear on the other contractors at the same building site."

I warned that common site picketing gave building trades a powerful and potentially dangerous organizational tool which "would encourage unionized employees who have long objected to the presence of non-union workers on construction sites, to strike and to ask other union workers to strike or protest the presence of non-union workers."

But, as logical and persuasive as I viewed the argument to be, it fell on deaf ears.

I decided that I needed help – lots of it – quickly. Within the Senate, such colleagues as Bob Griffin of Michigan, Dewey Bartlett of Oklahoma, Jesse Helms of North Carolina, Jim Allen of Alabama, Carl Curtis of Nebraska, Jim Buckley of New York and last, but certainly not least, Russell Long of Louisiana, all offered to help.

At our first meeting, it was clear we could form a conservative coalition of Republicans and southern Democrats. Then, here or there, we could also pick off a few Senators from right-to-work states.

After a head count, we came to the conclusion that on a "best case" basis, we could garner 40 to 45 votes – not enough for a floor victory, but perhaps enough to sustain a filibuster. (It takes 60 or more votes to shut down a filibuster.)

We also came to the conclusion that if we couldn't win on the floor, we should focus our strategy on President Ford (i.e., entice him to veto the bill).

Despite his public declarations in favor of the legislation, we felt that if we could marshal public opinion strongly in our favor, Ford would have to take that into consideration. After all, he would face a tough election in 1976.

Marshaling public opinion proved to be no problem. Immediately, the Associated General Contractors, with Jim Sprague and Warren Richardson, the Chamber of Commerce, the National Association of Manufacturers, the Business Roundtable and many others pitched in. These were all Washington pros who didn't need any pictures drawn for them.

The story on the floor was much the same as in the committee. As planned, we filibustered. In the old days, this procedural safeguard was used only in matters of great public interest, such as the Civil Rights Bill. Now, when an opponent doesn't have a simple majority, too often a filibuster is used to delay the process. After all, 41 votes are much easier to garner than 51.

We did have a temporary victory on November 14. The first vote to limit debate on the bill itself failed 58-31 — two votes short of the 60 needed to cut off the filibuster.

But on the second "cloture" vote, the Senate adopted the motion to limit debate by 62-37 vote. Labor obviously had gotten its act together.

Several "conservative" amendments were offered to the bill, but all were voted down.

Finally, on November 19, the Senate passed H.R. 5900 by a vote of 52-45. Our original vote count proved to be quite accurate and didn't change much during the floor debate.

Interestingly, the conference committee, which meets following the passage of similar bills by each house and is used to iron out differences in the two versions, centered not on the differences in the two bills, but on the question of whether the President would sign the bill.

Each side presented its own "spin," and eventually both

houses adopted the conference report, and the bill went to the President on December 15.

Our business allies had done their homework. As many as 750,000 pieces of anti-common situs mail flooded the White House, while only about 26,000 letters arrived in support of the legislation.

As significant as all this was, equally important was the fact that Ronald Reagan, then a Presidential candidate, announced his strong opposition to the measure and darkly hinted in the process that many Republicans would shift their campaign support to him if Ford signed the bill.

To the shock of organized labor, President Ford announced his veto decision on December 22. Quite a Christmas present for us!

In his veto message, he stated: "Unfortunately, my earlier optimism that this bill provided a resolution, which would have the support of all parties, was unfounded. As a result, I cannot in good conscience sign this measure, given the lack of agreement among the various parties to the historical dispute over the impact of the bill on the construction industry."

Ford's announcement was greeted with cries of betrayal from organized labor. To say the least, George Meany, AFL-CIO President, was not happy. He whined, "Now the President has shown what his word is worth." I learned later that George wasn't all that happy with a guy by the name of Laxalt, either.

Tip O'Neill justifiably criticized organized labor for insufficient efforts on behalf of the bill. "While opposition lobbyists were flooding the Congress and the White House with mail, labor let things slide until the last minute. When you get careless, the train goes off the track."

Labor went down fighting. They reintroduced the legislation in 1976. In a narrow vote, the House, on March 23, rejected common situs picketing by a vote of 217-205. Unbelievable!

That vote drove the last nail in the Labor's common situs casket. So far as I know, it's never been revived since.

Nevertheless, organized labor has a long memory. In 1979, when I was standing for re-election, Al Barkan, who was labor's chief political operative, came to Nevada and told our local press that I was a "double-plated, triple-sided, four-faced, five-ply rubber stamp for national anti-labor forces."

Other than that, Al must have thought I was a helluva guy!

The common situs experience was educational, enriching and satisfying.

My relationship with my Senate colleagues on both sides of the aisle changed overnight, mostly for the better.

It also established my credentials in Washington's conservative community, so much so that they turned to me to lead another highly controversial battle which came during the Carter years: the fight over the Panama Canal treaties.

A Memorable Lincoln Day

Not all the excitement in my early Senate career involved legislative battles on Capitol Hill.

In February 1976, I was invited to speak to a Lincoln Day dinner in Napa, California, in the heart of the wine country.

It has long been one of the duties of elected Republicans to speak at Lincoln Day dinners, which are held each February.

Soon after I arrived in Napa, I was advised by the Ford White House that there would be a critical vote the next day, and the President sorely needed my support. It was decided that after I spoke, I would be driven from Napa to San Francisco (about a two-hour drive) and then catch a "red-eye" flight back to Washington.

As Lincoln Day dinners are known to do, it lasted well past my scheduled departure time by car. "Plan B" was put into operation: A private plane would take me to San Francisco.

I was uneasy. There was a heavy rainstorm at the Napa airport, which made seeing beyond a few feet difficult. I was escorted to a strange plane with two unfamiliar pilots.

At that point, whatever concerns I might have had simply didn't matter. I'd convinced myself that this was an emergency. I had to make that "red-eye" or the Republic would be irrevocably damaged!

When we taxied to the end of the runway, a strange thing happened: One of the pilots turned off the engine. I didn't think much about it at the time.

Finally, we took off for San Francisco. The short trip — about 20 minutes — was uneventful until we were over San Francisco, when suddenly all was eerily quiet.

The engine had quit! And do you know why? We were out of gas! I now realized that they had cut the engine earlier in order to preserve fuel!

The pilots immediately contacted the San Francisco tower. The tower ominously replied, "You'll never make it to San Francisco. Oakland is shorter. You might make it there!"

So, with a sharp left turn, we were on our way to the Oakland airport.

One of the pilots turned to me and said, "Senator, we're awfully sorry, but we may not make it to Oakland. We may have to ditch in the Bay."

My reaction was one of total disbelief. How the hell could this have happened? A few minutes ago I was safely in Napa. Now, here I am gliding over San Francisco, in the dark of night, in a plane with an empty fuel tank.

I'd read enough about the perils of water landings to know that our chances of survival weren't all that hot.

Then suddenly, I had the strangest "out of body" experience.

I was a disinterested spectator looking at three characters who were about ready to "check out."

Still, we held on to a faint hope that somehow our long glide would bring us safely to Oakland. We passed over a San Francisco housing development, barely clearing the houses.

Finally, one of the pilots turned to me and said, "Senator, we can't make it to the airport. We're going to have to land in the Bay."

Then, he delivered the usual instructions about tightening the seat belt and leaning forward over my knees. (I have never figured out what good that does!)

Recovery of the plane in which I crashed into the San Francisco Bay in 1976.
Special Collections, University of Nevada, Reno Library

The pilots then gave the "May Day" call to shore, providing our general location.

We hit the water with an ear-shattering crash. Then, all was quiet. Not a sound. I didn't know whether we were dead or alive. Then came the realization that miraculously, we had survived the crash without breaking up.

Quickly, we could see flashing red lights on the shore. Our spirits rose. But no boat came.

There we were, with no communications whatsoever, with water beginning to seep into the cabin. The water was ice cold, which wasn't surprising since this was February.

As the water level rose, I told the pilots that the shore didn't look too far. "Rather than drown in this plane," I said, "I'd rather try to swim for it."

One of the pilots said, "You try to do that, Senator, and you'll be dead in minutes from hypothermia." I suspected he was absolutely right.

Gradually, the water continued to rise until I was sitting up on top of my seat.

Just then, a Coast Guard helicopter hovered over us and dropped a line with a bucket attached to it. The pilots insisted I go first.

Opening the cabin door, I jumped into the water and swam a few feet to a basket that was dangling from the helicopter. They hoisted me into the chopper, where they covered me with blankets.

Then the pilot was lifted, followed by the co-pilot. Just as they started to raise him, a gust of wind hit the basket and hurled him into the water, where he was quickly retrieved.

As we were being driven to the hospital, one of the medics told us he had heard our "May Day" call and didn't give us "a snowball's chance in hell" of surviving.

After being treated at the San Leandro hospital for exposure, a nurse lent me her boyfriend's clothes for the trip back to Washington.

I managed to make the vote, but I almost lost my life in the process. And, as it turned out, they didn't need my vote after all!

THE BATTLE OVER THE PANAMA CANAL TREATIES

My first recollection of a problem relating to the Panama Canal was when I was asked during my Senate campaign in 1974 whether I agreed with the plan "to give away the canal."

To be candid, I wasn't even aware there was a controversy involving the canal – a rather clear indication of how far I became removed from the political scene after leaving the Governorship.

In response to the question about the canal, I filibustered vaguely along the lines that I didn't think it was a very good idea, but I'd have to look into the matter further.

Good thing! The questioner, probably an avid reader of the conservative "bible," Human Events, would have had a field day proclaiming to her conservative friends, "That Laxalt is out of it. He didn't even know that the communists are trying to take over our canal!"

The question was a wake-up call and led to my having our research team go to work identifying hot-button issues, particularly those of interest to the conservative community.

When I went back to Washington after being elected, I found that some State Department types were indeed on one of their usual guilt trips, feeling that we had treated the Panamanians unfairly, and that it was time for us to expiate our guilt and return the canal to its rightful owners – the Panamanians.

Obviously, conservatives weren't too enthused about doing anything of the kind, but since Gerald Ford was President and would never go along with a "giveaway," it remained an "inside the beltway" issue, with very little, if any, attention paid to it.

But when Jimmy Carter was elected, it became a brand new ball game. Carter was a first-class breast beater himself, and the

State Department folks decided that now was the time to strike.

Immediately after the 1976 election, the Carter people entered into negotiations with the government of Panamanian President Omar Torrijos to settle on treaty terms.

FAT'S IN THE FIRE

On September 7, 1977, the announcement was made that the Panama Canal treaties had been signed. The "fat was in the fire!"

Many of my fellow conservatives were shocked. They just didn't believe that when "push came to shove," Carter would go along.

I remember thinking that the folks in New Hampshire were right when they claimed during the 1976 presidential campaign that if the Democrats won, they would move to give away the canal. Whenever Ron Reagan and I campaigned there, the people voiced concern about this subject. As so often is the case, the people were far ahead of Washington in their insight.

Under the terms of the treaties, the U.S. would gradually relinquish control over the 51-mile waterway until the year 2000, when Panama would complete the take-over.

Until that time, the U.S. would operate the canal, as well as the 14 military bases located in the Canal Zone. If, after the year 2000, the canal's safety were endangered, the U.S. would be free to intervene with military force.

Once the treaties were approved, the canal would no longer be operated by the old Panama Canal Company but by a nine-man board consisting of five Americans and four Panamanians.

Until 1990, the canal administrator was to be an American with a Panamanian assistant. Subsequently, until 2000, the roles were to be reversed.

Panama agreed to keep the canal open to ships of all nations. As soon as the treaties took effect, more than half of the 648 square mile Canal Zone would revert to Panamanian control.

The U.S. and Panama were supposed to retain joint responsibility for maintaining the neutrality and providing the defense of the canal.

THE CANAL'S HISTORY

The U.S. began construction of the Panama Canal in 1904 and finished it in 1914. The total cost was $352 million.

Under the original treaty (signed in 1903), Panama granted the U.S. "all rights, power and authority, which it would possess and exercise as if it were the sovereign" of the Canal Zone. The rights were granted "in perpetuity."

ANSWERING THE CALL

After the treaties were signed, representatives of several conservative groups in Washington contacted me. They expressed concern that too many Republican leaders were "soft" on the issue, and that in view of our successful common situs experience, they hoped I would lead the opposition.

I said that I would be pleased to do so, but that I wanted first to clear this with the Senate leadership. I did. As there was no objection, we, the opposition, went to work. Each of the conservative groups immediately began to marshal their supporters to mount a "grass roots" effort.

They also went to work raising funds, mainly through direct mail. Richard Viguerie, "king" of direct mail fundraising at the time, helped make sure this effort was successful. Ron Reagan signed a solicitations letter for the Republican National Committee which was also very successful.

My job was to organize the team that would lead the fight in the Senate, where all treaties of this kind must be approved.

Senator Jim Allen of Alabama agreed to be our floor leader

and strategist. He was highly regarded in the Senate and considered to be a superb parliamentarian.

Quickly, Bob Dole of Kansas, Jake Garn and Orrin Hatch of Utah, Jesse Helms of North Carolina, Strom Thurmond of South Carolina, John Tower of Texas, Pete Domenici of New Mexico and Bill Scott of Virginia all signed on.

Tower, Thurmond, Scott, Helms and Garn were all members of the powerful Armed Services Committee. This fact gave our group important "weight."

The Senate group's first assignment was to get a reliable "head count." Each senator was assigned a colleague with whom he had a personal bond so that when asked where he or she stood on the canal issue, the response would be accurate.

Each was asked to make contact personally rather than assign it to staff. It had been my experience during the common situs fight that on controversial issues, Senators rarely lie, but they can be masters of obfuscation and even "fudge" a bit.

If a vote-counter doesn't understand body language, he or she may conclude that someone is a "yes" vote when in fact the Senator is an "undecided" at best and maybe a "no."

We also well knew that the only reliable count was when the vote was actually cast.

From the beginning of my time in the Senate, I watched Senate leadership races with great interest. These are the contests for majority leader and the like, whereby Senators cast secret ballots to determine the fate of their colleagues who are running for the leadership posts.

Very often, the defeated candidates would express "shock" over the final count: "Why, I was certain that I had enough votes," they'd lament.

An easy explanation is that for many Senators it is awkward to tell a colleague you are going to vote against him or her. It is easier to say you're going to support someone, even if you don't intend to do anything of the kind, knowing that the "white lie" will never be discovered.

I may have been naive about the problem, but I could not bring myself to lie to a colleague — about anything. It made life less complicated, and very often my colleagues, even those I voted against, appreciated my candor.

On Panama, within days, we had a reliable count. We had 23 "hard" votes in support of our position, nine "probable" votes and five "possible." The rest were either solidly in support of the treaties or leaning heavily in that direction.

The constitution provides that for a treaty to be ratified, two-thirds of the members must vote in the affirmative. To defeat the treaties, therefore, we needed 34 of the 100 Senators.

With only 23 votes in hand, we had a lot of work to do. Since the White House was turning up the heat on undecided Senators, securing 11 more votes against the treaties became a huge chore.

In addition to organization, we moved aggressively on the media front. I appeared so often on television and radio that I felt as if I was back in the Reagan 1976 presidential campaign. Other Senators and various spokesmen for our groups spread all over the country.

Framing the Issue at Commonwealth

When major international issues are being debated in Washington, a key forum often has been the Commonwealth Club in San Francisco. I was invited to speak to the membership about the Panama Canal on December 9, 1977.

Ambassador Sol Linowitz, who had been the chief negotiator for the treaties, had preceded me and had very capably presented the Carter Administration's position on the issue. In my presentation, I simply took Mr. Linowitz's various arguments and tried to meet them "head on."

For weeks, the Carter team had been telling anyone who would listen that if the Senate rejected the treaties, the vote somehow would be a rejection of the President of the United States.

I said that that was a specious argument. The fact is that under our constitutional process, this President, as was the case for every President before him, had only the power to *negotiate* treaties. He had absolutely no power to *approve*. That is the function of the people through their representatives in the U.S. Senate.

Additionally, I pointed out that as far as the Senate's role was concerned, it should never be placed in the position of being a "rubber stamp," because that would be contrary to the Senate's constitutional responsibilities. The Senate's role is to apply its judgment, experience and constituents' concerns independently.

Mr. Linowitz had also dismissed the economic and security factors as being relatively unimportant. This observation elicited a question from the audience: "If it was not economically feasible for us to hang on to the canal, and if it had no strategic importance or other economic significance, why don't we simply just give the canal to the Panamanians now?" Not bad!

The Ambassador tried, unsuccessfully, to finesse the answer.

The fact was, I argued, that while the waterway lost money, it had done so because the tolls were unrealistically low.

I also pointed out, in reference to our Alaskan oil, that until we developed pipelines, and until we developed additional refiner capacity in California, it was essential for us to move Alaskan crude through the canal.

Also, I suggested that interruption in canal use would impair not only our economy but also those in Latin and South America.

About the canal's strategic importance, Linowitz contended that we shouldn't be concerned because a representative of the

Joint Chiefs of Staff had been at the conference table during the negotiations with the Panamanians. Nevertheless, those who know the workings of Washington understand that the Joint Chiefs are the President's men. Once policy comes down from the White House, they either sign on or ship out.

I pointed out that a more accurate assessment of the strategic problem would come from the flag officers, who weren't as constrained as the Joint Chiefs were.

A contemporary poll of 245 flag officers with experience in the Canal Zone revealed that 241 opposed ratification!

I noted also that four former Chiefs of Naval Operations had written to President Carter, vigorously opposing the treaties. They pointed out several reasons why the canal was of significant strategic importance to the U.S.

Linowitz contended that somehow we had shortchanged the Panamanians — "the poor-Panama syndrome." The response to that was this: Over the years, we had been generous to a fault to the Panamanians. We helped restore their country, offered employment opportunities, built their infrastructure and rid the country of yellow fever. I don't think anyone but a few left-liberal types took the "poor Panama" argument seriously.

One of the Administration's other weak arguments was that by being "nice guys," we would somehow improve our relations with Latin America. I felt strongly that our capitulating would not result in anything of the kind. In fact, there was deep division in Latin America on this issue. Many distrusted Torrijos, considering him to be a dangerous military dictator with questionable allies. These people wanted the canal to be open and operating efficiently.

Lastly, Linowitz contended that we should go along to improve our international relationships — that by doing so, we would qualify for some sort of "International Nice Guy" award. What a stretch! Internationally, people were aware of Torrijos' relationship with Castro who, in turn, was tight with the Soviet Union. That scenario made a lot of "internationalists" mighty nervous.

In closing, I pointed out to the members of the Commonwealth Club that it was "high time" for the U.S. to stop apologizing to countries that we had befriended and helped save.

DOLE AND LAXALT GO TO PANAMA

One of my more interesting international forays occurred in late December of 1977 when Bob Dole and I decided to go to Panama for a personal inspection of the canal. Bob had achieved national prominence as President Ford's running mate in 1976. Neither of us had been to Panama before.

By the time of our trip, we had been identified as two of the Senate's more vocal opponents of the treaties.

We were scheduled to be in Panama on December 30, and had hoped to have a low-key, brief visit. We were wrong! Somehow, word leaked out, and none other than the dictator himself, Omar Torrijos, insisted on meeting with us. He even offered his helicopter for an aerial view of the canal.

With Bob Dole visiting Panama in December of 1977. As leaders of the opposition to the Panama Canal Treaties, some questioned whether it was safe for us to travel to Panama. *Special Collections, University of Nevada, Reno Library*

General Dennis McAuliffe, commander-in-chief of the Southern Command at the time, and later the first administrator of the Panama Canal Commission, felt that taking the Torrijos helicopter was not a good idea. He either wasn't impressed with Panama's maintenance of its equipment, or he had other, more serious, concerns.

As a result, we traveled with him on a U.S. military helicopter. The trip proved to be both interesting and informative.

Dole, more used to helicopters than I, quickly took a seat up front with the General. That left me in the rear seat, which faced the side for better viewing. That was fine, but just as we were getting ready to take off, one of the enlisted men proceeded to take my door off!

I'm not ordinarily worried about heights, but sitting in that seat, with nothing but a belt holding me in, resulted in one terrifying trip. Dole has often said that he'd never heard me so quiet for such a length of time!

After meeting with our military people and the local officials, we were asked to visit with Torrijos himself. We were escorted into Torrijos' modest private home, where he warmly greeted us. For awhile, I thought he'd received faulty intelligence and believed us to be on his side.

When we asked him about his ties to Castro, he didn't back down, saying that Castro was a trusted friend and confidant.

After a few pleasantries and a cup of coffee, "El Presidente" abruptly got up and went into the street. We followed along, and the three of us proceeded to take a stroll down the streets of Panama City. Everywhere we went, Torrijos was hailed like a conquering hero. The people seemed genuinely to love him, and he them. After an hour or so, he suddenly called a halt to our walk and courteously bid us farewell.

Interestingly, wherever we went, there seemed to be a consensus among Panamanians about Torrijos: He was not, as depicted in the American media and by conservative politicians, a vicious, mean despot. Instead, he was described as a "good-hearted farm boy," who served his people well.

In 1981, three years after leaving office, Torrijos was mysteriously killed in a helicopter accident. Like many accidents in that part of the world, there were deep suspicions that he was the victim of foul play, but no one came close to proving it.

There were few, if any good feelings, however, toward the head of security in Panama at the time — Manuel Noriega. People were suspicious and fearful of him, feeling that he was a "CIA type." We never met him. Later, he became President and was widely feared until he unwisely challenged the U.S. in 1989, which led to his eventual arrest on drug charges. He was convicted in Florida, where he remains incarcerated to this day.

The Truth Squad

As the Panama Canal issue heated up in late November 1977, we concluded that the usual communications tools — direct mail, speeches, media interviews — were not enough to get the job done. We needed something more dramatic, something so novel that it would draw national attention.

After much brainstorming, we decided to put together a massive "Truth Squad" effort. Now, there was nothing new and novel about a "Truth Squad." They'd been used for years as a method in political campaigns to counter the opposition's assertions. Typically, they were composed of a handful of people.

We wanted to make ours grander, much grander, with a chartered airplane filled with Senators, Representatives and ex-military personnel. We calculated that it would cost about $125,000 to do the job effectively, no small sum at the time.

Naturally, we felt that the Republican National Committee

would be a good place to look for the money. After all, the committee had collected a lot of money from Panama Canal mailings, particularly one signed by Ron Reagan.

I wrote Bill Brock, our National Chairman, on November 30, 1977. I mentioned the party's general opposition to the treaties, the highly successful Reagan fund-raising letter and our plan to go to the people via the "Truth Squad." I concluded the letter by asking for $50,000 for the project. We all felt that Bill would be happy to join us.

To our amazement, a few days later Bill advised me that the RNC would not grant my request. To this day, I do not know why.

Coincidentally, Ron Reagan was in my Senate office when the Brock refusal came in. Now, in all the years I've known him, I've rarely – perhaps a half dozen times – seen Ron lose his temper, but he surely did that day! He went straight through the roof of the Russell Senate Office Building.

"Let's call the sonofabitch – now!" he yelled.

We did, and I'll bet that Bill Brock will remember to his dying day the "chewing out" he received from the Irishman.

Fortunately, the RNC's denial of our request did not slow down the "Truth Squad's" momentum. If anything, it motivated us all the more.

Beginning in late January, a chartered DC-9 jetliner carried us on a five-day, seven-city tour to alert the American people to what we felt were fatal flaws in the Panama Canal treaties.

As I said at the time, the central message of the tour was that "any treaty, amended or not, which turns over operational control of a hemispheric 'chokepoint' such as the Panama Canal, must be rejected." We also hoped "to arouse the public to tell the Senate clearly and convincingly that it will not stand for ratification of any document which gives up control of the canal."

As chairman of the group, I was honored to have with me, as fellow "Truth Squaders," such Senators as Bob Dole, Orrin Hatch, Jake Garn, Jesse Helms, Strom Thurmond, John Tower, Pete Domenici and Bill Scott.

Equally impressive were the ex-military officials on the trip. They included Admiral Thomas Moorer, former head of the Joint Chiefs of Staff, Lt. General Daniel Graham, former Director of the Defense Intelligence Agency and Adm. John McCain, former Commander-in-Chief of the Pacific and father of now U.S. Senator John McCain of Arizona.

We "spread the word" in Nashville, Atlanta, Miami, Cincinnati, St. Louis, Denver and Portland. In all the cities, we attracted huge crowds.

The Panama Canal Truth Squad in flight. PL chats with Paul Weyrich (center) and Congressman Mickey Edwards. *U.S. Senate photo*

One of our major concerns was that the Carter White House would attempt to convince the Senate to ratify the treaties after making "cosmetic" changes.

In October 1977, Panamanian President Torrijos and President Carter had issued a joint statement "clarifying" U.S. defense rights in Panama after the year 2000. We felt that the "clarifying" language was insufficient.

The Truth Squad also pointed out that in approving the treaties, the U.S. would be turning control of the canal to a government which was friendly to both the Cubans and the Soviets.

As I already noted, when Dole and I had met with Torrijos, we had asked him point blank about his views on Castro. Torrijos had acknowledged that Castro was a friend, advisor and supporter.

The Truth Squad received a lot of national press coverage and in my view helped turn the Senate vote on the treaties into a real cliffhanger.

Indeed, over the years, I've been involved in several "political exercises" throughout the country. None was more exciting or satisfying than the Truth Squad effort.

Everyone, particularly the military representatives, performed splendidly. It was so evident that these men had no political ax to grind. They spoke sincerely when they said the treaties, in terms of national security, were a huge mistake.

By March 1978, the debate over the Panama Canal treaties was the Number One political topic in the U.S. The Truth Squad effort had helped create the climate to make it so.

During all this time, our inside Senate group met regularly. Our head counts revealed that we now were within a few votes of securing the 34 votes we needed.

Undecided Senators such as Henry Bellmon of Oklahoma, Russell Long of Louisiana, Dennis DeConcini of Arizona, Sam Hayakawa of California, Wendell Ford of Kentucky and Ed Zorinsky of Nebraska were subjected to unbelievable pressure from both sides.

White House invitations to "discuss" the treaties were commonplace.

Two Votes Short

The day of the vote, March 16, 1978, could only be described as "wild." The galleries filled to the ceiling early. Majority Leader Robert Byrd insisted upon "order" in the galleries. He even ordered the "well" of the Senate cleared during the vote. (The well is ordinarily the favorite gathering place of Senators during votes.)

Shortly before the vote was called, there was bad news for our side from an unexpected quarter — my colleague from Nevada, Senator Howard Cannon. All along, we had assumed that Cannon was with us because of the overwhelming sentiment in Nevada against the treaties.

During the debate, I had talked with him several times. He always seemed to be on our side, although he had never formally committed himself.

Just before the vote, Senator Cannon, who was chairing the Senate at the time, signaled me to come to the chair. He asked, "How are *you* doing?" That should have been a tip-off to a close Senate watcher. "How are *we* doing?" would have been far more comforting.

I told him that it could go either way, and that we were at a hard 32 count and looking for only two more votes out of a pool of six "undecideds."

"How are you counting me?" he asked. "I'm counting you with us, of course!" I responded. To this, he gravely remarked, "I wouldn't, if I were you."

My heart sank. Without Cannon, that left us looking for three votes instead of two, which at that point was a huge difference.

In the closing hours, the time for debate, by agreement, was divided equally between the two sides. As floor leader, it became my questionable honor to parcel out the time to my colleagues and leave myself enough time to "close" with a summary of our position.

The competition for time was keen. After all, with the galleries packed and the country hearing the debate on national radio (television coverage of the Senate didn't start until the mid-1980s), it was an opportunity for unusually wide exposure. All along, I had figured I would need at least 30 minutes to close properly. But as time progressed to the last hour, it was clear that I would be lucky to speak at all.

Sure enough, time ran out and Laxalt's stirring close, which would not have changed a single vote anyhow, was lost forever.

The roll call vote started sharply at the appointed hour. Each Senator's name was called, and each one voted from his desk. (There were no women in the Senate at that time.)

The fact that the Senators voted as they did was historic in itself. Voting from the desk immediately upon the call from the clerk was very rare in the Senate. Usually, most voted while milling around the well, and many voted after the first call.

As the roll call proceeded, my hopes for victory dimmed. We needed three votes out of the undecided pool of Belmon, DeConcini, Ford, Hayakawa and Zorinsky. One by one, the undecideds went against us. By the time Zorinsky, who voted last, cast his vote, we were "toast." The final vote was 68-32.

The White House pressure on the undecideds proved to be too great. We had made it to the one-yard line, but couldn't push the ball over the goal line.

Although I've never been much of a believer in "moral victories," we opponents received excellent coverage in the media for having "fought the good fight."

I was flabbergasted, as were my colleagues, when Mary McGrory, the very liberal columnist of the Washington Post, wrote a glowing piece about me. After reading Mary's column, I have to admit that I was a little concerned about going to the Republican cloakroom. Any conservative who was complimented by Mary McGrory was automatically "suspect" in the eyes of some of my conservative colleagues.

As expected, I received a good "roasting," plus a taunt (unprintable) from Goldwater.

Curiously, the McGrory column led to better relations between conservatives and the Post. Not that the newspaper ever became a supporter, but at least they stopped describing us as "Neanderthals." And Mary and I continue to be good friends to this day.

The political friction at home, for those who voted for the treaties, was intense.

Both Howard Baker and Henry Bellmon asked us to come to their states to indulge in some "damage control." I went, for they were both good friends.

I indicated to their constituents that even good Senators are entitled to a mistake now and then, and that they should be evaluated by their entire record. I gave it my best, but came away feeling that, at least among conservatives, damage control was near fruitless for those who voted for the "infamous treaties."

Four years later, when he next faced the voters of Nevada, Howard Cannon was defeated. There were a number of factors involved in his defeat, and his Panama Canal vote was certainly one of them.

Sam Hayakawa decided against running for reelection in 1982. His vote for the treaties had enraged many California conservatives, and they never forgave him.

Over the years, the validity of our opposition to the treaties has been vindicated. Now we are faced with the possibility of serious problems with Panama in implementing the treaties. Some who are close to the situation cringe at the prospect of Panamanian operation of the canal from 2000 onward.

We have to do our best to make the treaties work, but in my opinion, the future of the Panama Canal is not all that promising.

Panama, Latin America and the U.S. would have been far

better served if we'd been able to pick up two more votes to kill a well-intentioned but misguided treaty.

MX FOR NEVADA?

When I was selected to serve on the Senate Appropriations Committee, I decide to try to get a seat on the Military Construction Subcommittee. Nevada had military facilities such as Nellis Air Force Base in southern Nevada and the Fallon Naval Air Station in north central Nevada

Little did I realize that this subcommittee would play a major part in the MX missile debate. Indeed, it became the focal point of hearings into the feasibility of the system itself.

The MX missile evolved in 1974 from the perceived need for us to meet the Soviet Union's nuclear capability — to close what was called "a window of vulnerability."

It was widely believed in the defense establishment that the Soviets, if they chose to deliver a "first strike" against the U.S., could destroy about 90 percent of our existing land-based force, which consisted of 1000 Minuteman and 52 Titan Intercontinental Ballistic Missiles (ICBMs).

The vulnerability arose because our ICBMs were based in silos. Our intelligence agencies were advising us that Soviet ICBM accuracy was increasing rapidly. The theory arose that if our ICBMs could be made "mobile," the Soviet threat would be reduced.

Over the years, the U.S. had considered some 30 mobile basing modes. Most fell into two categories: free mobile systems, in which missiles are moved on trains, trucks, aircraft and submarines over large areas without being tied to fixed shelters; and Multiple Protective Structure (MPS) systems, in which missiles are shuttled among a large number of shelters.

The debate over which of these modes should be used went

on for years. Finally, on September 7, 1979, President Carter announced his decision to base the MX in the so-called "racetrack" MPS system.

Under this plan, each missile would be deployed on its own closed-loop roadway and would move among 23 shelters attached to the road. The Carter plan contemplated building 200 race-tracks with 4,600 shelters. The shelters would resemble underground garages. The missiles would be stored horizontally in them. The Air Force's preference was to base the system in the Great Basin area of Nevada and Utah, with most of the missiles being deployed in Nevada.

The racetrack system was expected to have a substantial impact on Nevada's land, water, environment and people. Preliminary estimates were that it would require some 50,000 construction personnel, fencing off 250 square miles of land, a deployment area of roughly 30,000 square miles, and the use of 121 billion gallons of water.

Seemingly, this could have been an economic boon for Nevada. Some members of my staff strongly hoped that Nevada would be the new home for the MX system. However, the more we dug into its impact, the less appealing this "economic God-send" became.

The reaction to the Carter announcement in 1979 and thereafter in Nevada and Utah was quite negative, with many influential groups strongly opposing it.

On June 16, 1980, Utah Governor Scott Matheson argued that the MX/MPS was "fatally flawed." On May 16, 1981, the Mormon Church, taking a rare political position, asked the nation's leaders not only to keep the MX out of Utah and Nevada but also to find an alternative plan altogether.

Spencer Kimball, President of the Mormon Church, made the MX a moral issue. He said that the world was engaged in a "terrifying arms race" that had to be stopped.

The church's opposition was unusual and strong, and it carried exceptional political weight. Utah Senators Jake Garn and Orrin Hatch – both Mormons – were walking a political tightrope. After all, they were both strongly pro-defense, and they did not want to reject MX out-of-hand. Thus, instead of taking a fixed position at that time, they both said they wanted to await the results of a "final" government study before adopting a firm position.

During the 1980 presidential campaign, Ron Reagan raised serious questions about the Carter basing proposal. Shortly after he was elected, he named Caspar "Cap" Weinberger to be Secretary of Defense. At that point, both had been thoroughly briefed on the status of MX.

Reflecting the skepticism he had expressed during the campaign, President Reagan decided that Cap should gather a panel of disinterested experts to examine thoroughly the proposed MX basing mode, then report its findings with deployment options and recommendations by July 1, 1981. To head this group, Cap named a renowned University of California physicist, Dr. Charles Townes.

During this period, there were many MX hearings on Capitol Hill, including a series before our Military Construction Subcommittee. The more hearings we held, the more questions were being raised about the feasibility of the proposed basing mode.

In April 1981, Jake Garn and I appeared in a closed session before the Townes panel. We pointed out our constituents' dissatisfaction with the MX basing mode. We asked the panel to visit Nevada and Utah so they could learn first-hand about the social, environmental and economic effects MX would have on our states.

The panel listened courteously and asked us a number of questions. After the meeting, Dr. Townes told the press that we had presented "very thoughtful views."

After the hearing, though, Jake and I could not accurately gauge the effect of our testimony on the panel. We decided that, as a result of two years of hearings, briefings, public discussions and intensive study, the time had come for us to compile our own report – our "white paper" – and present it to President Reagan and the Department of Defense.

We released our report on June 26, 1981. The news coverage was extensive. Essentially, we called on President Reagan to discard the racetrack basing mode for the MX missile.

We contended that a multiple-shelter system of 200 MX missiles and 4,600 shelters would be inadequate to meet the likely Soviet Union threat in the 1990s. We noted that the Soviets could legally build enough warheads to overwhelm the entire "racetrack" system. Not only would the vulnerability problem be unresolved, but also the Air Force would be inviting an open-ended race between Soviet warheads and U.S. concrete shelters.

U.S. Senator Jake Garn. We were the only two Republican "rookies" elected to the Senate in the "Watergate election" of 1974.

As an alternative, in the interest of national security, we made several recommendations. Most importantly, we recommended that at least 200 MX missiles be placed in modified Minuteman III silos, protected by a limited anti-ballistic-missile system. We felt the time had come to renew debate on an ABM system, which had been defeated by a single vote some years earlier.

In addition, we recommended strengthening U.S. bomber

capability and the development of a new strategic bomber – the B1.

Senator John Tower of Texas wasn't overly enthused with our plan. One press report characterized his reaction as "a stinging rebuke." Although John, as chairman of the Armed Services Committee, had great credibility in defense matters, his statement at the time – that we offered no clear program and were recommending a "dangerously destabilizing strategy" – seemed to have little effect, much to our relief.

During the time that the Townes panel was constituted (including the period just after the panel's report was issued on July 17), there was no indication as to where the White House was leaning. I suppose they were occupied with other matters and were in a "hold" mode until all the studies were in – until "the hay was in the barn," so to speak.

THE TOWNES REPORT

The Townes panel of experts recommended in its report that, at least initially, the MX program should be halved from 200 missiles to 100, and that the 100 missiles be placed in vertical silos rather than hidden among thousands of horizontal shelters. After the 100 MXs were in place, the panel decided, several additional options should be pursued:

• The MX, as originally planned, could be extended by building an additional 2,200 vertical sites, among which the 100 missiles could be shuttled to make their location uncertain and thereby reduce the risk of a surprise Soviet attack.

• Explore thoroughly the development of an ABM system to provide a "screen" to protect the MX system.

• Undertake the development of an air-launched MX system.

• Reject the idea of "stuffing" MX into Minuteman.

Reaction to the report varied. Some felt it was not so much a consensus as a compromise. And on the critical siting issue –

where the MX should be based — they "punted." We guessed that issue was just too hot for the panel.

The basic problem of the vulnerability of the proposed system was also left unresolved. One hundred MX missiles in 100 shelters just didn't make sense, as far as we were concerned.

Many cynics concluded that the Townes recommendations would be irrelevant anyhow. The panel had served the purpose of giving Cap Weinberger "political cover" and badly needed time for the President and him to come up with an alternative plan.

After the Townes report was released, the city buzzed with rumors about the fate of MX. They ranged all the way from speculation that the President had concluded that perhaps "race track" wasn't so bad after all, to the "all out" approach Jake Garn and I had recommended in our "white paper."

On July 31, Ed Meese indicated strongly that the Reagan Administration would scrap the multi-sheltered basing scheme for MX in favor of an alternative to be announced in 30-45 days.

No one had more credibility on such an issue than Ed Meese. As Counsellor to the President, he handled the flow of both national security and domestic issues to the President's desk, and the President trusted his judgment completely.

Ed indicated in his statement that President Reagan, during the 1980 campaign, had considered the Carter basing plan to be a "bad idea," which was dictated by that Administration's "slavish adherence" to SALT II, and that this was not a good reason for "drilling 4,600 holes in the ground."

The Meese statement was good news indeed. At least "race track" was dead. But we still worried about the new basing mode and its location.

Reagan's MX Decision
On Friday, October 2, 1981, President Reagan made one of the

most significant announcements of his presidency.

He stated that he would seek Congressional approval to build 100 MX land-based missiles and 100 B1 Bombers under a $180 billion program to upgrade the nation's nuclear forces.

The plan called for the first of several MX missiles to be placed in existing missile silos. Reagan also pledged to push ahead with the Stealth bomber and to put the silo-busting D5 missile aboard Trident II submarines as soon as it was ready late in the decade.

The President's rejection of the Air Force basing plan, as expected, drew the most fire.

Secretary Weinberger insisted that the political opposition, most notably from Senators Garn and Laxalt, along with the Mormon Church, was not what killed "race track."

Instead, he said, the administration concluded that the Soviets could build enough warheads to hit all the shelters built for MX and easily blow them up in a war. That was the principal point we had raised in our "white paper."

This meant that deployment in Nevada and Utah was unlikely.

As soon as the Reagan announcement was made, our offices were flooded with calls from the news media. Rather than deal with them individually, Senator Garn and I decided to hold a joint news conference.

Usually suspicious, the reporters at the conference were downright cynical! From the tone of their questions, it was apparent they felt a political "fix" was in. Because of my closeness to the President and the fierce opposition of the Mormon Church, President Reagan, in their view, had simply caved in.

Anticipating such charges months before, Jake and I had decided that we would do a thorough job in evaluating the proposed "race track" basing mode by holding several hearings, which we did. Further, at the end of the process, we decided to issue a substantive report, which we did.

For the press to feel that we would abuse a relationship with the President and risk impairing our national security was ludicrous.

Although I had expressed to candidate Reagan the reasons for my strong opposition to the Carter basing plan during the 1980 campaign, I had assured Jake Garn that I would not discuss MX with President Reagan. When I indicated this at the press conference, the reporters seemed to calm down.

Senator John Tower, as expected, was unhappy and said so. He said that the proposed system was "enormously vulnerable" to Soviet attack and pronounced himself "gravely disappointed" in the President's decision.

Majority Leader Howard Baker backed me by saying that he was sure the President's decision against basing the MX in Nevada and Utah had "nothing to do with politics and nothing to do with geography and certainly nothing to do with friendship."

President Reagan's decision was met with jubilation in Nevada. From the cattlemen in the north to the Duckwater Shoshone tribe in central Nevada, people were overjoyed. The same was true in Utah.

Eventually, 50 MX Missiles were deployed at Warren Air Force Base in Wyoming. They were placed in upgraded Minuteman silos. If the Russians ratify the Start II Treaty, the existing MXs will be "deactivated."

Going forward with the MX added greatly to our bargaining power with the Soviets and contributed to the Soviet meltdown.

Nevadans will always be strong supporters of national defense, but we are also relieved that the MX racetrack system, which would have overwhelmed a good portion of Nevada and Utah, was scrapped.

CHAPTER 15

❖ *Traveling to Learn* ❖

Before coming to the Senate, my view of the travels of members of Congress was probably typical: These "junkets" were pleasure trips at the taxpayers' expense. When you think about it, though, all of us in Congress come from different backgrounds and experiences, and very few come to Washington with detailed first-hand knowledge of many foreign countries.

That was certainly true in my case. We'd had vacation travel to Europe, but that's not the same thing as gaining an understanding of the political situation within a country or current aspects of its relations with the U.S.

I soon learned that a "CODEL" (the bureaucratic acronym for "Congressional Delegation") could provide valuable experience with which to deal with the kinds of global issues Senators are often asked to address.

For example, traveling to Israel, meeting its leaders and talking with a number of its citizens is much different from reading a book or receiving a briefing from an expert. Such a visit gave me a badly needed "live perspective," and I was much better informed as a result.

After participating in a CODEL, I would report my experiences to my constituents in Nevada about such places as the Soviet Union, Africa and the NATO countries. People in the audience would often tell me their perspective had been broadened, too.

No matter where these travels took me, they made me appreciate "home" all the more. I'd often say in Nevada that it was too bad that every Nevadan couldn't take a sabbatical every two or three years to some foreign country so that we won't take our own country for granted.

The Air Force provided the planes for the CODELs. That made the "nuts and bolts" of travel easy: no tickets, no baggage check-in, no crowded airports. Once aloft, we roamed at will through the cabin, which provided us Senators with many opportunities to get to know one another better on a personal level.

Once on the ground at our destinations, however, the schedules weren't for the vacation-minded. The days began early and ended late, crammed with meetings, briefings and visits to various facilities that related to the purpose of the trip. Now and then a little free time was included for relaxing or seeing tourist sights, but not much and not often.

Here's a sample of the issues agenda of a CODEL. This one is from a trip to the Soviet Union in 1978, and these are the topics we discussed with Soviet officials: the USSR's strategic build-up; weapons verification; the Backfire bomber; Minuteman missile vulnerability; the cruise missile; the role of the U.S. Senate in the treaty-making process (they couldn't believe we could veto a President's signature on a treaty!); China; transfer of the MIG 23's to Cuba; the Korean withdrawal; Soviet naval activities in Vietnam; economic relations; agriculture; energy; human rights and refuseniks.

Talk about a crash course in Soviet-American relations!

CODEL RIBICOFF-BAKER
ISRAEL

Looking back, I think our first trip in 1976 was the most exciting and one of the most productive.

The groups of Senators comprising the CODELs were always bipartisan, with the senior Republican and the senior Democrat usually "co-chairing" the trip. The staff competently handled the details.

The chairmen had the social responsibility of doing reception line duty, opening and closing meetings and handling toasts and responses at receptions and dinners.

On this trip, we had Senator Abe Ribicoff of Connecticut and Senator Howard Baker of Tennessee as our co-chairmen. Carol and I were the "juniors" of the delegation.

To be invited so soon after being elected was an honor for me. Howard and Joy Baker were our sponsors. We came to know them well on this trip, and we became close friends, as was the case with Abe and Casey Ribicoff.

The trip began at Andrews Air Force Base in suburban Maryland. Within eight hours we were in Vienna.

The next day, after a briefing at the International Atomic Energy Agency, we were off to Jerusalem, about a three-hour flight.

Some in the delegation had been to Israel before, but for most it was a "first" visit to the small country that always had such an impact in the U.S.

Landing in Tel Aviv, we traveled by bus to Jerusalem. The country and trip reminded me of western Nevada. The bus trip, traveling uphill on a winding road to Jerusalem, might just as easily have been from Reno to Virginia City.

We were housed in the King David Hotel, which had a "Casablanca" flavor to it. Our room overlooked the Old City with its famous landmarks, including the Wailing Wall.

I was amazed at how "un-Christian" our tour of Jerusalem was. I shouldn't have been, for it's obvious that Jerusalem consists almost entirely of Israelis and Arabs. Nonetheless, I was surprised by the scant recognition Jesus Christ received – usually a mere reference to the effect that he was a "famous prophet who had died in Jerusalem."

There were conflicting reports about where he had been crucified and where he had been buried. The "Way of the Cross," where we were taught Jesus painfully carried his cross to his crucifixion, was buried several feet beneath the existing thoroughfare.

I'd often thought that one day it would be nice to take Momma Laxalt to Jerusalem and the "holy places." After seeing them, I'm glad I didn't. She had a Roman Catholic's "blind faith" – in every good sense. If Momma had seen how the holy places – even if they could be identified – had been commercialized, she would have been crushed.

It seems to me that the Christian community could do more to restore some order in what now seems to be chaos. But the political situation is so tricky, it might well never happen.

GOLAN HEIGHTS

We traveled to the Golan Heights by Israeli helicopter. When one looks over the adjacent barren land, with the Lebanese and Syrian borders only a stone's throw from Golan, you realize how vulnerable Israel is.

From where we observed, it appeared that it could be a target even for short-range mortar fire. Before the trip, we Senators often wondered why Israel was so ferocious about preserving the security of its borders. After our Golan visit, we wondered no longer.

The longer a person is in Israel, the more one appreciates how small it is. (All of Israel would easily fit into many of Nevada's counties.) After Golan, Carol and I traveled by car all the way from the Lebanese border to Jerusalem in about three hours, visiting along the way the Dead Sea, Nazareth and Bethlehem.

On our last night, Defense Minister Shimon Peres held a dinner for us in the King David Hotel. We had met previously with Prime Minister Yitzhak Rabin, who was later assassinated. We'd also had a meeting with Golda Meir, who had made history as the first woman Prime Minister of Israel, serving from 1969-1974. Peres eventually became Prime Minister himself in 1984.

One gets the feeling at times, watching Israeli politics, that it's one grand game of musical chairs between key members of the Labor and Likud parties.

Carol and I meet former Israeli Prime Minister Golda Meir in 1976. *Photo by K. Weiss. Special Collections, University of Nevada, Reno Library*

That night, as usual, people were seated according to rank. Being junior, I was seated well in the back. It was there that I met Menachem Begin, who was way down in the political pecking order at the time. A year later, however, he was elected Prime Minister. Later, on a few occasions, Begin reminded me of the Peres dinner "when we were both in the back of the political bus."

JORDAN

Our flight from Tel Aviv to Amman, capital of Jordan, took about 30 minutes. We were scheduled to meet King Hussein and the Queen for lunch. The King was on time, but there was no Queen. She arrived a good half-hour late. It seemed that she'd been shopping and simply lost track of time. A recent young bride of the King, she tended to be rather independent.

The King was obviously irritated, and he virtually ignored her during the lunch. Unfortunately, she was killed in a helicopter accident some years later.

After the lunch, the King invited the Senators to his library for brandy and cigars. Mix some jet lag, several glasses of luncheon wine and a poorly air-conditioned room, with a touch of Jordanian brandy, and you have all the ingredients for "nap time" instead of a productive meeting.

There we were, eleven U.S. Senators seated around a magnificent table with the King of Jordan. I was one of the first casualties and awoke just before the "briefing" concluded. When I awoke, I was the only Senator who wasn't asleep! The King cheerfully concluded his briefing as if nothing had happened.

King Hussein was the ultimate political survivor in the Mideast (although in early 1999 he died of cancer).

EGYPT

We left Amman after the lunch (the King probably sighing with relief) for our next stop, Cairo, a two-hour flight.

Riding into Cairo from the airport, I don't think any of us expected the masses of people we saw. On the way, we passed the famed "City of the Dead," a huge cemetery where thousands of families actually live.

As we approached the city, people were everywhere, like ants on a hill. We saw young mothers with three or four children with another "in the basket." On buses, people hung off the sides.

The Pyramids and Luxor, not to mention a trip down the Nile, were all interesting, but most fascinating to me were the people. Seeing those families on the streets and in the parks, I wondered where they went at night and whether they had any semblance of housing.

The climax of our Egypt trip was the meeting with President and Mrs. Anwar Sadat. We were told in advance that "the President does not set appointments in advance of VIP's arriving in

Egypt." Even then, years before he was assassinated, security concerns were high.

Meeting with Egyptian President Anwar Sadat in Washington in 1978. I had first met him in Egypt in 1976. Sadat was a great statesman whose assassination in 1981 was a tremendous loss for the world. *Senate Republican Conference photo. Special Collections, University of Nevada, Reno Library*

We met the Sadats at their beautiful home in Alexandria, on the water. They were cordial and gracious. President Sadat and I hit it off right away. It had nothing particularly to do with me. It was my cowboy boots. He fell in love with them. I was told later that he was an avid horseman and the proud owner of many pairs of boots.

During the meeting, the President described how dire the situation was for the people of Egypt, including its rampant poverty. He pointed out, too, that the continuing tension with

Israel created a huge financial burden. He had to spend large amounts of money on national security to defend against what he viewed as a constant Israeli threat.

At one point, I asked him to tell us the one thing he would wish for his people. He quickly replied, "I would like to have the means to provide every child in Egypt one glass of milk per day." On citizens of an affluent and wasteful country, his observation made a deep impression.

It was no surprise to me that he was so conciliatory in the Camp David talks. I felt a real loss when he was killed in cold-blood in 1981. It was a great blow not only to Egypt but to the entire free world as well.

The fanatics had never forgiven him for making peace with Israel.

IRAN

From Cairo, we flew to Tehran, a flight of some four hours.

Dick Helms, who was the Ambassador to Iran at the time, met us at the airport. I'd known Dick in Washington. His years as Director of the Central Intelligence Agency gave him an aura that makes him particularly interesting.

He pointed out at the embassy, where later our hostages were held, that Iran, under the leadership of the Shah, was enjoying great prosperity. That seemed clear to us, since the landscape was covered with construction cranes. High-rise buildings were sprouting up everywhere. "What a difference a little oil makes," someone in our party exclaimed. It was certainly a marked contrast to the poverty we had just seen in Egypt.

We were told that the level of education was high in Iran. Dick Helms also told us that Iran, before long, would be the power, militarily and economically, in that part of the world. He noted that Americans should be reassured in having a powerful, loyal ally in such a vital region of the world.

Most of us in the delegation agreed, but Senators Tom Eagleton of Missouri and John Culver of Iowa had reservations. They saw the Shah as less than benevolent, as someone who was taking advantage of the people of Iran and who was shamelessly exploiting the U.S. in order to have us pour billions into a defense force that he didn't need. In short, they felt the Shah was on a "first-class ego trip."

Since Tom and John weren't shrinking violets and were two of the most effective liberal voices in the Senate, I'm sure Dick Helms shrunk at the prospect of a sharp exchange when our delegation met with the Shah. I admit that the rest of us, since we weren't personally involved, actually looked forward to what seemed to be a potentially exciting confrontation with the Shah.

Before that happened, though, we were treated to interesting visits to the cities of Isfahan and Shiraz. In those cities, as was the case everywhere in Iran, there were life-size photos of the Shah. After several days, Culver had had enough: "You know," he told us, "I'd think twice before I ran against this Shah guy!"

After Shiraz, Senator John Glenn of Ohio and I decided to take a side trip by small plane to fly over the Strait of Hormuz, the narrow passage through which the Mideast oil is shipped out by tankers. The Strait was (and is) the energy lifeline for much of the industrialized world.

We had seen maps and photos of the area, and our flight confirmed our worst fears: If the Strait of Hormuz were ever endangered, the seeds of a third world war would be quickly sown.

Fortunately, that hasn't happened yet, but the basis of our concern was confirmed by the Gulf War. If the industrialized nations' supplies had not been threatened by Saddam Hussein's invasion of Kuwait, there is little likelihood that President Bush would have been able to organize the coalition he did to fight the war.

Our dinner with the Shah and the Empress was held on our last night in Iran at his palace in Tehran. Our visit earlier to view the crown jewels should have conditioned us to the opulence of the Shah's regime, but it didn't prepare us for this.

The grandeur of the palace and the dining hall was breathtaking. The dinner, with gold service, exquisite crystal and individual waiters for each of us, was unlike any we'd ever attended. And of course, the finest wines of the region flowed freely.

After dinner, the Shah led the men to his library for the customary cigars and brandy. (Equal rights for women hadn't reached Iran yet, and still haven't as I write this in 1999.)

The Shah told us of his admiration for the United States and how much he appreciated our help over the years. That compliment caused Eagleton and Culver to flare. They took strong issue with the Shah, stating that they had come to Iran with suspicions that Iran was well able to defend itself without billions of dollars in aid from the U.S.

Furthermore, they contended, there didn't seem to be any imminent threat to Iran in the region. They also noted that they had personally observed the prosperity in Iran, and after several defense briefings, they were now convinced that their original suspicions were well-based and would so report to the Congress.

With that, the Shah blew up. "How could you possibly arrive at the conclusion that we are not threatened? To make that statement, you've shown that you're totally ignorant of our history!"

He added, "We in Iran have constantly been menaced by the Soviets. They've even invaded us! Since they're positioned on our northern border, there's never a moment when Iran is not concerned about their striking again. The United States' technical help and funds have provided me with the resources to repel the bastards!"

The congenial mood had changed in an instant, and the Shah

had made his point.

In 1979, the Shah was deposed by a cleric, Ayatollah Ruhollah Khomeini. During our briefings in Iran, Khomeini had been depicted as "some kook in Paris" who wanted to oust the Shah and his western ways, but that "this will never happen."

Khomeini's overthrow of the Shah gave the Islamic fundamentalists control over Iran, which they maintain to this day. Our relations with Iran, exacerbated by the hostage crisis, have been badly strained for most of the time since.

Our intelligence reports about Iran in those years had been faulty. Khomeini had been vastly underestimated. The Islamic influence in Iran was waiting to be energized, and Khomeini did it. In some respects, the Shah had been too successful in his educational efforts. Young people were trained for high-level technical positions, but the economy didn't grow at a rate sufficient to create the necessary jobs.

As a result, millions of young, educated Iranians, who should have been natural allies of the Shah and the West, became disillusioned and bought the Islamic fundamentalist line that our ways were not for them and, indeed, were corruptive.

Someday, I hope that a reconciliation can be made between the U.S. and Iran. The Iranians are an exceptional people, and we should be friends again, to our mutual benefit.

CODEL RIBICOFF-BELLMON
LONDON

"CODEL Ribicoff," as it was called, chaired by Senator Ribicoff and Senator Henry Bellmon of Oklahoma, was organized in November 1978, with twelve Senators and their wives in the delegation.

The trip received a great deal of press, since it was the largest U.S. Senate delegation ever to visit the Soviet Union. I had never been to the USSR. Because arms control and other issues were under intense discussion in the Congress at the time, Senators John Glenn of Ohio and Sam Nunn of Georgia – two of the acknowledged arms control experts – were included in the delegation.

First, there was a stopover in London for a meeting with then Prime Minister James Callaghan at No. 10 Downing Street, that historic building where Winston Churchill had presided during the darkest days of World War II. I was impressed by the lack of ostentation of the place.

The Prime Minister was in excellent spirits, having the day before received a vote of confidence in the House of Commons.

SOVIET UNION

The next day we left for the Soviet Union. Our first stop was Leningrad, originally named St. Petersburg for Peter the Great. After the revolution in 1917, Lenin modestly renamed the city in his own honor. With the breakup of the Soviet Union, the name once again is St. Petersburg.

Peter the Great loved the West and incorporated into the culture and architecture of his city a substantial western influence. It remains to this day one of the most beautiful cities of the world.

From there, we traveled to Minsk, and for the first time were exposed to the hard-line Soviet politicians – the Belorussian Supreme Soviet Deputies. They were downright ornery and showed their contempt for the U.S.

They contended that the U.S. had wrongly claimed credit for winning World War II; that the Soviets had really turned the tide by repelling the German army at a cost of some 25 million lives. They were also critical of the U.S. for carrying on what they viewed as a hugely expensive arms race, depriving the Russian people of critical needs.

Ribicoff and Bellmon answered them as diplomatically as

they could, stating that the American people fully understood the sacrifice of the Soviet Union in the war and gave them full credit for contributing greatly to the Allied victory. Since these were second-level officials, we all agreed the "discussion" was a good warm-up for the "main event" in Moscow.

After a 90-minute flight to Moscow, we were taken to the Hotel Sovetskaya, supposedly one of the best. In its day, the hotel had been elegant, but over the years it had deteriorated. Because we were only going to be there four nights, we resigned ourselves to hard beds, cold water, drafty rooms and, of course, Soviet listening devices.

Before leaving Washington, we had been admonished to be extremely careful in our discussions, particularly in the hotel. In the past, the Soviets had taken great delight in "bugging" foreigners, especially Americans.

I'm confident that we were being monitored. One night in our room, we talked about my socks coming back wet from the laundry service. When we returned from dinner, my socks had been dried and replaced where they were!

During the next few days, we did some ceremonial things, such as laying a wreath at the Tomb of the Unknown Soldier, but most of our time was spent in spirited exchanges with members of the Supreme Soviet.

On the issues of the day, such as arms control, verification, SALT II, China and human rights, we and they were poles apart. They viewed us in the same light as their Minsk counterparts but were a bit more diplomatic in saying so.

Many of the meetings were held inside the Kremlin in plain rooms with long, narrow, felt-covered tables. One day, though, they gave us a tour of the "public" rooms. These had been created in Czarist days and were magnificent. The grand reception room, which was used as a ballroom by the Czars, is surely the most beautiful I've ever seen.

The meetings started to become tedious and repetitious. Abe Ribicoff and Henry Bellmon renewed our earlier requests to meet with President Leonid Brezhnev and Premier Aleksei Kosygin. The answer was always that it was unlikely we would meet with either because they were deeply involved in a "vital international matter." Before we left Moscow, we learned that they in fact were involved in a crisis relating to Cuba.

Finally, Kosygin consented to meet with Senator Ribicoff. Although we were told that Kosygin was a disagreeable sort, Abe, who could get along with anyone, had a reasonably pleasant meeting with him.

Then, on our last day, we were told that the President would meet with us after all – late in the afternoon.

Our briefing on Brezhnev indicated that he was a tough peasant who had risen through the ranks in the Stalinist tradition. We also learned, ominously, that late afternoon meetings were chancy because that was usually well into "Vodka time," which we were told was not a happy time for visitors, particularly American politicians. Therefore, I didn't know whether we were going to a meeting or an hour of mud wrestling.

Faced with that uncertainty, we did the noble thing, insisting that our leaders, Ribicoff and Bellmon, lead us into the meeting room, which was one of the bare rooms we had met in before. The only decoration was the enlarged photo of Lenin, whose portrait was as ubiquitous in these parts as the Shah's was in Iran.

When we were ushered into the room, Brezhnev was all by himself – no staff – just him! When it came my turn to shake his hand, I was impressed by his physique. He was short – about 5'6" – but he had shoulders like those of a Brahma bull. He easily could have been a linebacker for the Chicago Bears!

And his hands were rough and huge, like some of the hard-rock miners I'd represented in Nevada. His eyes were hard and cold. He would have been a great warden at Alcatraz. With a practiced Nevada eye, I looked for evidence of vodka, but came up short.

Through an interpreter, he quickly established that he was not pro-American. His points included the following: The Soviets had made the greatest sacrifice in World War II by far, for which they had received very little appreciation; the U.S. was forcing the USSR into a costly nuclear arms race, which they didn't want and couldn't afford; President Jimmy Carter was dragging his heels on SALT II.

At one point during his diatribe, Brezhnev pounded on the table fiercely and exclaimed, "Don't you men realize that I have the ability to destroy your whole country in 20 minutes?!"

His "official" statement, when reading it today, is relatively benign. To hear it expressed aloud, however, was the most chilling I've ever heard. This man was not only capable of pushing the button, he had the means to get the job done! Thank God we don't have to deal with the likes of him any more!

When we flew out of Moscow, we clapped and cheered as one. The oppression, the subservience of the people – the whole scene was suffocating.

We mused: How can we be so concerned about a country that is so backward, decades behind us in terms of its infrastructure and its economy? We feared them, and should have, because they had been so traumatized by World War II. It had scarred the Soviet psyche. Never again would they be unprepared to defend themselves, even though to do so would produce untold hardships on them.

My colleagues and I agreed that facing that sort of national paranoia, we had to keep our guard up at all times, maintaining a healthy lead in the arms race. Ronald Reagan called it "peace through strength." It worked — to the ultimate benefit of both countries.

HUNGARY

After Moscow, we looked forward to Hungary and its capital, Budapest. Although it was inside the "Iron Curtain," it continued to chart its own course domestically.

From the moment we landed, we knew things were different in Hungary, beginning with the shiny new Mercedes-Benz which took us from the airport. After the hearse-like vehicles we'd been subjected to in Moscow, it was, to say the least, a pleasant change.

During our time in Hungary, we learned how they had finessed the Soviets over the years. While being subservient in matters of foreign policy, they had ingeniously established a free market system and made it work.

CODEL LAXALT
FRANCE

In July 1982, I had the opportunity to lead my own CODEL. CODEL Laxalt was charged by the Senate to participate in the "American Week Celebration" in Biarritz, France, to visit the Mediterranean Fleet in Italy, combined with a visit to Pope John Paul II, and to make an official visit to Budapest, Hungary, to meet with government officials.

Accompanying Carol and me were Senator Fritz Hollings of South Carolina and his wife, Peatsey, Senator Bennett Johnston of Louisiana and his wife, Mary, and Senator Walter "Dee" Huddleston of Kentucky and his wife, Jean.

Some of my key staffers — Eileen deLatour, Pat Dondero and Ed Allison — accompanied me. This was their first trip to Europe.

Particularly pleasing to me was that the American Week Celebration was held in Biarritz, France, in the heart of my beloved

Basque country. When our jet landed, we were met by a huge delegation that included several young Basque dancers.

We were housed at the Hotel du Palais, the beautiful castle built by Napoleon III for his wife, Eugenie.

Carol and I had been to the Basque country a few times before, both to my mother's birthplace in Baigorry and to my father's at Tardets. But to see the magnificent countryside and the wholesome, friendly French Basque people through our friends' eyes gave this visit special meaning.

ROME

On July 6, we traveled to Rome for our visit with Pope John Paul II. We had a private audience with him.

He responded beautifully to our American Senatorial delegation, engaging in animated conversation with us. We were impressed by his knowledge of the United States.

Meeting with Pope John Paul II at the Vatican in July of 1982. *Photo by Felici of Rome. Special Collections, University of Nevada, Reno Library*

When I reminded him that my sister, Sister Sue, was still serving as a nun, he asked me to convey his blessing to her and graciously agreed to my being photographed with him — a picture that Sue still proudly displays in her Henderson, Nevada, home. Although she was proud of other happenings in her big brother's life, they paled in comparison to my being with Pope John Paul II.

While there, we were hosted by Ambassador Max Rabb and his wife, Ruth, at the American residence in Rome in the core of the city.

For the tennis players of the group (and there were several), we took particular pleasure in playing on the Ambassador's court. In the midst of one match, we were surprised to hear cheers rise from the surrounding high-rise apartments. They weren't cheering us but rather the news that Italy had just won the World Cup. All night long the Italians rejoiced.

It was our first exposure to the importance of soccer and the World Cup in the lives of fans throughout the world. And we thought the World Series and Super Bowl generate excitement. Not even close to the World Cup!

CODEL HATFIELD-EAGLETON
AFRICA

Senator Mark Hatfield of Oregon and his wife, Antoinette, invited Carol and me to join them and Senator Tom Eagleton and his wife, Barbara, on a CODEL to Africa in October 1982. Aside from Egypt and Morocco, none of us had ever been to Africa.

We were charged by Senate leadership and the Reagan Administration to give them an evaluation of conditions in the Ivory Coast, Zimbabwe, Tanzania, Kenya and Tunis. We were to concentrate, however, on South Africa, whose internal policies, particularly apartheid, were hot topics in the U.S.

Other than South Africa, we found the condition of the countries to be directly related to the length of time since they had achieved independence from the Europeans. The longer they had been independent, the worse their condition appeared to be. Governments were inefficient, rife with corruption and unresponsive to the needs of the people.

A clear example was the Hotel Kilimanjaro in Dar Es Salaam in Tanzania. Built a few years before our visit, it was a shambles. Nothing worked: power, plumbing – nothing!

We found leaders to be well-educated and gracious but quite impressed with their own importance. They didn't speak; they intoned from on high. And once they started talking, there was no way to stop them. We decided they would have been capable additions to the filibuster teams in the U.S. Senate!

South Africa was a different story. Whatever else might be said about their deficiencies in human rights, the country worked.

In our travels to Durban, Cape Town and Johannesburg, the most interesting meeting was with then Prime Minister and Mrs. P.W. Botha in their residence in Pretoria.

Hatfield and Eagleton were two of the most noted and respected liberals in America, I could hardly wait for the fireworks when they locked horns with P. W. Botha.

But the fireworks never materialized. Instead, each treated the other respectfully.

Botha pointed out, at times near patronizingly, that the Afrikaners had originally settled the country (contrary to the widespread belief that they had displaced the blacks). He further pointed out that, economically, South African blacks were far better off than elsewhere in Africa.

Then he pointedly said that were it not for misguided liberals flying the civil rights flag, all would continue to go well in South Africa, and that seriously to consider turning over the country to the blacks would result in a bloody civil war. In effect his message was: "Butt out. Your boycotts won't seriously affect us. We'll get along just fine!"

Mark and Tom said that world opinion was rapidly turning against South Africa. They predicted that before long, South Africa would be isolated, and they advised Botha to recognize reality and gradually remove apartheid policies.

They also predicted that one day, before too long, one-man-one-vote would be instituted in South Africa, and the black majority would elect one of their own to head the government.

How prophetic! Little did any of us realize that in a few short years, Nelson Mandela would be free, one-man-one-vote would be invoked and Mandela would be President of South Africa by 1994.

And no civil war occurred.

South Africa, no longer a pariah, today appears to be getting along reasonably well. Now, as Mandela leaves the scene, we can only hope for the best.

CODEL GARN
CHINA

On November 7, 1984, the day after Ron Reagan was comfortably re-elected as President, Carol and I joined my Senate seatmate Jake Garn of Utah and his wife, Kathleen, Senator Jack Danforth of Missouri and his wife, Sally, and Senator Alan Simpson of Wyoming and his wife, Ann, for a trip to China, Hong Kong and Taiwan.

Jake was the only one of us who had been to China. Getting there, with stops at Elmendorf AFB in Alaska and at Yakota Airport in Japan, was a long and tiring trip.

After some 20 hours of flying, we arrived at Beijing, China. Our hotel was the Beijing Hotel, where many movies had been made. It had an historic aura about it, particularly in terms of musty odor. Nevertheless, the staff was gracious.

We went to bed around 10 p.m., Beijing time. With the time difference, it was about nine in the morning, Washington time.

The next day, bright and early, we went touring, first to the Great Wall, a 45-minute drive. The Wall is more dramatic than the pictures we'd seen over the years. Almost every recent U.S. President had been there. Our Chinese guides pointed out to us that President Carter had traveled farther on the Wall than any of the other Presidents, a testament, I guess, to the fact that his jogging had paid dividends.

Walking along the Wall, we reflected how dramatically warfare had changed over the centuries. When it was completed in the Third Century (although it has been modified repeatedly), it was deemed the ultimate defense. It was built to protect the Chinese against their nomadic enemies of the day. It was an ancient equivalent to the Maginot Line which the French built along their eastern border before World War II to stop German invaders. The German forces simply outflanked it by attacking through Belgium, and Hitler's Panzer divisions overwhelmed the Line in a short period of time, leaving the ill-prepared French essentially defenseless.

With today's technology, such fixed defenses are of little value. Now the challenge is to construct defenses in space or on the ground to intercept incoming missiles.

After the Wall, we visited the Ming tombs and the Summer Palace. As they say, "you can't take it with you," but those Chinese ancients gave it a good shot with their fantastic tombs. All we have are presidential libraries!

In the Ming Dynasty (1368-1644), the general population lived at subsistence level, while the leaders lived in regal splendor at the Summer Palace and the Forbidden City.

Returning to Beijing in late afternoon, we saw a sight that shall remain with me forever. Thousands and thousands of bicycles ridden by Chinese men, women and children, almost all of whom were dressed in the traditional blue and gray of the time, riding home from work on Beijing's main drag. And so quietly! There were scarcely any automobiles in sight — just a few for high officials of the government.

Since then, the volume of automobile traffic in Beijing has risen dramatically. The introduction of capitalism has permitted millions of Chinese to increase their earning power and enabled them to buy such things as television sets and even cars. The eerily quiet bicycle traffic in Beijing will be only a memory before long.

From Beijing, we traveled to Shanghai, which was described to us as the "Paris of Asia." A cosmopolitan city, it had attracted many Europeans prior to the Communist revolution.

Our visit there confirmed the Chinese assertion that Shanghai was by far the most Westernized city in China. In a tour on the Huang Pa River, we saw a thriving seaport next to an imposing skyline. I haven't been back, but I'm told that in the past 14 years there has been a huge infusion of foreign capital into Shanghai. It has apparently once again become "the Paris of Asia," both culturally and economically.

After a number of formal meetings with Chinese officials, we concluded that they were well-informed, liked and respected Americans, but at the same time were wary of us. The Nixon rapprochement in the early 70s had helped greatly, as had visits of groups such as ours.

This huge country, with a billion citizens, was in the throes of a dramatic transformation. In part, it was manifested by what people wore. Although most still wore the traditional blue or gray, we often saw western clothing, particularly among the young. Some wore blue jeans. In later visits, I was amazed to see how the people dressed more and more like westerners. Now, to the distress of American textile people, more and more "western clothing" is being produced in China.

Hong Kong

On Thursday, November 15, after six days in China, we flew to

Hong Kong. Although our Chinese hosts had been courteous and hospitable, we were ready for a change.

Landing in Hong Kong after a two-hour flight was the difference between night and day. To me, it felt like traveling to Hungary after several dismal, near-depressing days in the Soviet Union.

Hong Kong, still under British rule, was a thriving, exciting city, with one of the most vibrant economies in the world. It was firmly rooted in free-market economics with a minimum of government regulation and a low tax rate. The unemployment rate was near zero, and Hong Kong had beautifully-constructed, modern buildings.

We stayed at the Shangri-la Hotel, which was palatial compared to our hotels in China. Not only were the accommodations luxurious, but they served American food! Carol and I remember with great satisfaction ordering cheeseburgers and french fries. No gourmet meal ever tasted better!

Politically, the arrangements were underway for the eventual transfer of Hong Kong to China, which occurred in 1997. The politicians — and particularly the business community — expressed concern about how two radically different systems, capitalism and communism, could be successfully merged.

Some felt it would never work and proceeded to leave Hong Kong. In the early 1990s, there was substantial "capital flight" overseas, much of it to Vancouver, British Columbia. Many stayed, feeling correctly that China's rulers were too pragmatic to alter the Hong Kong economy.

In 1997, the transition was made peacefully. Although it is too early to tell, it appears the "marriage" will work.

TAIWAN

Our last stop was in Taipei, the capital of the Republic of China on Taiwan. It was there that Chiang Kai-shek and his followers fled in 1949, when it was clear the Communist revolution was going to succeed. In the intervening years, Taiwan grew into a prosperous country. Taipei, its capital, is a thriving metropolis, although it suffers from the usual air pollution and traffic problems. But, in our discussions with its leaders, it was apparent they were aware of the problems and were serious about addressing them.

The principle concern of their officials was U.S.-China relations. This had been a thorny problem for years and continues to be one to this day. The U.S. values Taiwan as a trusted friend but doesn't want to alienate China.

In time, China and Taiwan may fashion a settlement of their problems. Younger generations may not feel the animosity the old-timers did.

Our final meeting was with President Chiang Ching-Kuo, the son of Chiang Kai-shek. After our delegation meeting, the President asked me to remain. Because I had chaired the Reagan campaign, he wanted to know about the recent Presidential campaign between the President and Walter Mondale. It was apparent from the outset that he was well-informed about American politics.

After I briefed him on the strategy of the campaign, in which we had won 49 of the 50 states, he asked pointedly, "Why didn't you pour more money into Minnesota? If you had, you'd surely have won it."

My kind of guy!

Nonetheless, I tried to explain to him that President Reagan, knowing he was comfortably ahead, felt we should hold back on Minnesota, since that was Mr. Mondale's home state. In fact, we'd had trouble even having Ron attend a closing rally in Minnesota.

President Chiang listened patiently and then said, "Believe me, Senator, if I had been the candidate, I wouldn't have held back one bit."

From his earnest tone, I knew he wasn't kidding.

CHAPTER 16

❖ *The Marcos Mission* ❖

It was in early October 1985, that I ran into my old friend, Senator Dan Inouye of Hawaii, on the floor of the Senate. A World War II hero who'd lost an arm fighting for the U.S. as a Japanese-American, he had befriended me from the time I first entered the Senate.

In a near conspiratorial tone, he asked, "Got your bags packed?" I said, "Hell, no, Danny. I'm not going anywhere until the end of the session. Like you, I'm traveled out."

Suddenly, I sensed that he was deadly serious. Since he was a power on both the Armed Services and Intelligence Committees, my instincts told me that something important was afoot. And, as it turned out, it surely was.

He confided to me that he had just participated in a National Security Council briefing in the War Room of the White House. He told me that the meeting had been called on a top-secret basis to discuss the "Philippine situation."

Our intelligence sources had advised the council that the Philippines were on the verge of a Communist takeover, and that President Ferdinand Marcos, our long-standing, loyal ally, was ignoring State Department admonitions to attend to the precarious economic and political state of affairs in his country.

According to Dan, the National Security Council had

decided that I would be the logical person, in view of my close friendship with President Reagan, to deliver a stern message to Marcos.

My reaction was mixed. On the one hand, I was surprised that the President hadn't contacted me directly. We had discussed the Philippines from time-to-time, but both of us felt that Marcos, who was as smart an inside politician as there was anywhere in the world, would handle the situation.

I was also apprehensive in view of the fact that I'd had very little diplomatic experience.

The word came quickly from the White House that the President wanted me to meet with the NSC on a matter of "urgent importance." I met with the group in the War Room immediately. Rather than risk creating problems for Dan, I didn't allude to our floor conversation.

After the President opened the meeting, Cap Weinberger immediately took charge. As Secretary of Defense, he and his department were concerned about the military aspects of the Marcos problem. Cap contended that unless corrective steps were taken quickly, there could be a Communist military takeover, which would create huge security problems for the U.S. in that part of the world.

Secretary of State George Shultz said that his State Department people had attempted to impress upon Marcos the seriousness of the situation, but to no avail. It was clear that Marcos had no particular respect or regard for the "striped-pants crowd."

Shultz added that although personal diplomacy was dangerous, even the State Department people who had dealt with the problem agreed that sending me as the President's personal emissary was worth trying.

President Reagan closed by stating that his "experts" had satisfied him that this was the proper course to follow. He recognized that this would be a difficult mission, but he felt confident I could handle it.

The next several days were spent in intensive briefings with intelligence agencies. They made the point that Marcos had been a faithful and reliable ally in a very volatile part of the world, and that the U.S. would prefer to keep him in power. Nevertheless, they feared he had lost control. He was in poor health and disappeared from public view for long periods of time. In addition, the economy was in peril, and the Communist insurgency was growing stronger, threatening his rule.

Bill Casey, director of the Central Intelligence Agency, suggested it might be helpful if I was also briefed by Hank Greenberg, the CEO of American International Group, an insurance giant with interests throughout the world. They had a large presence in the Philippines as well. Bill was right.

Hank had an insightful businessman's perspective of the situation. He indicated that he was a close friend of Marcos and admired him. He also noted that Marcos was a "health nut" who always tried to stay in shape by punching heavy bags, skipping rope and the like.

Hank felt that Marcos badly needed a "wake-up call," and he was fearful that "the little man" was gradually becoming a spectator rather than an active player.

Finally, the appointment with Marcos was arranged, and our party left Andrews Air Force base for Manila on a Department of Defense plane. The mission was staffed by the Air Force.

State Department, National Security Council and CIA representatives accompanied me. Tom Loranger and Ace Robison of my Senate staff made the trip as well. The dozen or so of us rattled around the plane, which could have easily carried about two hundred passengers. There were also sleeping compartments, which were a godsend on such a long trip.

I left Washington feeling relieved that the secrecy of the entire mission had been carefully guarded. The last thing we wanted was any appearance that President Reagan was trying to apply pressure publicly on President Marcos.

Philippine President Ferdinand Marcos.
Special Collections, University of Nevada, Reno Library

After we were safely aloft, one of the NSC staffers confided to me that he had leaked the story to a friend of his at The Washington Times in order to frame the subject properly. The press was all over the story by the time I arrived in Manila. So much for our secret mission! One report went so far as to suggest that I was going to the Philippines "to kick ass and take names." Just what I didn't need.

I hadn't been to the Philippines since the war, which was almost 41 years earlier to the day.

During my stay, I met twice with Marcos in the presidential palace. At the outset of our conversations, I mentioned to him that I was involved in the Leyte campaign at the same time that he had been part of the Philippine liberation force fighting the Japanese occupation. This helped to establish a linkage between us that probably later contributed to the strength of our relationship.

As I noted earlier, the primary purpose of my mission was to communicate President Reagan's personal concerns about the general political and economic instability in the Philippines. The specific "concerns" included a declining economy, questions about whether Marcos continued to enjoy the popular support of his people, and whether the Philippine military was taking the steps necessary to deal with a growing Communist insurgency.

I delivered a hand-written "Dear Ferdinand" letter from President Reagan that outlined these concerns. Marcos did not agree with the message contained in the letter, but he knew enough about my relationship with President Reagan not to pass me off as just another meddling American diplomat.

With the help of his military staff, including Deputy Chief of Staff Fidel Ramos, who would later join the opposition forces, Marcos attempted to paint a rosy picture of how he was dealing with the Communist insurgency.

Marcos, generally speaking, was upbeat and optimistic – unrealistically so, as it developed. I believe he had the interests of the Filipino people at heart, but over time he had become isolated from reality and surrounded by cronies who told him pretty much what he wanted to hear.

President Marcos had been twice elected to his nation's highest office in the 1960s. It was obvious to me that he was a very capable politician. In some ways, he reminded me of Richard Nixon in that he loved the craft of politics and political strategy. He was well informed and knew the U.S. and how its political institutions worked, including the limitations of our presidency.

Unfortunately, he had allowed a number of his friends – his wife's friends – to develop an economic cartel that had a stranglehold on the Philippine economy. There really wasn't a free-market economy, at least for the country's major products.

Likewise, the military, although staffed by capable individuals such as Ramos, became more concerned with protecting its interests rather than dealing with the serious threat posed by the Communist insurgency.

To address the question of whether Marcos enjoyed the support of the Filipino people, it had been suggested by CIA Director Bill Casey, during a previous visit, that a "snap election" be called to prove his strength or lack thereof. He had waved off these suggestions.

After my return to the U.S., however, I told Marcos by telephone that most Americans, including those in Congress, felt strongly that he no longer enjoyed the support of his people.

At that point, which was in late October, he said that he was reconsidering his position on a snap election. We were both scheduled to appear on the David Brinkley Sunday morning television show in a few days. I told him that it would be dramatic for him to announce his decision about a snap election on the Brinkley show, which is what he did.

I think he figured that he would easily win the election over any challenger, including Corazon Aquino, the wife of the assassinated leader of the Marcos opposition. Marcos vastly underestimated her strength. He probably also assumed that the opposition would be fragmented.

This was a major miscalculation because an ad hoc coalition between Aquino and another opposition candidate, Salvador Laurel, was achieved, thus solidifying the anti-Marcos movement.

During the pre-election period, critics of the Reagan Administration said it was more concerned with preserving our military bases in the Philippines than with building democracy. I didn't believe these objectives were mutually exclusive because maintaining the bases was in the interests of both countries.

In addition, we had to be careful to preserve the distinction between making constructive suggestions to a long-time ally and stepping over the line and intruding on another nation's sovereignty. We certainly never said, "We think you should hold an election now!"

I had told President Marcos previously that if he decided to go forward with an election, it would have to be fair and open. I said that an election was of no use if it were deemed to be fraudulent.

I had also told Marcos that it would be helpful if he were to allow international election observers into the country. To his credit, he agreed to do so.

The election took place on February 7, 1986. Unfortunately, the results, which initially showed Marcos to be the winner, were completely undermined by the massive fraud that was perpetrated by government authorities, particularly the military. I received a number of top-secret briefings which led me to conclude that this was a dishonest election.

Marcos' position began to deteriorate rapidly after Defense Minister Juan Ponce Enrile decided to break from him. Soon thereafter, General Ramos did the same. Before long, tens of thousands of Filipinos had taken to the streets to "protect" Enrile and Ramos. It appeared as if a bloody clash between the opposing forces was imminent.

On February 24, 1986, at around noon Eastern time, our office received what turned out to be an historic call from Malacanang Palace, the Presidential home in Manila. The call came into my press secretary, Tom Loranger, who was eating lunch at his desk. One of the Philippine embassy officials had Tom's number, and he must have passed it along to his colleagues in Manila.

When an operator in a faint voice said, "This is Malacanang Palace – President Marcos is calling for Senator Paul Laxalt," Tom could hardly believe his ears.

Earlier in the day, with the Philippines teetering on the brink of a civil war, the White House had taken the extraordinary step of issuing a statement calling for a "peaceful transition to a new government."

Tom called for my secretary, Eileen deLatour: "Eileen, would you please transfer this call to the Senator. I don't feel like cutting off Ferdinand Marcos."

Eileen sent the call to an office in the Capitol where a few of my colleagues and I were receiving a top-secret briefing from Secretary George Shultz and Ambassador Phil Habib. During the briefing, they were speculating about Marcos' next moves when the meeting was interrupted by a staff member entering the room to say, "Senator Laxalt, President Marcos is calling for you."

You can imagine the expressions on the faces of Shultz and Habib as I left to take the call.

Marcos immediately asked me if the statement calling for a "peaceful transition" had really come from President Reagan. I told him that it had, but when he asked several other questions, including one about whether there might be a chance for a "power sharing" agreement with Aquino during the transition, I told him that I would have to call him back.

In that first conversation, which occurred at 3:00 a.m. Manila time, Marcos was in a frightened and pugnacious mood. He told me that he and his family, including his grandchildren, had holed up in the palace. He was terrified by reports that our Marines were planning on joining the rebel forces. (I checked this out with Cap Weinberger immediately and was assured that it was ridiculous.)

The conversation frightened the daylights out of me. The last thing we needed was a civil war in the Philippines. At the end of our conversation, I implored him to avoid any unnecessary bloodshed and assured him that I would speak to the President.

Shultz, Habib and I traveled immediately to the White

House, where we met with President Reagan and key national security staff members.

President Reagan shot down the idea of "power sharing," and he told me to tell Marcos that "he would be welcome in the United States, if he saw fit to come here."

I then called Marcos back from the office of National Security Adviser John Poindexter. It was 5:00 a.m. Manila time.

President Marcos asked me at the outset whether President Reagan wanted him to resign, and I indicated that I wasn't in a position to "make that kind of representation."

Then Marcos asked me the "gut question": "Senator, what do you think I should do?"

Although I felt a rush of sympathy for him, I quickly decided to tell him what I thought he needed to do in order to avoid bloodshed in the Philippines.

"Cut and cut cleanly. The time has come," I said.

There was the longest pause. It seemed to last minutes – so long that I finally asked, "Mr. President, are you still there?"

In a weak, sad, defeated voice, he said, "I'm here, Senator. I'm just so very, very disappointed." And then he hung up the phone.

Sixteen hours later, Ferdinand Marcos, after 21 years as President of the Philippines, departed the country, never to return.

The biggest lesson I learned from my dealings with President Marcos is the value of personal diplomacy. I cannot weigh in the total equation how important was Marcos' call to me, but it may have prevented a civil war in the Philippines.

I know that if I had gone to Manila and tried to lecture Marcos, I doubt that his last call to me would ever have been made.

President Marcos didn't call a State Department bureaucrat or even the Secretary of State. He called me because he trusted me and knew that I would level with him.

Thankfully, and to his great credit, he left the Philippines peacefully and thus avoided a bloodbath.

CHAPTER 17

❖ *The Reagan Years* ❖

W hat turned out to be a unique personal and political friendship with Ronald Reagan started perfunctorily in 1964,
during Barry Goldwater's ill-fated campaign for the presidency.

I was Nevada's Lieutenant Governor at the time and became
the first state official in the West to announce my support for
Barry. Ron was well-known because of his television and movie
work, of course, and was stumping for Barry. Our paths crossed
occasionally on the campaign trail in California and Nevada.

At that time, Ron was still thought of as little more than an
entertainment figure, a movie star, although one active in his industry's internal politics and willing, as a concerned citizen, to
use his name and connections to help candidates in whom he
believed. Then, as now, the "household name" value of show
business personalities was very valuable to any candidate, regardless of the office he or she was seeking.

It had been mentioned that Ron might run for public office,
but in 1964 it was still in the early discussion stages.

My recollections of Ronald Reagan in those days are hazy,
because we didn't really become well-acquainted until a few years
later. I remember him as a stylish, charismatic individual, always
smiling, with an instinctive ability to relate to an audience and to
attract the interest of a crowd.

He was a natural campaigner, appearing totally at ease in any type of setting or situation. In observing him, I was impressed, but I had my doubts about whether he was "real." After all, any accomplished actor could deliver a ringing speech from notes.

NEIGHBOR GOVERNORS

In 1966, we were elected Governors of our respective states. Ron defeated Pat Brown, the father of future Governor Jerry Brown, and I defeated Grant Sawyer who, like Pat Brown, was seeking a third term.

This election marked the official start of our political association and personal friendship. We had frequent common problems as Chief Executives of neighboring states, and as we dealt with them, we became good friends.

Nevada and California have a relationship unlike that of virtually all other bordering states. On the surface, two more dissimilar states would be hard to find.

California, of course, is first among the separate but equal states of the Union – packed with people, loaded with natural resources, fat with things to do, places to go, people to see. It's the "land of milk and honey."

Nevada, on the other hand, is a land-locked state rich only in the barrenness of its high desert, poor in most natural resources and sparsely populated.

To many Californians, that which Nevada holds dear – the sagebrush wilderness of its interior – is nothing more than wasteland. To many Nevadans, the hustle, bustle and fervor of California is repugnant, representing a foreign way of life.

But Nevada has legalized gambling which, for more than six decades, has kept Nevada well-populated on a temporary basis with visiting Californians. It has drawn heavily on an influx of tourists from across the state line. Millions of Californians have left billions of dollars in Nevada casinos over the years.

During our Governorships, Ron and I would kid one another about this unique "love-hate" relationship between Nevada and California. Ron would jokingly threaten to close the borders and thus "bankrupt Nevada in 24 hours."

The 1968 Republican Convention

While Ron and I were closely involved on a bi-state basis in the late 1960s, our only involvement on a broader political scale came at the 1968 Republican convention in Miami. Something that happened at that convention told me a lot about the character of Ron Reagan.

Richard Nixon was the overwhelming favorite for the nomination that year. He had it virtually locked up as a result of his hard work and the accumulation of many political IOUs. It was a textbook case of a political comeback after Nixon's painful defeats in 1960 and 1962.

He worked tirelessly on behalf of Republican candidates everywhere, which resulted in a lot of grateful individuals who felt they "owed" Nixon.

While he enjoyed strong support overall, Nixon had very few "true believers" – the types who would jump off a cliff for his candidacy.

At any rate, Ron had asked me to nominate him as a "favorite son" candidate at the convention. Initially, it was intended to be only a means by which to avoid a nasty California primary between Nixon and Rockefeller, although, looking back, I'm sure some of Ron's supporters saw it as a chance to secure a significant bloc of delegates in case the candidacy became "real."

Anyway, I assumed that Ron had no intention of challenging Nixon for the nomination. As a result, I consented to nominate him, as a courtesy only, because he knew I was committed to

Nixon. Everything was fine until we got to Miami.

There, Ron switched gears and decided that he was actually going to run for President. The favorite son idea went out the window. He was going for it all, which left me in an uncomfortable position with some of my fellow Republicans.

Some Nixon supporters feared that his support was evaporating, pointing out also that the delegate commitments were only for the first ballot.

One can imagine the psychological impact of a Governor, even one from a small state, coming to the convention and appearing to switch from Nixon to Reagan. It could have started a momentum shift.

John Mitchell (the future Attorney General and then a Nixon political adviser) and I had some strong words. Senator Strom Thurmond was all over Bob Mardian, who was in charge of the western states for Nixon. Bob assured Strom that I was going to stay put, but it was starting to circulate like wildfire that I was going to nominate Reagan.

At that time, however, I thought that Nixon was the best man for the presidency, and I had made a commitment to him and a different commitment to Reagan. To stop all the speculation, I went to Ron's hotel suite and asked to be relieved of my nominating duties.

"Ron," I told him, "I made my commitment to you based on a certain set of circumstances, purely on a favorite son basis. If you tell me you're a serious candidate, I'm just going to have to be relieved of that commitment."

Lyn Nofziger, one of Ron's key people then and throughout his political career, wasn't happy with that news.

"Oh, no you don't, Governor," he erupted. "A commitment's a commitment."

Ron, to his credit, said, "No way. A commitment's a commitment only under a set of circumstances. If Paul feels he has to be relieved, we're just going to have to let him go. And with no hard feelings."

Lyn choked down his exasperation, but the boss had spoken.

Ron showed nothing but style, in what for him must have been an awkward situation. It caused me to appreciate him all the more.

The Reagan effort at that convention was, in all honesty, quite amateurish, and the favorite son effort went nowhere.

Ron served another term as Governor after he was re-elected in 1970, while I chose not to run again after serving a single term. During the next few years, I was almost completely occupied with running our family hotel, while Ron was busy running California, so I saw him infrequently.

I really don't think Ron had that many close personal friends in those days, probably because he had left one career as an actor and started another as a politician. He had left one set of friends and a lifestyle behind and wasn't yet completely immersed in the other.

I suppose I was as close to him as anybody in political life, but I don't think anybody was what could be considered intimate with him outside of a handful of his buddies in California. At the various Governors' conferences, I had been pretty much his link to the other politicians, most of whom he was uncomfortable being around.

LOOKING TOWARD 1976

I knew that Ron harbored some Presidential aspirations, but I wasn't involved at that stage and really didn't give it any thought until I went to Washington in late 1974 as Nevada's newly-elected U.S. Senator. That's when I first realized that Ronald Reagan offered something that this country needed desperately.

I had always felt that the political talent that drove this country was in Washington. Looking at national politics from my Nevada perspective, perhaps with a little bit of gullibility and awe, I had wrongly assumed that Washington had a virtual monopoly on people with presidential qualifications.

When I came to Washington, however, and was exposed to the so-called "heavyweights" of politics, I quickly changed my mind. The longer I was in Washington, the more attractive Ron Reagan became, not only in terms of how he handled difficult situations and his magnificent personal qualities, but also by virtue of almost everything that I felt was important to the presidency.

Although I liked and respected President Ford, I thought the country, particularly after Watergate, needed new blood and a fresh perspective.

Already in early 1975, people such as Lyn Nofziger, Mike Deaver and John Sears were laying the foundation for a Reagan presidential campaign. Because they were "plotting" against a sitting Republican President, a lot of this work was of the "cloak-and-dagger" variety.

In May 1975, I received a call in my Senate office from Mike Deaver, asking me to meet Ron for dinner at the Madison Hotel in downtown Washington, to discuss "informally" the political situation. Looking back, I'm sure they weren't seeking a political commitment from me, any more than I was prepared to give one.

But they felt I was the closest person to Reagan in Washington, and they felt my presence would be helpful. They probably knew that I would level with them about the prospects for a Reagan Presidential campaign without pulling any punches.

The meeting, with Ron, Deaver, Nofziger, Sears and myself, took place in a suite at the Madison, just a few blocks north of the White House. We sat around after dinner and shot the bull, talking mostly about a potential campaign.

After Ron asked me to sum up my feelings, I said, "It's been my brief experience around town, and in particular in dealing with the President and his people, that Ford isn't going to be all that strong." That assessment was quickly endorsed by the others.

"I think you should give some serious consideration to getting into this thing," I went on, "irrespective of the obvious problems of running against an incumbent President, and the possibility that it might cause some divisiveness."

Ron expressed some interest, but it seemed to me that he was somewhat reluctant, unlike John, Mike and Lyn, who were 100 percent in support of a run. We left it with Ron agreeing to give the matter further consideration.

Not too long thereafter, John Sears and Jim Lake, Reagan's young and talented press adviser, came to my Senate office and laid on me the possibility of forming a committee to promote a Reagan candidacy, with my serving as chairman. I was both flattered and surprised, but I gave them a quick turn-down. It was just too early.

Hugh Scott, the Senator from Pennsylvania and the Republican leader in the Senate, had attempted to circulate a letter on behalf of President Ford that was, in effect, a commitment to Ford. It was a bad idea that many of us resented, and it was shot down rather quickly. Again, it was too early to get committed to anyone.

After our meeting, Sears and the others decided to go forward with the Reagan committee. I agreed to provide them with names of potential supporters. They kicked around the names of some possible chairmen with me, but they repeatedly came back to me as the best choice.

I explained to them that it was premature, and that I didn't think that I was prepared to handle a national campaign. We left it there, with Sears and Lake saying they would report my decision to Ron and would keep looking for a chairman.

During the Senate's Fourth of July recess in 1975, Ron called me at the Ormsby House in Carson City.

"I don't know if I'm going to do this thing," he said, "but if I form a committee, I just absolutely have to have you as my chairman."

"Ron," I said, "I don't think I can do it. I'm not qualified, for one thing. I have no experience in a national campaign."

"That's not the important thing, Paul. From a personal standpoint, I need someone in there I can trust. Someone I can talk to in complete confidence. Someone who is loyal. You're the man for the job."

"Ron, I'm just getting started. I've got a lot of projects, and I haven't any experience..."

"I know all that," he interrupted, "and I still want you to do it."

Turning pragmatic, I said, "I don't want to walk off a political plank on this thing. You have a sitting Republican President, and I'm a rookie Senator from the same party. There are some damn tough people in this administration. If we form a committee and this doesn't result in a candidacy, you can imagine where that leaves me."

Ron said, "I appreciate where you're coming from."

"I don't want any assurances," I went on. "I know the committee would have to go out and explore something. But I've got to know where the hell I am, Ron, to some extent. I just have a couple of questions."

"Go ahead," he replied.

"You've got a fire burning in your gut to do this, don't you?" I asked.

"Yes, I have to tell you I have," he said quietly.

"Well, tell me, on a scale of one to ten, if the committee should come back with a positive result, where would you place yourself in terms of a candidacy?"

He hesitated, and then said, "Oh, right about eight."

"That's good enough for me," I said. "I guess I'm your man!"

"Paul, all I can say is thanks. I hope you never regret this."

I hung up the phone after that conversation wondering whether I'd done the right thing. I was convinced that Ronald Reagan should be our next President, and the more I thought of that, the stronger I became in my belief that it was only proper that I "come out of the closet" politically.

THE 1976 CAMPAIGN

The 1976 campaign officially started in Washington, D.C., on November 20, 1975, when Governor Reagan announced his candidacy for President of the United States at the National Press Club.

The place was jammed with supporters and the national press, all feeling that history was being made. Although an exploratory committee had existed for several weeks, many felt down to the last moment that Ron would finally pull out.

I was backstage before the announcement and witnessed Ron and Nancy in a long embrace before he stepped on stage.

The announcement and subsequent press conference went well. The reaction was generally positive, although several of my staff and political supporters thought I'd "gone over the edge" in chairing a campaign against a sitting Republican President as a very junior Senator. It "broke all the rules," and they simply couldn't understand. Fortunately, they eventually did.

My colleagues in the Senate treated me gently (perhaps as one would treat a colleague who is heading for the political gas chamber). I remember Senator James Eastland, after learning of my decision to go with Reagan, jokingly saying in his southern drawl, "You're a radical!"

But then the polls started coming in, with many of them showing Ron substantially ahead of Ford. Suddenly, my desk on the floor began to be surrounded by Senators from both sides of the aisle trying to assess what the hell was going on. I loved every minute of it!

John Sears, who was our chief strategist, and Lyn Nofziger, who handled the political side of the campaign, decided on "blitzkrieging" our opponent through solid victories in New Hampshire, Florida and Illinois. They reasoned that if we won big in those opening states, the Ford campaign would quickly crumble.

So off to New Hampshire we all went, to places such as Nashua and Concord, which were just names on a map to all of us, save for John Sears, who had worked New Hampshire for Richard Nixon.

New Hampshire then, as now, was campaigned on a "retail" basis. Yes, there is the usual media advertising, but the most effective political work is done on a person-to-person basis.

And so it's one meeting hall after another, with a service club appearance wedged in. A rally with several hundred people is a rarity.

For several days, we traveled New Hampshire from Massachusetts to the Canadian border. As westerners from large states, Ron and I found it unusual to attend an event at one end of the state, and then another on the other end a couple of hours later.

Some days, I'd campaign with Nancy. Anxious at first, she quickly blossomed into a world-class campaigner. Ron and Nancy were as effective a campaign team as I've ever seen.

On the weekend before the New Hampshire primary, John Sears decided that we were in good enough shape to move Ron to Illinois for a few days of campaigning in that important state. After all, our polls showed us well ahead. What a mistake that turned out to be!

On election day, Ron returned to our New Hampshire "home" in Concord, the Highway Hotel. This was, and had been for many presidential primaries, the favorite watering hole for the national press and the political operatives.

We decided to have dinner together in the Reagan suite, fully confident that the evening would be a happy and productive one vote-wise.

After dinner, the early returns started to trickle in. From the outset, they were disappointing. Instead of being comfortably ahead, we were slightly behind.

Around 10 or so, Ron went to the adjoining meeting hall to bolster several hundred supporters who had gathered there. His message was simple. "Be patient. We'll win out at the end."

But it didn't happen that way. When the votes were counted, we had lost — by fewer than a thousand votes! We couldn't believe it. Ron Reagan had never lost a race.

As the evening wore on, the rationalizations grew. "This wasn't that important." "We'll recover in a few days in Florida." After all, our chairman there, Tommy Thomas, had predicted that week that Reagan would win Florida by a two-to-one margin.

But again, it didn't happen that way. We lost Florida, badly. Then Illinois.

We learned first-hand what a domino effect a New Hampshire loss can have.

Then the money started drying up!

Very early in the morning of the day the Reagans were to fly to North Carolina for their final campaign swing in the Tar Heel State, their charter plane sat on the tarmac at Los Angeles airport, filled with the campaign team and reporters.

Time dragged on. The delay, it turns out, was necessary for the Reagan campaign staff in Washington to open the mail to see if there would be enough money to pay United Airlines for the flight. There was — barely.

The word spread like wildfire that we were "sucking air." Without a win to breathe life into a badly crippled campaign, this contest might be over.

Then a lifeline came our way. Jimmy Lyons, a staunch conservative and a Houston banker, called to say he could furnish $100,000 to keep the campaign moving. It was like "manna from Heaven."

So we went into North Carolina on a do-or-die basis. Ron asked me to come down for a few days to campaign with him. The day I arrived at the motel where the Reagan camp was staying, we were advised that several Republican office holders released a statement to the press demanding that Reagan, in the interest of the party, withdraw!

Instead of intimidating him, the message had just the opposite effect. In profane terms, which he rarely used, he told us what the Republican politicians could do to themselves.

For the next several days, we worked all of North Carolina. I don't think we missed a single shopping center. To add spontaneity to his appearances, I induced him to give up his 3x5 cards. The results were spectacular. I've never seen him better.

Allied with us in North Carolina were Senator Jesse Helms and his legion of supporters. Without Jesse and his people in North Carolina, Ron would never have been President.

Election night in North Carolina came with our feeling "cautiously optimistic." After New Hampshire, how could we be anything more!

When the votes were counted, we were overjoyed. By a 52-46 percent margin, we'd won! I don't recall ever seeing Ron happier! Who can blame him? We now had a "second life."

Utilizing our newfound momentum, we decided to do a national telecast with Ron making an appeal for funds. As a result, we raised more than $1 million which qualified us, in turn, for another $750,000 in matching federal funds. We were now out of the hole financially.

On the heels of our "must win" victory in North Carolina, we zeroed in on Texas, which had 100 delegates at stake. The Texas Republican establishment was solidly in favor of President Ford. They were led by my Senate colleague, John Tower, the first Republican ever elected to the U.S. Senate from the Lone Star State.

He was a prodigious campaigner, who covered the state "killing us with kindness." He'd say, "Governor Reagan is a hell of a guy, but unseasoned nationally. We Republicans should stick with Ford."

To offset John as best we could, it was decided that I would campaign Texas. I'd served there in the Army, but had no idea how gigantic it was or how diverse it was politically. So we worked Texas from one end to the other, appearing at countless television and radio stations and political rallies.

The message was two-fold: Ron was a solid Texas-like conservative, and he had the best chance to win in November.

Gradually, we came to a pleasant conclusion. Although the establishment was for Ford, the rank-and-file voters were looking for a conservative alternative, and Ron looked good to them.

Jimmy Lyons of Houston and Ernie Angelo of Midland were invaluable. They had statewide credibility as successful businessmen. More important to us, they had been pioneers in the Republican Party effort to establish itself as a political force in Texas. To be sure, there were many more who helped Ron in Texas, including stalwarts like Diana Denman and Ray Barnhart.

Out of any campaign come great stories, and Texas was no exception. My favorite was when one of our county chairmen, a 6'6" sheriff, was interviewed on television. He was asked about

John Tower's efforts in the campaign. John was about 5'6" in his elevator shoes. The good sheriff stood up, pointed to his belt line, and proclaimed: "I've had it with John Tower up to here."

We left Texas for Indiana on election day — May 1st — feeling that we would get a healthy slice of the 100 delegates, perhaps 60 or 70.

That evening, after concluding a campaign appearance, we went to our hotel in Indianapolis. The place was swarming with the national press. A reporter shouted to us: "Have you heard the results from Texas?" When we replied that we hadn't, he contended that we'd won "75 or 80" of the delegates. We didn't dare comment.

We went upstairs to our room and waited a couple of hours, while taking calls from allies in Texas.

Finally, the results were confirmed. We hadn't won just "75 or 80" but all 100 delegates!

It was unbelievable in terms of impact. As one of our campaign guys said the next day, "It just made everybody feel so goddamned good!"

For the first time since New Hampshire, we felt we had a real shot at the nomination. From that point on, we continued to accumulate votes in all the convention states. The huge Ford lead had dissipated to the point that it had become an exciting horse race.

We went on to California in June. A great deal was at stake in that primary, not only because of the number of delegates at stake, but also because it was a "winner-take-all" situation. Even though it was Ron's home state, he worked hard for the votes he could get. We won, getting all 164 delegates.

After the California primary there were only a few caucus states left. When these were concluded, we were done in terms of primaries and convention states.

At that point, there was a small pool of uncommitted delegates.

The "magic number" – the number of delegates needed to win the nomination – was 1130. Each camp had between 900 and 1,000 committed delegates going into the convention in Kansas City. The pool of 150-200 uncommitted delegates would determine the nomination. Everyone was treating the "uncommitted" like royalty.

We soon realized that competing for these delegates against the White House wasn't a fair fight. Ron would call them – even visit with them personally – and did reasonably well. But then Jerry Ford would invite them to a meeting in the Oval Office. It was like a guy with a Volkswagen vying for the attention of a girl against a competitor who has a Rolls Royce.

Something drastic had to be done. Once the news media decided the Ford campaign had reached the magic number of 1130, it would be all over. John Sears, ever the tactician, came up with a possible solution.

Although it was unprecedented, Sears proposed that Ron select his Vice Presidential candidate before the convention. This might "freeze" the uncommitted delegates, who were mainly from the northeast. A freeze would prevent our being counted out prior to the convention. Once we made it to Kansas City, anything was possible, or so we reasoned.

Ron signed off on the idea immediately. The big question was: Who would be Ron's running mate?

Since the delegates we were wooing were from the northeast, we decided to look there for prospects. Sears and I pored over lists – Senators, Congressmen, businessmen.

Finally, John came to my office one day in an excited state, which was rare for him, and told me that he had a recommendation to make: Senator Richard Schweiker of Pennsylvania.

The geography couldn't be better; Schweiker voted pretty much "middle-of-the-road"; he had a telegenic wife, Claire, who used to have her own television show; they had a beautiful family; and, like frosting on the cake, he was very close politically and personally to Drew Lewis, the Ford campaign chairman in Pennsylvania.

The word was that Drew was unhappy with the Ford campaign. We thought that with Schweiker's urging, Drew might switch, which could lead to several more in the northeast, particularly in Pennsylvania, where the delegates were not bound by law to support Ford, even though they were supposedly committed to him.

My immediate reaction to the Schweiker idea was one of near shock. Dick was my seatmate in the Senate, and we were good friends. But a running mate for Ron? I thought, "No way. Dick is too liberal, he supports Ford and wouldn't switch, and besides, Ron would go into orbit!"

After kicking it around for awhile, John convinced me that Dick might be a natural. After all, his philosophy would "balance" the ticket. The media would love it. It was all so "off the wall" that it might just work. At the very least, it might achieve the "freeze" we were seeking ahead of the convention.

So we had a political marriage in the works. Now, who was going to notify the principals?

Since John didn't know Dick well, he asked me to be the "John Alden" to convey the proposal to him. This came to a head during Congress' July 4 recess. Dick had told me at some point before that his family spent the Fourth at the Jersey beach.

I drew a deep breath and called him. From the outset, I could tell that he thought "something was up," and it probably had to do with the Reagan campaign.

"Dick," I said, "I've got a very important matter to discuss

with you." He said, "Well, what does it relate to?" "Politics,"
I replied.

So Dick came off the shore in a helluva hurry.

John Sears and I met with him and his assistant, Dave
Newhall, in my Senate office. John gave him the history of the
campaign and where matters stood. He then outlined our strategy about an early running mate, and that we had decided that he
was the right man.

Dick was surprised, to put it mildly, but quickly recovered as
most good politicians do when confronted with a dramatic
change in circumstances.

Former U.S. Senator Richard Schweiker of Pennsylvania, Reagan's running mate in
1976, watching coverage of the convention with "The Gipper."

He was interested, but he said that he'd have to discuss the
matter with his family and Dave. Also, he would have some questions for Ron.

We told him that time was of the essence, and it surely was. The convention was just a few days off.

Within hours, Dick reported back, saying that, subject to talking to Governor Reagan, he was "ready to go."

Since security was absolutely essential, John and I traveled separately to Los Angeles so John could brief the Reagans before Dick's arrival. Dick and Dave traveled separately as well.

The "conditioning" by John was essential, since Ron didn't know Dick, other than when his political people would tell him that Schweiker was "liberal as hell."

I was apprehensive, but my concern disappeared as soon as Dick and Ron met. Their "chemistry" couldn't have been better.

Before the meeting, which took place on Saturday, July 24, I had briefed Ron, telling him that Dick was a good, honest man and an effective Senator. I also said that the liberal tag was tied to Dick principally because he had a pro-labor voting record, which wasn't surprising since he came from a state in which organized labor was very strong.

The discussion on issues went well. To the surprise of both Ron and Dick, they were in basic agreement on fiscal discipline, national security, gun control and the federal-state division of power.

Dick was principally concerned about having a meaningful role in the decision-making process in the campaign and thereafter. Ron assured him that he would, and that satisfied him. The fact that Ron delegated freely reassured Dick.

Finally, a decision was reached that henceforth they would run as a team. A simple handshake sealed the bargain.

We decided to make the announcement the following Monday. Meanwhile, we had to protect against "leaks." Any leak would diminish the effect of a surprising and exciting announcement.

On the way to the airport before our departure for Los Angeles, I had asked Dick whether he was going to call his close friend, Drew Lewis, in Pennsylvania. After all, the strategy was in great part based on the assumption that Dick's "signing on" would quickly bring Lewis, the Ford Pennsylvania state chairman, on board, too.

Dick assured me that a call wasn't necessary because Drew was like a brother to him and that when the announcement was made, Drew, who was disenchanted with the Ford crowd, would defect to the Reagan campaign.

Unfortunately, it didn't turn out that way. After our announcement, Drew was contacted. He advised us that he was deeply offended that he hadn't been contacted in advance and wouldn't make a change now. This was proof positive that you can't take anything for granted in politics.

I've often wondered what would have happened had Dick made the call prior to the announcement. If Drew had switched, perhaps a snowball effect would have developed, causing the northeast states to go to Reagan. Perhaps not. In any case, Ron refused to indulge in such speculation.

Upon my return to Washington following the initial Reagan-Schweiker meeting, I went immediately to my Senate office. Other than knowing I had traveled to California to visit with the Reagans, no one on the staff had a clue as to what had transpired. I called them in and advised them of Governor Reagan's decision to select Senator Schweiker as his running mate, and that we were going to make the announcement in the Senate Caucus Room.

On the heels of my announcing that I was going to chair Ron's campaign, this was simply "too much!" One staff member, Dick Moore — wide-eyed — said, "Senator, do you realize what's going on here?"

Although they didn't say so, I'm sure my staff felt that the announcement would result in my political annihilation both by my conservative colleagues and the press.

Fortunately, and to my staff's great relief, the press conference went well. The fact that it was a complete surprise (with absolutely no leaks) made the announcement particularly dramatic. The reporters were so shocked that their questions were benign.

Dick handled the situation beautifully. The fact that he was an "old pro" with many difficult press conferences under his belt helped greatly.

When the conference ended, as luck would have it, a vote on the Senate floor was announced. Talk about facing the conservative lions in their den!

The first person I ran into was Strom Thurmond, who wailed, "But Paawwll, he's ah librawl!"

On the floor, Senators Jesse Helms, Jim McClure and others were waiting for me. Rather than risk being chastised on the floor, I asked them to meet with me in the cloakroom.

After we adjourned to the cloakroom, I patiently explained to them our reading of the situation: There were only about 100 uncommitted delegates; we were losing in our efforts to secure their support because the White House simply had too much horsepower; we needed to come up with something dramatic now or else we'd be dead before the convention; we picked Dick because he came from the area of the country where many of the "uncommitteds" were from; Ron had met with Dick over the weekend and was comfortable with him personally and politically.

I told them that the decision was final: "There's no other way, dammit, that we can go to Kansas City with any chance of securing the nomination."

I said that if they chose not to go along, which they had every right to do, it would be over. To their credit, all of them, however reluctantly, decided to support our new ticket. Their collective decision, I'm sure, was the result of pure pragmatism.

In the days before the convention, we showcased Dick as best we could. He was remarkable. Everywhere we went, we caught hell from conservative delegates, particularly the Mississippi delegation, where the criticism at times rose to the level of insult. Through it all, Dick handled the situation with complete dignity.

THE CONVENTION IN KANSAS CITY

By the time we arrived in Kansas City, we knew the Schweiker strategy had worked. Ron Reagan came to the convention with his candidacy very much alive. The Ford momentum had been stopped. The national media were excited about the prospect of a dramatic – perhaps historic – convention.

I arrived in Kansas City a week early, accompanied by Carol and my daughter Michelle.

The schedule was non-stop from early morning until late at night. There were press conferences, planning sessions and meetings with our delegation leaders to make sure there wasn't any slippage. We had delegate leaders from all 50 states, which meant that we were able to secure accurate head counts.

Shortly before the convention started, we again came to grips with the reality that going head-to-head with the White House and its horde of aides was very difficult. As had been the case in the running-mate selection, we decided at the urging of our chief strategist, John Sears, that a dramatic tactical move at the convention was needed.

Our polls had consistently indicated that any Vice Presidential selection would lose votes for President Ford. It followed that if he could be compelled to announce his running mate, regardless of who it was, it would lose him votes. In a race in which every vote counted, we reasoned that if we could carry this off, it might work.

We knew it wouldn't be easy. It had not happened before in

either party. Presidential nominees had always selected their running mates after they had been nominated, not before.

We turned our parliamentary procedure experts loose to research the matter. They reported that rule 16C of the party rules set forth the procedure of nominating Vice Presidential candidates.

It provided for nomination after the presidential nomination. To change the procedures, a majority vote of the delegates was needed.

Within our camp there was deep division. Many felt this would be a radical departure from traditional procedure and might cost us votes. Others of us contended, as we had in the Schweiker case, that we had no alternative. We had to try to change the rule.

Ron agreed, and that was that.

When we announced what we were going to do, the excitement rose by several decibels. Since the media thrived on the unexpected, they loved it. There was no backlash from our own delegates; they sensed we were hanging on by a thread, and 16C might just work!

As we worked the various delegations, it became clear that the Mississippi delegation was key, and that they were in doubt about what to do.

Coming into the convention, we had counted Mississippi as being ours. After all, Clark Reed, the delegation chairman, was a long-time Reagan friend and supporter and seemed to be in control. Unfortunately, our intelligence was flat-out wrong.

The Ford White House had courted the Mississippi delegation energetically and that work was paying off. Even Clark Reed was wavering, and the delegation was split.

We told them that the nomination of the next President was in their hands. We pointed out that if they supported Reagan, necessary votes from the northeast were pledged to us, and the nominee would be Reagan.

So, the victory on 16C came down to 59 Mississippi delegates. We heard that they might vote as a bloc to insulate individual delegates.

Finally, they ended up caucusing outside the convention hall. No one knew for certain what the delegation would do.

We held our breath.

Finally, the bad news came.

We lost the fight to change Rule 16C by a vote of 31-28.

Although we had 24 hours before the actual nomination vote the next night, we knew we had been dealt a very damaging blow.

While the sophisticates quickly counted us out, we could not surrender in fairness to our loyal delegates. Besides, anything can happen in politics. The only vote that counted would occur the next night.

And so, exhausted physically and drained emotionally, it was off to bed for a few winks.

We knew we had to put a positive spin on the situation to our delegates and the media, but the reality was that, in all probability, we had been counted out by three measly caucus votes!

The next morning, we met with the Reagans to assess the situation. We decided to rework Mississippi and other "uncommitted" delegates, but our prospects weren't all that bright.

Just then, Dick Schweiker came into the meeting. He told the Reagans that he felt very badly about what had happened. He said that he felt that he was the problem with the Mississippi delegation, many of whom thought he was "too liberal." He wanted to call an immediate press conference to announce his withdrawal from the ticket in the hopes that this would change votes in the Mississippi delegation.

Ron, without a moment's hesitation, said, "Dick, we came

into this together, and we're going out together!"

Since then, I've wondered how many politicians would have reacted the same way. It would have been easy for Ron to say that "circumstances have changed" and "perhaps Schweiker should step aside," but he didn't.

As Ron told the press later that morning, he regarded his commitment to Dick to be a matter of principle, and it was.

Later that day, prior to the vote, we worked and reworked the uncommitted delegates right up until the time of the nominations.

Ron had asked me to place his name in nomination, and I was proud to accept. As it turned out, I was so busy working the delegates that I didn't have time to prepare my speech, much less rehearse it. At the very last moment, I scratched out a few notes on the back of a three-by-five card and proceeded to the podium.

On the way, I ran into Sam Donaldson of ABC News, who asked for a copy of the text of my speech. "Didn't have time, Sam," I replied, showing him the card. "Oh, my God," was his only reaction.

Funny thing, I was so busy, so consumed with the task of securing delegates, that I hadn't really reflected on what I was going to say. Under the circumstances, speaking to 25,000 people in Kemper Arena and millions more on television was an intimidating prospect.

But the reception the delegates gave me was immediately reassuring. Each sentence I uttered was met with thunderous applause and cheering. I knew that what was happening was all about Ron, and had very little to do with me, but it was still the most exciting evening of my life.

After I placed Ron's name in nomination, the hall literally came apart. Waves and waves of applause coincided with a demonstration that seemed to last forever.

Finally, the balloting was conducted, but we lost — as expected.

After the balloting, there was a sticky meeting with President Ford to deal with. There was already a lot of press speculation about Ron's being on the ticket as Vice President.

As I feared, Ron asked me how I felt about the subject.

"Ron," I said, "this is a tough one. Politically, there's no question that you'd be a great asset to the ticket, and it could make the difference. But on a personal basis, I think you'd detest the job and so would Nancy."

Although I was Chairman of the Reagan for President campaign against incumbent Gerald Ford in 1976, President Ford never held it against me. He is truly a world-class man. *Special Collections, University of Nevada, Reno Library*

Ron then said, "Only the lead dog gets a change of scenery. Please get word to President Ford that I'm not available." The word was dutifully passed along to the Ford camp.

At the meeting, President Ford was very gracious. Having already been told that Ron wouldn't entertain the idea of being on the ticket, the President discreetly avoided the subject. Instead, he asked for Ron's reaction to a list of prospects. Ron was generally noncommittal.

Lyn Nofziger weighed in heavily for Bob Dole. The next morning, President Ford advised Ron that his selection was "a Senator from the Midwest."

Ron replied, "It seems to me it's got to be Bob Dole," to which Ford replied, "That's right."

Throughout the rest of the convention and the campaign, President Ford couldn't have been more decent to me. To this day, I'm grateful to him. A lesser man could have made it mighty difficult for a rookie Senator from Nevada.

Of course, thereafter, President Ford lost the general election to Jimmy Carter by a whisker. The Nixon pardon certainly contributed to Ford's defeat.

At the convention, President Ford asked me to join him in announcing Bob Dole's selection at a packed press conference. Although Bob had had trouble with the press ever since serving as Republican National Chairman during Watergate, he was treated well and, of course, rose to the occasion.

After the press conference, I felt the convention was over for us. All that remained were the Vice Presidential and Presidential acceptance speeches. Our family group joined the Reagans in their box.

After the conclusion of his well-delivered speech, President Ford did the most unexpected thing: From the podium, he extended an invitation to Ron to join him. The place went wild. Ron, caught totally by surprise, at first was reluctant to go, but the people in the hall solved that problem for him. With their cheers and applause, they insisted that he go. As he walked down the aisle, he said to Nancy, "This is so unexpected. I don't know what to say."

President Ford, traveling that extra mile, then asked him to speak. Again, bedlam.

Then, for a magical few moments, Ron delivered the finest, most moving speech I've ever heard. He spoke of the realistic aspirations of all Americans, that America should be the "city on the hill."

One never knows for certain, but that speech, thanks to Jerry Ford, might well have launched the Reagan Presidential campaign of 1980.

After the closing night, a "going away" breakfast for the Reagans was arranged. It was in their suite, and just a few of us attended.

The whole mood of the breakfast was somber. We had fought the good fight but hadn't quite made it. The Reagans plainly felt that their political days were over and didn't seem to be all that unhappy about the prospect of a politics-free future.

So that the experience wouldn't end on a negative note, I cautioned Ron and Nancy to "keep your powder dry." I added, "You never know in the crazy business of politics, but there might be another shot at the presidency."

They thanked me, but from the looks on their faces it was plain that they felt their pursuit of the presidency was over for all time.

1976-1980

A few months into the presidency of Jimmy Carter, he granted several of us western Senators a meeting at the White House to discuss water problems. The Carter Administration had announced the cancellation of several water projects in the West, and the West was up in arms.

Admittedly, this was a difficult meeting for a new President. He tried to justify the policy, but failed miserably. It was clear that he didn't understand the importance of water to the West. Beyond that, several of us came away feeling that this intelligent, well-intentioned man was in over his head.

Returning to my Senate office, I called Ron and told him of the meeting. I again suggested that he keep his options open, adding, "My gut tells me that I've just met with a one-termer."

Ron laughed and was his noncommittal self. But I also sensed that my call had piqued his curiosity.

Fortunately, by early 1977, we had a political vehicle called Citizens for the Republic. Lyn Nofziger was heading up its operation. This political action committee (PAC) gave us the means to provide Ron the funding to travel around the country, to meet with key supporters, to advance the conservative message and support like-minded candidates for various offices. Looking back, it was an ideal vehicle to launch another presidential campaign, although it hadn't been created for that purpose.

By 1978, it was clear that President Carter was vulnerable, and that Ron should seriously consider running.

In the summer of 1978, I convinced Ron that it would be a good idea to come to Washington. I said that I would set up key meetings with Republican leaders in my office. The meetings would be for the purpose of talking strategy concerning the future of the party and also to take some soundings for another Reagan candidacy. We made it clear, however, that he was only in the "consideration stage."

One of these meetings was with Phil Crane, the young Congressman from Illinois who had been so helpful in the 1976 campaign. We considered him to be a staunch Reagan supporter. Ron advised Phil that he was seriously considering the race and would probably announce his candidacy in a timely fashion.

To our great surprise, Phil, instead of being elated by the news, told Ron that he had decided to run for President himself! I've had my share of awkward moments, but none has ever matched this scene. Ron was completely flabbergasted – speechless.

When he later declared for the presidency, Phil indicated that he was afraid that Reagan really wouldn't run, and the conservatives would be left without a candidate. Giving Phil the benefit of the doubt, he obviously didn't believe Ron's assurances in my office – or didn't want to.

This was unfortunate. Phil's campaign went nowhere, and a serious personal breach was created. Phil had been badly advised. Fortunately, he continued to serve in the House and now, having served with distinction these many years, is a powerful force on the Ways and Means Committee.

As disagreeable as the Crane meeting was, it had one beneficial effect. Ron realized that he was going to have to make a decision, sooner rather than later. After all, who really knew how many Phil Cranes were out there?

THE 1980 CAMPAIGN

In March 1979, the Reagan exploratory committee was formed, and the campaign was officially kicked off in New York in November of that year.

By the time of the Iowa caucuses in February of 1980, the Republican field was crowded. Besides Reagan, the candidates were George Bush, Senators Howard Baker of Tennessee and Bob Dole of Kansas, Congressmen Phil Crane and John Anderson of Illinois and former Texas Governor John Connally.

As this is being written in 1999, Republicans shrink at the prospect of several candidates vying for the presidency in 2000. They needn't. The 1980 race should be proof positive that a multi-candidate presidential field – coupled with a fair and issue-oriented campaign – can be beneficial to the eventual nominee.

The 1980 campaign started with the same basic campaign team

that we had in 1976. John Sears was the campaign manager. The Reagans, over the objections of several of us, decided to stay with him. We objected because John, although a brilliant strategist and tactician, as demonstrated in 1976, was distrusted by conservatives, and because he wasn't a proven manager of campaign funds.

Iowa was the first caucus state. To our amazement, John decided against having Ron campaign there. He reasoned that Ron was already well known in Iowa, pointing out that he had been a sportscaster there and was known affectionately as "Dutch." John argued that skipping Iowa would permit more time and resources for New Hampshire and Florida. I guess he was still traumatized by the 1976 New Hampshire debacle, when Reagan was upset by President Ford.

The Iowa decision proved to be disastrous. Not only did we lose, but George Bush achieved a momentum early in the process that he could never have gained otherwise. Overnight, he moved from being a dark horse to a formidable contender in New Hampshire.

As the primary loomed, it was clear that we were locked in a tough race with the Bush forces. Obviously, a loss in New Hampshire on the heels of a surprising Iowa defeat could prove lethal.

Then, an unexpected break came our way. A debate between Reagan and Bush was arranged by the newspaper in Nashua, New Hampshire. But when Bob Dole protested about being excluded, and after the Federal Election Commission ruled that the debate, as proposed, would be an illegal campaign contribution to the Bush and Reagan campaigns, Reagan decided his campaign itself would pay for the debate. It was to be held in a local high school gymnasium.

Ron and George Bush arrived, and so did four of the other candidates, who had been invited by Ron. Before the debate got under way, several conferences were held in an attempt to fashion a compromise, but George Bush remained opposed to having the other candidates included.

The debate moderator sent a message to the room where Reagan and all the other candidates, except Bush, were waiting. The message was: "Bush is on the stage, and if Reagan isn't there in three minutes, the debate will be forfeited to Bush."

At that, Reagan, Baker, Dole, Crane and Anderson made their way to the stage, facing a packed hall. Bush, uncharacteristically, sat stony-faced, ignoring the others. When Ron asked to speak, the moderator threatened to cut off his mike. Ron grabbed his mike and emphatically and angrily reminded the M.C. that he had paid for it, and he was going to speak!

The crowd erupted in applause. The debate, totally anti-climactic after Ron's outburst, went forward.

Ron, by showing his disgust, had dramatically demonstrated his leadership. That episode could well have been the turning point of the New Hampshire campaign and probably helped propel Ron to the presidency.

Ron easily overwhelmed the field, and New Hampshire became a launching pad, not an obstacle, as it had been in 1976.

Just before the returns in New Hampshire came in, Ron made a startling announcement. He was terminating John Sears, Charlie Black and Jim Lake from the campaign. The decision was long in the making.

Since Iowa, Sears had lost the confidence of the Reagans. Although they liked Black and Lake, they felt they were totally dominated by Sears and had to go, too.

What brought matters to a head was an unwise power play by Sears designed to get rid of Ed Meese, in much the same manner as he had previously done with Lyn Nofziger and Mike Deaver.

Ron, with the full support of Nancy, told Sears in effect that he had outlived his usefulness to the campaign.

During the several hours this was all taking place, I was in Washington tending to senatorial business. Peter Hannaford, a trusted Reagan aide dating back to the Sacramento years, and who was present while all this was taking place, briefed me in his usual fair and understated fashion as to what had happened.

I was proud of the Reagans for having made such a difficult decision.

Shortly after, Bill Casey, future Director of the CIA in the Reagan Administration, was selected to be campaign manager. Thereafter, under Bill's steady hand, the campaign was free of the internal divisions that had plagued the campaign, and he guarded our money, too much of which had already been squandered.

After the New Hampshire primary, John Connally appeared to be our principal opponent. He had decided to make South Carolina his test state. Well-funded, Connally was worrisome to the Reagan camp, but he ended up running badly in the South Carolina primary. His campaign spent several million dollars and got only one delegate!

That left only George Bush. After intense negotiations, which centered on the protection of his delegates, George, through the assistance of Jim Baker, withdrew in May 1980.

George's exodus was timely. His characterization of the Reagan economic plan as "voodoo economics," along with other slights, had offended the Reagans. Had he held out much longer, George might well have been vetoed as Vice President at the upcoming Republican convention, to be held in Detroit at the Joe Louis Arena.

Most of the pre-convention time was spent in forming advisory groups to unify the various factions that formed during the campaign. This "outreach" proved successful, so that by the time of the convention, we were essentially a unified party.

Choosing a Vice President

Picking a Vice Presidential running mate proved to be a chore, particularly for me.

Before the convention, Ron asked me to permit him to include me as a candidate for Vice President. I implored him not to do it. First, I preferred to stay in the Senate. Secondly, it didn't make political sense to have the ticket composed of candidates from adjoining states and having the same political philosophies. (Clinton and Gore did just that twelve years later.)

Ron said he understood, but that he and Nancy would appreciate it if I would stay in.

Looking back, I think they were hoping that lightning would strike, thus permitting me to be on the ticket, despite the obstacles.

So I reluctantly filled out the required forms and sent them in, satisfied that it was a waste of time.

At Detroit, the media pressure started building. They were regarding me more and more as a serious candidate. A Los Angeles Times article suggested that Ron was going to pick me, adding fuel to the fire.

I phoned Ron at his hotel and asked him to permit me to withdraw my name from consideration. The situation was becoming embarrassing. Also, as long as I was on the list, I was unable to participate in the deliberations. Again, he said that he would prefer for me to stay in.

As the convention started, another bizarre development took place. The media started reporting that aides to Ron and Gerald Ford were working on the feasibility of a Reagan-Ford ticket. Serious negotiations took place, and Reagan and Ford discussed it, but finally the idea fell of its own weight. How to assign office space in the White House, much less the division of policy responsibilities, was simply too much to overcome.

As to the Vice Presidency, I had no idea what Ron would do.

George Bush was a logical selection, but the primaries had left deep wounds.

On "decision night," I went to the convention hall totally in the dark. Before long, I had an urgent call from Ron, which I took in a trailer outside the arena.

At the 1980 Republican National Convention, against my objections, Ron Reagan kept my name on a short list for Vice President, eventually selecting George Bush. Once again, I delivered the nominating speech.

"Paul," Ron said, "I've decided to go to George Bush. I know that many of the delegates will be unhappy, so George and I are coming to the arena together. Will you please join us?"

In a few minutes, George and Barbara Bush and Ron and Nancy Reagan arrived. Nancy rushed to me and took my hand. "I'm so sorry, Paul. I wish it had been you."

"Nancy, it's probably for the best," I responded.

When we all climbed the platform at the convention hall together, some of my youngsters watching on television throughout the country thought their Dad had been selected.

Ron handled the situation beautifully. Before he was through, the vast majority of the delegates felt that the Reagan-Bush ticket was a natural.

After all these years, I still feel that George Bush was the right choice. He proved to be a loyal and helpful Vice President. Of course, he succeeded to the presidency, where he served with distinction. It's a shame that he and his people didn't recognize in time that a severe recession was hurting millions of Americans in the early 1990s.

REAGAN IS ELECTED

The month of October 1980 was one of my most frustrating. Here I was chairing the Reagan campaign, while campaigning for my own Senatorial reelection in Nevada. Talk about competing priorities!

Ron's campaign went well, although the polls were tight up to the final days. The Presidential debate in Cleveland between Ron and President Carter seemed to satisfy millions of Americans that Ron was a responsible, decent man who, contrary to his critics' suggestions, wouldn't blow up the world.

President Carter couldn't overcome the recession problems, which were caused mainly by the oil cartel in the Middle East. In addition, he had bungled the Iranian hostage crisis. And underlying it all was the gnawing concern that several western Senators felt after meeting him early in his term that he simply wasn't up to the job.

Bright and early on election day, Bill Casey, who had taken over the campaign after John Sears was fired back in February, called me in Reno. We had been in regular contact the month leading up to the election.

"Paul," he said, "you might not believe this, but looking at the exit polls back here, I think we've got a landslide in the making."

Bill asked me if I wanted to call Ron, to which I instantly said, "Hell, no! He's so superstitious he wouldn't listen anyway."

That morning, I went to a campaign meeting to thank my workers. After expressing my gratitude, I boldly told them, "I don't usually predict how a race will come out, but this time I'm going to make an exception. Before the day is out, Ron Reagan will win in a landslide."

That evening, we watched the election returns at the home of Bob Berry, a good friend and former law partner, in Reno. Not only did Reagan win the Presidency, but also Republicans had taken control of the United States Senate for the first time in 26 years.

After Carter's concession speech (which occurred at 5:30 p.m. Pacific Time), phone calls poured in to Bob's house. Ron called to thank me and congratulate me on my reelection to the U.S. Senate. I asked him, "Ron, do I have to call you Mr. President now?" "Only in the presence of others," he said.

He then asked me to fly to Los Angeles the following morning for a press conference.

I also heard that night from the Republican leader in the Senate, Howard Baker. He called to ask if I would nominate him for the position of Majority Leader. There had been some speculation that I might be a candidate for Senate leader. But the truth was that I had no desire to be Majority Leader. I told Howard that I would be pleased to nominate him.

The next day, I met with Ron and Nancy in their hotel suite. Everything seemed the same, except for one ingredient: Ron already had "the Presidential aura" about him, something he would never lose.

As I left Los Angeles, Ron said, "I'm going to need your advice putting together the staff and cabinet. Will you help?"

"Of course, Mr. President," I said. "I'll be glad to help."

Little did I realize at the time how difficult it would be to staff a new administration, from the cabinet on down.

Ed Meese was selected to head the transition. No one was more deserving and better qualified. At the time, we thought it was a natural prelude to his becoming Chief of Staff in the White House.

I became involved principally by becoming a member of the "kitchen cabinet" to make recommendations to the President-elect for cabinet positions. Other members of this group included several of Ron's "insiders" from his Sacramento days.

William French Smith, Ron's private lawyer and close friend, headed the group, with the strong support of the President-elect. Others in the group were Justin Dart, Holmes Tuttle, Earle Jorgensen, Ted Cummings, Bill Wilson, Henry Salvatori, Jack Wrather and Cap Weinberger. In addition, Bill Simon, Charlie Wick, Dan Terra and others sat in from time-to-time.

Pen James was our official "head hunter." Helene Von Damm, who had ably served in Sacramento in the Governor's office, was the only woman included in the deliberations. She often was the glue that held together a disjointed and frequently volatile group.

Ron had asked Pen James for three recommendations for each cabinet position. Out of this process, within a relatively short period of time, came the first Reagan cabinet. Actually, it turned out to be less controversial than I thought. Many of the positions were settled in Ron's mind before the "kitchen cabinet" went to work.

We all knew that William French Smith would be Attorney General. Cap Weinberger and Bill Casey could have pretty much anything they wanted. Eventually, Cap opted for Secretary of Defense, while Casey became Director of the CIA.

Ron so admired Ray Donovan of New Jersey, a construction company executive, that no one else was seriously considered as

Secretary of Labor. Ray's original FBI reports indicated some questionable associations, but they turned out to have been based purely on rumor. Nonetheless, Ray was later indicted on the basis of some questionable racketeering allegations, but he was eventually acquitted. He then made his famous statement, "What office do I go to to get my reputation back?"

Ray, a good man, was just one of many political victims in the Reagan Administration.

Malcolm Baldrige, a Connecticut businessman and an accomplished rodeo rider, which certainly appealed to the President, was named Secretary of Commerce. Drew Lewis, who had made amends for his decision to stick with Ford in 1976, was named Secretary of Transportation. Jack Block, who had been Director of Agriculture in Illinois and who was pushed strongly by Bob Dole, was given the Secretary of Agriculture post. Jim Watt was supported by several Rocky Mountain Senators, including me, for the position of Secretary of the Interior.

Naming persons to fill the positions at Treasury and State wasn't nearly as easy.

Bill Simon, who had served as Secretary of the Treasury in the Nixon-Ford Administration, was the early favorite for the same post in the Reagan Administration, but Bill wanted to be the "economic czar," which would have given him control of both Treasury and the Office of Management and Budget. That proved to be unacceptable.

Finally, Don Regan, CEO of Merrill Lynch, the huge investment firm, surfaced. He was unknown to most of us. I've never figured out who his sponsor was. He was controversial with the political types, who claimed that he was cool to Ron's candidacy and had even contributed to Jimmy Carter.

Nonetheless, Ron finally decided that he was the man for the job. Don served the President loyally and well as Secretary of

Treasury. Later, when he became White House Chief of Staff, he ran aground when he had well-publicized differences with Nancy Reagan.

The most coveted position in the Reagan cabinet was Secretary of State. During our "kitchen cabinet" sessions, I sensed that George Shultz, Cap Weinberger and Bill Casey all would eagerly have accepted the post if offered.

Finally, after many names were considered and discarded, we settled on Al Haig, former Commanding General of NATO and Nixon Chief of Staff, subject to an interview. The President-elect asked Jim Baker, Ed Meese and me to meet with Al, which we did at the Jefferson Hotel.

In answer to our queries about whether he had any presidential ambitions of his own, he answered, "None at all." He pointed out that he felt the worst position someone running for President to hold would be Secretary of State. That proved prophetic when he had a brief run for President in 1988.

I came away from the meeting impressed with Al's knowledge of foreign affairs and the workings of the presidency, as well as his self-discipline.

Ed and Jim were a bit more reserved about him, worrying that Al's strong personality might lead him to be unresponsive to the White House. Their concerns later turned out to be true, for it wasn't long before Al and the White House staff were in near total war.

The problem was principally about a strong feeling on the part of Al Haig that Jim Baker was restricting his access.

One day he called me to express his concerns. We had lunch together at the State Department. When he told me his concerns, I suggested to him that he simply call the President directly. "Hell," I said, "you're the Secretary of State! He'd be pleased to talk to you anytime!"

Walking away from Marine One with President Reagan after a horseback ride at Quantico, Virginia in 1981. *White House photo*

Al, still very conscious of protocol from his military days, asked, "Do you really think I should?" I said, "Hell, yes! Do it!"

And he did, which started a great personal relationship between Al Haig and Ronald Reagan. Ron often remarked later of the calls Al was making, and how much better all was going as a result.

I suppose the cabinet appointments, particularly Haig's, were a surprise to some, but not nearly as much as when the White House staff was announced.

Ed Meese had handled the transition smoothly, and most everyone assumed he would be named "Chief." It didn't happen. Jim Baker was named instead.

Ed was bitterly disappointed but didn't show it. Later, the position of Counsellor to the President was created, and Ed was appointed. Had Ed Meese not been totally devoid of ego and completely loyal to the President, he would have been tempted to play the leak game, but he didn't. There was some speculation about his being shunted aside, but not a word came from Ed that might hurt Ron.

Actually, what happened was probably best for the President. Ed admittedly was not a "management type." He found it hard to say "no," and as a result, his "plate" was constantly overloaded. The position of Counsellor, where he was able to advise the President on policy, was perfect.

Jim Baker proved that he was an excellent manager, saying "no" frequently. And he was masterful in dealing with Congress and the press. Along with Mike Deaver, who handled "imagery," they were an excellent team.

"First Friend of the President"

After many years of being described by the Nevada press as "the son of a Basque sheepherder," I became known in the media after

Ron was elected as "the best friend of the President," or simply "the First Friend."

Seemingly, that would be a major asset in access-minded Washington. In many ways, it was good, for it provided me with a perspective on the Reagan presidency that was unique. In effect, I had "one foot in the Congress and one foot in the White House."

At first it was exciting – and quite flattering – to have the attention that I did. Complete access to the White House, the state dinners, the Presidential Box at the Kennedy Center, Camp David, Air Force One – it was all heady stuff. But it was the substantive aspects of my position that I relished most.

One day I received a call from Anatoly Dobrynin, the Soviet Union's canny Ambassador to the U.S. This led to several interesting private meetings.

The Soviets were greatly concerned about President Reagan. His reputation in the Soviet Union as an irresponsible "cowboy" with his finger on the nuclear button had frightened the Kremlin. Reagan's speech in 1983 calling the Soviet Union an "evil empire" added to their anxiety.

Dobrynin, wise to the ways of Washington and recognizing that media images were often false, wanted to know more about Ronald Reagan as a person. He wanted to be able to assure his Moscow colleagues that they needn't worry about Reagan being reckless.

After many conversations with the Ambassador, I think he had a picture of the real Ronald Reagan, rather than false characterizations gleaned from media stories. I hope that these conversations help the Soviet leadership better understand President Reagan.

JOINING THE SENATE LEADERSHIP

Shortly after he was elected Senate majority leader, Howard Baker asked me to join him in his office. He told me he had talked to others in the leadership, and they would like to include me as a "non-elected member of the leadership," which apparently was unprecedented.

I told Howard that I would be honored to serve. From that point on, I regularly attended leadership meetings within the Senate and with the President at the White House.

To be able to participate in these meetings with a full voice was due to my Senate colleagues. To this day, I feel greatly indebted to Howard Baker and my colleagues for the privilege.

WHAT HONEYMOON?

New Presidents normally have a "honeymoon" period with the press, but if the Reagans had one, I missed it.

From the time of the inauguration, the press dwelled on the Reagans' "fat cat, California crowd." During the inauguration, the limousines, fur coats and the so-called "opulence" received as much publicity as Ron's policy planning, or so it seemed.

At one point, Nancy Reagan decided to buy a new set of china for state dinners. Even though the china was paid for by a tax-free foundation, Nancy took an unfair hammering. She was depicted in the press as an uncaring, materialistic person, interested mainly in being a socialite.

Within the Washington press establishment, however, she recovered greatly when she appeared at the annual Gridiron Dinner in 1982 dressed in tatters and sang "Second Hand Rose." She was a huge hit for poking fun at herself, and the press temporarily loved her for it. Throughout the presidency, however, she never really connected with the mainstream press.

Nancy could take solace in the fact that she wasn't alone. Aside from Jackie Kennedy and Barbara Bush, the press has been very hard on First Ladies.

President Reagan didn't fare much better. The media elite regarded him as an amiable and pleasant "lightweight" who really didn't measure up to what they expected of a President.

Since the press was overwhelmingly liberal ideologically, that wasn't really all that surprising. Goldwater, as an outspoken conservative, would have been battered, too, had he been elected President.

Actually, as Governor of California, Ron had good practice in dealing with the liberal press. The Los Angeles Times and the Sacramento Bee took great delight in lampooning him.

So, when the Washington Post or the New York Times worked him over, he'd "been there, done that."

Lou Cannon, a fellow Nevadan and the Washington Post's White House reporter during the Reagan presidency, was an exception. I suspect he secretly admired Ronald Reagan, and Lou always did his best to report objectively. Of all the books written about Ron by reporters, I thought Lou's, "Ronald Reagan: The Role of a Lifetime," was the most insightful. Having reported on Ron both as Governor and President, Lou had a perspective that was unique.

An Early Moment of Truth

The first few months of any presidency often set the tone for the entire term.

After Ron was elected, there were serious questions raised about how he would react when confronted with tough political decisions.

He was tested during the summer of his first year when the Professional Air Traffic Controllers Organization (PATCO) decided to strike. Ironically, PATCO was one of the few unions which had supported him during the Presidential campaign.

Ron could have easily finessed a settlement, but quickly he decided that wasn't the right thing to do. The air controllers were public employees, and they had no right to strike. In fact, they had signed a sworn affidavit agreeing not to strike.

Ron gave them this ultimatum: Either come back to work within 48 hours or be fired. Few in the union took the threat seriously. Surely, they must have felt, Reagan wouldn't fire them. Wouldn't there be a huge air safety problem if they were fired? Union leaders, of course, predicted doomsday.

Oval Office meeting. (L. to R.) PL, Senator Howard Baker, President Reagan, Vice President Bush, Rep. Bob Michel and Budget Director David Stockman. *White House photo*

But Ron didn't deal with the situation in a predictably "political" manner. So far as he was concerned, the issue was clear: Either the controllers shaped up or he would ship them out.

When the 48-hour period expired, Ron directed Transportation Secretary Drew Lewis to fire them and hire replacements.

Seemingly, he had dealt with the situation in an arbitrary manner. But he hadn't. He had been reliably informed that replacements, along with those who had returned to work, could handle the job responsibly and safely. And they did. There were no accidents. PATCO, for its part, went into bankruptcy.

Ron's display of guts favorably impressed the public.

After the showdown, the word went out: "Don't mess with the Irishman! He means business!"

THE REAGAN AGENDA

On the policy front, Ron moved aggressively in three areas: cutting taxes, beefing up our defense forces and balancing the budget.

As to taxes, he was able to achieve the largest tax cut in American history. The centerpiece was the 25 percent income tax cut, to be phased in over three years.

At the outset of the debate over taxes, it seemed doubtful that there would be the votes needed to pass the tax cut legislation. Little by little, however, the moderates in the Senate decided to support the President.

Then came the "boll weevils" – a group of conservative Democrats in the House of Representatives. They were led by then Congressman Phil Gramm of Texas, who now serves in the U.S. Senate as a Republican.

That gave us the majorities we needed in both houses.

Shortly before the votes were taken on the tax cut package, the President made a dramatic television appeal to the people to support him. The response was incredible. Any waverers in the Congress could see that there was abundant public support for the President. That helped a great deal in securing the necessary votes.

In one fell swoop, Reagan demonstrated to Speaker Tip O'Neill and the other power brokers that he could get the job done, even if it meant going over their heads to the people by way of television.

Regarding the defense program, Cap Weinberger was the "point" man, and the defense budget from 1980-1989 rose by more than 50 percent.

When Cap went to Capitol Hill to argue for more defense spending, he went with the enthusiastic support of the President.

At White House budget meetings, I noted with amusement that when Cap's proposals were challenged as being excessive, he would inevitably pull out his charts, proceed with his "the-Russians-are-coming" speech, which Ron loved, and that would end the debate.

There is no question in my mind that Ronald Reagan's defense build-up, as costly as it was, was responsible in great part for our winning the Cold War. And the President's Strategic Defense Initiative, laughed at by the elites when it was proposed, certainly played a valuable role.

While we did well on the tax cut and defense fronts, we failed on the balanced budget. In order for the tax cuts and defense increases to be justified, many of us felt that we should drastically reduce domestic federal spending, and that the President should send to the Congress a budget that was balanced.

We even pleaded with him to send up a balanced budget for appearances sake, knowing that the Democrat-controlled Congress would quickly consign his budget – even if balanced – to the waste basket. We also appealed on the basis that not submitting a balanced budget would be a breach of an important campaign pledge.

But he just wouldn't do it – not for his entire presidency. It was quite a disappointment. Instead, he settled on sending up budgets that reduced the level of the projected increase in spending.

Ironically, we never paid a price for running large deficits. During the Reagan years, the national debt tripled, a result that we conservatives had firmly believed in previous times would have constituted a disaster.

True, there was a deep recession in 1982, but it was not the result of tax cuts or the deficits. It was due mainly to the restrictive monetary policies of the Federal Reserve under Paul Volcker, a Carter holdover whom Reagan supported. Ron felt that we had to curb runaway inflation, and Volcker's policies were the painful but necessary cure.

It worked. Inflation came down dramatically and has stayed down over the years. But as inflation came down, unemployment rose from 7 percent to nearly 11 percent. Millions of Americans were out of work. Reagan's critics began to refer to his economic policies scornfully as "Reaganomics."

Despite strong urgings from those who wanted dramatic spending increases, Reagan refused to go along and asked the people to be patient and to "stay the course."

Nonetheless, Ron paid a heavy political price. His approval ratings plummeted to the low 30s. The 1982 elections produced significant Republican losses in Congress.

By early 1983, things looked bleak for the Reagan Presidency. The country seemed to be in worse shape than it was under Carter. The pundits began to talk about another "one-term presidency."

But things turned dramatically in Ron's favor during 1983. Actually, in late 1982, the economy had begun a seven-year period of uninterrupted growth. Ron used to quip that "the best sign that our economic program is working is that they don't call it Reaganomics anymore!"

The wisdom of his policies extended throughout the world. His economic program combined with a red-hot private sector to establish the U.S. as the economic and industrial heavyweight of the world.

BLACK MONDAY

On Monday, March 30, 1981, I was having lunch with journalist Elizabeth Drew, then with The New Yorker magazine, when an emergency phone call came. It was from Ed Hickey, head of security at the White House.

Breathlessly, he said, "Christ, Paul, some son of a bitch just shot the President!"

Ed, who was on Capitol Hill for a budget hearing, said he'd pick me up at the corner of Constitution and Delaware Avenues. I ran all the way from the Senate dining room, leaving a perplexed Elizabeth Drew in my wake.

In the car, I asked Ed if he had any details. "No, other than the fact that he caught a bullet," Ed responded. He added, "We don't know how bad it is. They're taking him to the closest hospital, George Washington."

We decided to find out where Nancy was so we could take her along with us. We learned that everyone at the White House was in shock. In checking the White House computer, we discovered that Nancy was already on the way to the hospital.

So, with sirens and lights blazing, we raced to George Washington University Hospital. By the time we arrived, it was already bedlam there. Had I not been with Ed, it would have been far more difficult getting through the emergency entrance.

As we entered the emergency area, we ran into Mike Deaver, the White House Deputy Chief of Staff and long-time Reagan aide, who had a deeply worried look. Mike had been at the scene of the attempted assassination. He said that he had reserved a small room in the area for Nancy, and asked if I would go there. Ed went to meet with his security people.

Poor Nancy. She was disconsolate with fear and worry, but managed a wan smile of welcome when I entered the room. She fell into my arms. I held her as I would one of my children. She trembled.

Then the ordeal began. It lasted for several hours. The false reports and rumors were among the most difficult issues to deal with. The room where Nancy was located became a sort of communications center.

As to the condition of Ron, the first report we had was that he had taken a bullet in his chest area, but since the tap into his tummy revealed no blood, the bullet "would take care of itself." There might not be a need for surgery.

We all breathed a huge sigh of relief. Ron appeared to be out of danger.

Then the signals from the attending physicians changed abruptly. There were "some disturbing signs," and they were going to take him into surgery after all. We stepped out into the hall when Ron was wheeled by on a gurney. That's when he looked at Nancy and made the famous "Honey, I forgot to duck" line.

All he said to me was "Don't worry, I'll be all right." But for the first time since I'd known him, I saw a frightened look in his eyes. It scared the hell out of me.

Back to the room we went. After a while, we decided that we needed more space. The small room was becoming suffocating. We moved into a larger room, which had a television set. Watching television only heightened the urgency of the situation.

In addition to the reports on Ron, the reporters were following the condition of the White House press secretary, Jim Brady. Most reports indicated that he had been shot in the head, and that his chances of survival were not good.

Then came the report that Jim had died. We knew the report was false because one of his doctors had already told us that he was going to make it. Sarah, his wife, was brought into the room, and she and Nancy consoled one another.

Ron's surgery seemed to last forever. After awhile, we decided to go to the chapel for several minutes. The visit was comforting to all of us. I'm sure the Good Lord heard all of our prayers to help Ron.

Finally, the surgery was over. The surgeons reported that it had gone well. The bullet had come to rest only an inch or so from his heart.

His recuperation went unusually well. The fact that he exercised regularly in the White House with equipment helped greatly. Within a few weeks, the President was "good as new."

The "revisionists" have stated from time to time that President Reagan was "never the same" after the shooting. As one who saw him regularly throughout his presidency, let me state unequivocally that after Ron's recovery, I saw absolutely no evidence that he was less capable of performing the duties of the presidency than before.

GENERAL CHAIRMAN OF THE GOP

After Ron Reagan assumed the Presidency in 1980, I decided to take a hiatus from party politics. The campaigns – his and mine – had been wearing, and I simply wanted to be free of the stresses and strains of party fights.

In Nevada, I had been a county chairman in my early days, but had never aspired to the position of state chairman, which over my years had been handled by such men as Emery Graunke, Jac Shaw, George Abbott and Frank Fahrenkopf.

The position of National Chairman, since I'd been in Washington, had been filled by notables such as Bob Dole, George Bush and Bill Brock. In the 1970s, it was decided by the Republican Party to make the chairmanship a full-time job. Formerly, it had been done part-time. Bob Dole, for example, was Chairman during the Nixon Presidency, while also serving Kansas in the Congress. As the party grew, so did the job. As a result, the chairmen worked on a full-time basis.

It should also be noted that a national party's function is lessened when it has a sitting President. Usually, the White House staff wants to keep the main political people in the White House.

The Reagan White House was no exception. Such pros as Lyn Nofziger and Ed Rollins quickly established an effective political shop in the White House.

This arrangement worked reasonably well during the first two years, but at about the time of the disastrous 1982 elections, the Chief of Staff, Jim Baker, along with others, sought to strengthen the Republican National Committee. Working with White House official Rich Williamson, a Reaganite from Illinois, Jim asked me to take over as National Chairman of the party.

When I reminded them that this would necessitate my resigning as a U.S. Senator, which I would not do, they felt that the problem could be "fixed" by going back to the "old system" of letting a Senator serve as RNC Chairman simultaneously.

With President Reagan in the Oval Office. *White House photo*

Because I felt that

the Chairman of the RNC should be full-time, I told the White House that I didn't think this was a good idea.

The next thing I heard was that the White House had contacted Roger Allan Moore, the counsel of the RNC, to find a creative solution.

Roger did exactly that. He proposed creating the new position of General Chairman of the Republican Party.

When the White House contingent came to me with the suggested solution, I still was reluctant. There were too many unanswered questions. For instance, what would be my relationship to the other "chairmen" at the Republican National Committee, the National Republican Senatorial Committee and the National Republican Congressional Committee? I certainly didn't want to have any operational responsibilities at these committees; that should be up to the respective chairmen.

I indicated I would be willing to help in coordinating the committees' activities (particularly with respect to fund-raising), doing some fund-raising mail and arranging for the chairmen to meet regularly with the President.

With the 1984 presidential campaign approaching, I felt it was essential for the various Republican campaign organizations — particularly the Presidential campaign — to work in a cooperative and coordinated manner. Historically, that had not always been the case.

But even assurances from the White House on these issues were not enough for me. I wanted to have a personal understanding with the President, first to establish the fact that I hadn't hustled the job. I also wanted him to tell me personally why he felt that I should take the job of General Chairman of the Republican Party.

A lunch was quickly arranged in the garden near the Oval Office on the day of the 1982 elections. It was on a particularly beautiful day.

Ron had been briefed on the situation. He asked if I'd made up my mind. I told him that I had some questions.

First, I wanted to know from him why he felt I should do this. He said he really didn't know the national party scene, but that I did. He didn't want a party blow-up to arise, which might distract him. In effect, he wanted a "friend in court," as we used to say in my law days.

I said I viewed the position as being a coordinating one, and also serving an intelligence function, to keep him fully informed on party matters. I also suggested that it would be useful from time to time to bring our party leaders into the residence on a social basis. He readily agreed.

In addition, I asked if I could have authority to name the new chairman of the Republican National Committee. He said that I could and asked if I had anyone in particular in mind. I told him that I'd be comfortable with Frank Fahrenkopf, the Nevada chairman who was also serving at the time as chairman of all Republican state chairmen. Ron said that he remembered Frank and thought he'd be a good choice.

Lastly, I reminded him that ahead of the 1976 election, he had asked me to chair a campaign against a sitting Republican President whom I liked. At that time, I wanted to know, on a scale from one to ten, whether he would actually run against President Ford. "Eight" was his reply at the time.

Likewise, before I accepted the position of General Chairman, I wanted to know whether he was in the same range to run for reelection. With a twinkle in his eye, he said, "Yes."

With all that in place, I agreed to serve.

My term as General Chairman extended from January 1983 through January 1987. Ollie Kinney, a good friend from Nevada, and a retired Air Force Colonel, consented to come to Washington to run my office at the RNC. As I expected, Ollie did an excellent job. To this day, he maintains contact with the many young people he helped at the RNC.

When the other political committee chairmen realized I wasn't there to poach on their turf but rather to assist in their efforts, they were greatly relieved.

For four years, they kept me posted on their activities, and we met regularly with the President. During all that time, the Republican Party progressed, and there were no "blow-ups."

Frank Fahrenkopf proved to be a dynamic, effective Chairman of the RNC. He and his family, like so many others, have remained in the Washington area and are enjoying it thoroughly.

As for me, I enjoyed the position of General Chairman. I think I was able to do some good, not only for the President but for the party as a whole. One aspect of the job that I didn't find appealing was signing so many fundraising letters. In my frequent travels around the country during this period, I would inevitably have someone tell me, "We hear from you often."

Roger Allan Moore's "creative idea" worked. In fact, it worked so well that the position of General Chairman is now used frequently by both parties.

CHAPTER 18

❖ *Reagan's Re-election, 1984* ❖

Although Ron went through his usual pre-candidacy "tease" as to whether he would run for re-election in 1984, those of us close to him felt strongly that he was going to run. And, of course, he did.

By that time, the prospects were bright — certainly brighter than 1980 when there was a group of contenders for the Republican nomination. And we were thankful that he didn't have to run in 1982, when the economy was in recession. By 1984, the economy was humming.

Ron asked me to chair his campaign "one more time," as he put it. After the struggles in 1976 and 1980, this race looked like a cakewalk. I talked to Bill Casey about playing a role in the campaign, but he was not enthused about undergoing the rigors of another one. Besides, he was thoroughly enjoying being Director of the CIA.

After I was named Chairman, I thought it would be helpful to hear from that ultimate political strategist, Dick Nixon. When I proposed a personal meeting with him, the "nervous nellies" objected. I relented and asked President Nixon to send me his thoughts on the campaign in the form of a memo. The following was his response:

RICHARD NIXON

PERSONAL

Memorandum to: Senator Paul Laxalt
Subject: 1984 Election

Prospects

The best thing Reagan has going for him are the Democrats. In a nutshell, they have six candidates for Vice President. No one of them is a heavyweight in Reagan's class and even more fatal as far as their chances are concerned is that no one of them has a solid issue which Reagan will not be able to preempt from his position in the White House.

But even assuming the accuracy of this evaluation, the erosion of Reagan support among blue-collar voters, Jews, and women as compared with 1980, while it can be halted, can not be reversed significantly. What we face, therefore, is the necessity of running as near perfect a campaign as possible so that we can win the close ones as we did in holding the Senate in 1982.

Target States

This must be a fifty state campaign. We must disabuse ourselves of the formulas that have proved successful in the past – whether a southern strategy, a sun belt strategy, or a heartland strategy. We must take no states for granted and concede none to the opposition.

The traditional Republican heartland in the Midwest is our most vulnerable area. Even with the economy coming back, unemployment in heartland states will still be unacceptably high and a potentially good issue for a candidate like Glenn. In past elections, we could pretty well count on winning Ohio and Illinois. In this election, while we must try to win them all, we have to assume that because of the economic issue we may lose Ohio, Illinois, and of course Michigan.

If Glenn becomes the Democratic candidate, as Connally, for example now predicts, he will hold most of the South. Mondale would lose it all as would Cranston. Barring a major victory for one of them in an early primary, none of the others has a chance.

A successful Republican strategy requires that we win at least three of the big eight and possibly four if we lose the South. California and Florida are our best bets. From reports I receive from Clements and Connally, Texas is tough but we have to consider it a virtually must state in any successful strategy. While most people I talk to disagree, I think New York has to be put in the priority column. Because New York, in view of the stock market surge and the lack of dependency on heavy industry, will be better off economically, I think it is a good possibility assuming we have an effective campaign.

Organization

In 1980, as it turned out, Reagan would have won regardless of what kind of an organization he had and regardless of who was on the ticket for Vice President. This is not to say that Bush did not campaign well or that the organization did not perform reasonably well. But when the tide is running with you, you can afford to have deficiencies, disagreement, and just plain incompetence in your organization. In 1984, while we hope the tide will be running as strongly for Reagan as it did in 1980, we must assume that this will not be the case. This means that it is vitally important to hope for the best and plan for the worst. Reagan deserves to have the best possible organization in recent political history.

Above all, heads have to be knocked together. There can be only one Chief Executive Officer. While you will play an indispensable role as National Chairman, we have to realize that as 1964 demonstrated so vividly, a Republican candidate for President needs an organization which reaches out far beyond the hard-core Republican support that the National Committee can generate.

It is absolutely essential to keep the campaign out of the White House. This, incidentally, is a way you can bypass the White House infighting. Meese, Baker, and Clark must recognize that their only responsibility as far as the campaign is concerned is to serve the President in an above the battle non-political capacity.

I strongly urge that you keep the campaign organization lean. One of our major mistakes in 1972 was that we had too much money and too many over paid second raters throwing their weight around and getting us into trouble.

You are in an excellent position to insist on another objective: a new team across the country where possible. Don't use burned out hacks even though they are loyalists in any state that really matters to your victory strategy. Don't insist on a litmus test requiring that whoever has a top position must have been for Reagan before New Hampshire in 1980. Concentrate on getting young, pragmatic, fire in the belly regional and state chairmen. What is more important is for you to get across the idea that in a close election, we can not afford to go with what Disraeli called "exhausted volcanoes." The older people who have been around the track before should not of course be shunted aside. They can render invaluable advice as consultants but where it counts, choose the young bucks who have the energy and the drive to map out and implement a victory strategy.

Surrogates

When the President was the challenger he had to carry on the battle directly. It was his responsibility both to attack and to defend. In 1982 the President had to be both attacker and defender. He did a splendid job but it is not in his interest or in the country's for him to get in the partisan pits in 1984.

He should be President of all the people as Eisenhower presented himself in 1956 and as I did in 1972. But he is not going to be able to play this role unless others take on the responsibility of attacking the opposition and defending the President when he comes under inevitable assault.

We have a problem here. Bush has demonstrated complete loyalty and is excellent as a positive propagandist for the Administration. But he can not do for Reagan what I did for Eisenhower in 1956. Attacking is simply not his bag. He is not comfortable doing it and he should not be asked to do it. The same is true of the Cabinet. Putting it in the vernacular, there simply isn't one nut cutter in the Cabinet with the possible exception of Watt whose constituency is too narrow to be of any assistance in the big key states essential to victory.

Here you will have to look over the field and pick some people who can take the attack. But beyond big names, there should be truth squads in both the House and the Senate who will go to bat for the President when he comes under attack and take on the opposition. Of course you can do some of this as National Chairman. But the very fact that you are National Chairman does not make you as credible in this role as others might be.

White House Guest Lists

I have left to the last what would seem to be an insignificant issue but one that has been raised in talks I have had with good Reagan supporters across the country. It is vitally important that at State Dinners and other White House events from now until the election, the emphasis on having the beautiful people be sharply reduced. I think people are fed up to the chin with all the talk about Calvin Klein gowns and Gucci shoes, etc. Beyond that, however, the White House events can and must be used to bring to Washington the people across the country who have worked in the vineyards for the President even though they may not make the best dressed list or appear in Suzy's or Liz Smith's columns. Selected labor leaders, leading Mexicans, Italians, Poles, outstanding women leaders come to mind. You will have a tough time getting this through at the White House because of the great pressures to include the VIP types. But the President has done more than enough for the so-called upper class. He was not nominated and he was not elected by the people from that class. They will never in their hearts really be for him. They will always be for anyone who will be so stupid as to invite them to the White House. Get more people in who may not know which fork to use or who might even make the mistake of drinking from the finger bowls. It will be a mountain top experience for them, but even more important the reports that such people were there can have a positive effect across the country and will avoid the negative effects of simply continuing to have the same beautifully gowned women and properly manicured men gracing the White House table.

Richard Nixon

July 14, 1983.

Ed Rollins, a Californian who had served capably in previous campaigns, and whom I'd grown to like and respect, consented to be campaign manager.

Ed and I felt that putting together a campaign team would be easy. Were we wrong! Ron wanted us to expand the political base. That meant replacing some of our old Reagan hands, which they didn't like one bit!

Two particularly difficult states were Texas and Illinois. Don Totten of Illinois had been one of our earliest supporters in 1976 and took pride in being "Reagan's man" in Illinois. Our suggestion that Governor Jim Thompson replace him as chairman in 1984 went over like a lead balloon. Totten heatedly pointed out that Thompson had long been a political rival of his and that Thompson had never really been a Reagan supporter.

Texas was even worse, if that was possible. We floated Senator John Tower's name to be Texas chairman. Our loyalists in the Lone Star State went up in smoke. After all, Tower had led the Ford campaign against us in 1976, they noted. If we went ahead with John, they threatened to "bolt." Knowing their resolve from past campaigns, I knew they were dead serious.

We finally settled the matter by indicating our choices were the President's wish. Thompson and Tower were "in."

Working with campaign officials such as Ed Rollins and Lyn Nofziger, who had impeccable "Reagan credentials," we were able to overcome these problems and maintain campaign harmony.

A DISASTROUS DEBATE

Most people today would characterize the 1984 Reagan re-election campaign as "never in doubt." True, it turned out to be a landslide. But at the outset, we had a scare.

It arose out of the first Reagan-Mondale debate in Louisville, Kentucky, which took place on October 7, 1984. For days before the debate, there had been dress rehearsals at the Old Executive Office Building. Dick Darman, a White House aide, headed up a group involved in preparing Ron for the Louisville debate.

To be candid, Ron performed poorly at the debate. Mondale was never a great debater, but that night, by comparison, he sounded like Clarence Darrow.

In contrast, Ron appeared stiff, humorless and ill at ease. Unlike his usual spontaneous self, he spewed out statistics like an accountant. Worse than that, he looked and sounded like an old man.

At the end of the debate, we insiders were crestfallen. Ron clearly had been defeated. He was nearly embarrassing.

I was asked by some of our press types to go out to the media and do the usual "spinning" to the effect that Ron was great.

"No way," I said. "You wouldn't like what I'd say," I added. That was the end of that.

During our "debriefing session" the next day, I was astonished. The "debate team" thought that Ron had done very well. The "campaign team," of which I was a part, thought he was a disaster.

Worse than that, real doubts were starting to creep in that Ron Reagan might be "spent," and that one term as President was enough. Simply put, some contended that he was too old for another term.

Although the debate team staunchly denied it, a consensus quickly developed that the problem was the debate preparation, not the candidate. Ron had been overprepared and in the process had lost his spontaneity – his greatest strength.

We decided to go forward with the next scheduled debate, which was two weeks later in Kansas City. To do otherwise would have sent out bad signals. But this time, we were going to use a whole new preparation format.

The final and most difficult item on the post-Louisville agenda: "Who was going to fly back to Washington with

Nancy?" We'd heard that she was "mad as hell" about the debate. She'd insisted to Jim Baker and Ed Rollins that she wanted to find out what had happened.

Since there were no volunteers, I decided I'd best go with Nancy. We flew in a small jet she used from time to time.

The reports were right. She was, to put it mildly, mighty distressed. I told her that my opinion was that the debate preparation was the problem, and that we would change the format drastically. Further, I assured her that I'd go public and place the blame where it belonged soon after we returned to Washington.

The Washington press corps, it turned out, was eagerly awaiting my reaction. Four days after the debate, several Republican Senate colleagues and I scheduled a press conference to "rebut" Mondale's various campaign statements.

No sooner had we concluded our prepared remarks than several reporters sprang to their feet asking me to recognize them. It was clear that they weren't the least interested in our attacks on Mondale. They wanted to get my reaction to the Louisville debate.

With Nancy at the site of the Louisville debate in October of 1984. We won the campaign by a comfortable margin, but the President lost the debate to Walter Mondale. The First Lady criticized the debate preparation and made sure changes were instituted for the debate in Kansas City two weeks later.

Without dancing around, I decided to hit the issue head on. In effect, I told them that our candidate had not done well, but it wasn't his fault. I said, in fact, that he'd been "brutalized" by those who'd prepared him for the debate.

"Brutalized" captured the fancy of the media. The response was widely covered, which helped diffuse the growing perception that Ron wasn't "with it."

But there was a strong negative reaction from the White House staff who were involved in the debate preparation. They felt betrayed. Normally, that might have bothered me, but not this time. If sides had to be taken between Dick Darman and his crowd versus Ronald Reagan, that was an easy call for me.

In some ways, the Louisville debate was a blessing in disguise. It clearly showed that Ron did not respond well to structured debate preparation. For the second debate, we adopted a wholly different preparation routine. In short, we "let Reagan be Reagan."

Ron was fabulous in Kansas City, laying to rest any lingering questions about the "age issue." When the inevitable question about the issue arose, Ron was ready: "I will not make age an issue in this campaign. I am not going to exploit, for political purposes, my opponent's youth and inexperience."

The audience roared!

A Landslide in the Making

During the last several days of the campaign, I went with him on Air Force One, campaigning across the country.

What a difference from our campaigns in 1976 and 1980! When we arrived in Air Force One, it was a major event. The perks of a sitting President, as we learned in running against Gerald Ford in 1976, cannot be underestimated.

Many of the President's campaign appearances in 1984 were on college campuses. Imagine conservatives like us, who cut our political teeth in the 1960s, looking forward to going to a college campus! In the 60s, when we were Governors and Vietnam was a hot issue, it wasn't deemed safe to go to a campus without security.

Now, a few short years later, here was Ron being lionized by the students. The college rallies had an energy level that could not be duplicated in the usual political rally. Ron enjoyed them greatly, and there is no doubt that these rallies contributed to the success of the 1984 campaign.

For me, the most memorable experience occurred near the end of the campaign. We were working the upper Midwest states, and the response to Ron was overwhelming. The people there just loved him.

What we found on the hustings was matched by the findings of our pollster, Dick Wirthlin. Everything pointed to a landslide. Only Minnesota appeared to be leaning toward its favorite son, Fritz Mondale.

Since we were in the neighborhood, and it was near the end of the campaign, we asked Ron if he would reconsider his past refusals to campaign in Minnesota. In the past, he had consistently said that he didn't feel comfortable going to Mondale's home state to campaign against him. On the final morning of our campaign swing, a group of us went and asked him one last time. The schedule showed that otherwise all we had to do that day was return to Washington.

He resisted, saying it was too late to stage an event. He said the event organizers would need more than a couple of hours to prepare. He also asked how we could get the word out on such short notice. In short, he was full of questions and objections.

Finally, we told him that it wasn't fair to the people of Minnesota not to make at least one visit. We added that we could announce an arrival at a convenient rural airport, and let radio, television and word-of-mouth do the rest.

He relented, and what happened next was one of the most moving experiences I've ever had.

As we approached the airport, we could see that several dirt roads were clogged with vehicles, mostly pickups. The airport was in a farming area, and thousands of Minnesotans wanted to see and hear their President.

At the rally, the energy and intensity were on the same level as our college rallies. They cheered Ron, and he responded by delivering one of the finest speeches of the campaign.

When we left for Washington, we all felt that the Minnesota "drop in" was a fitting close to a campaign, which would conclude in a few days with another landslide win for Ronald Reagan. Of the 50 states, he eventually lost only in Minnesota. Based on the reception that last day, if Ron had worked the state even for one full day, I believe he would have carried Minnesota, too.

CHAPTER 19

❖ *Last Terms for Reagan and Me* ❖

THE IRAN-CONTRA MATTER

Some two-term Presidents have complained of boredom during their second terms. President Eisenhower comes to mind. His golf buddies at Augusta said his golf game surely seemed to improve between 1957 and 1961!

But Ron Reagan never complained about not having enough to do in his second term. Iran-Contra took care of that.

I first learned of the problem directly from him when he called me in Bermuda right after the 1986 elections. I was there playing golf with Indiana Senator Dan Quayle, Wyoming Senator Malcolm Wallop and Washington lobbyist Tom Korologos.

The call came while we were at U.S. Consul Max Friedersdorf's residence. (Max headed the legislative liaison office in the White House during the first term.)

When told that the President was calling, I was prepared for bad news. Rarely did he call to just chat.

He opened by saying, "Paul, I think we've got a bit of a problem. Some Beirut newspaper has just run an article indicating that we're exchanging arms for hostages in Iran." He told me he had no knowledge of any such arrangement, and that he was having Ed Meese check it out.

When I confided to my golf mates what the President said,

they were dumbfounded. If the allegation was true, and the President was implicated and then lied about it, we could have a replay of the Nixon impeachment ordeal.

After all the statements he'd made vilifying the Iranians and stating that his administration would never negotiate with terrorists, if the truth were otherwise, Ron's credibility, his greatest strength, would be shattered, and his presidency imperiled.

In rapid order, Ed Meese reported his findings on November 25. He indicated that arms had in fact been traded for hostages in an effort to open lines of communications with so-called moderate elements in Iran. To make matters worse, it turned out that the proceeds from the arms sales had been diverted to the "Contras," who were engaged in a civil war with the Communist government in Nicaragua.

Ron originally denied knowing of the hostage/arms exchange, and he later strongly denied knowing of the Contra arrangement.

A special review board, headed by former Texas Senator John Tower, after extensive investigation, faulted the initiative and how the administration had handled it.

Later, Congress held hearings and was critical, too, although a then-unknown National Security Council staffer, Oliver North, used the Congressional hearings to catapult himself into international celebrity.

Finally, on March 4, 1987, Ron, in a short speech from the Oval Office, made a brave but difficult acknowledgement. He said, "A few months ago I told the American people that I did not trade arms for hostages. My heart and my best intentions still tell me that is true, but the facts and evidence tell me it is not."

The diversion of money from the arms sales to the Contras did not involve Ron at all. Even independent counsel Lawrence Walsh acknowledged after years of investigation that he found no proof that Reagan directed or even knew about the transfer of funds.

Throughout, Ron maintained his innocence, even after his Oval Office speech.

Undoubtedly, Iran-Contra was by far the most severe crisis of the Reagan Administration, but Ron still survived. A President with less credibility with the people would have been destroyed.

A sidelight: One weekend during the height of the crisis, while at my cabin in Virginia's Shenandoah Valley, I received a surprising phone call. To protect my privacy, I had opted not to have a phone in the cabin. The owner of the development, a former CIA agent, knocked on my door. He said anxiously that CIA Director Bill Casey was trying to reach me. Although Casey was a close friend, he rarely called me. Thus, his calling me at the cabin was particularly worrisome.

When I returned the call, Bill opened by saying, "Paul, I'm sorry to bother you, but I just have to get something off my chest to you as a friend. There's been a lot of loose talk around town that I masterminded the arms for hostages deal. I want you to know that I wasn't involved at all. If I had been, I would have put a stop to it in a helluva hurry."

Within days of this call, Bill suffered a collapse. He died of a brain tumor not long thereafter, in May 1987 – without ever testifying. His involvement, or lack of it, remains one of the unsolved Iran-Contra mysteries.

How Howard Baker Became
White House Chief of Staff

In the wake of Iran-Contra, a lot of people were calling for major changes in the White House structure, starting with the Chief of Staff, Don Regan. In February 1987, when it became apparent that he would be leaving as Chief of Staff, there was concern about who would succeed him.

At that time, I was just getting into the saddle at Finley, Kumble, the law firm I joined after leaving the Senate, but I had nonetheless stayed in touch with the White House.

The whole Regan scene had been unpleasant. I liked Don's tough, Irish, Marine-like style, but many others did not.

From the time that he swapped jobs with Jim Baker — Don to White House Chief of Staff and Jim to Secretary of the Treasury — I had the uneasy feeling there would be problems. And there were — with the press, Capitol Hill and, most importantly, with the First Lady.

Don got along well with the President. Ron, in turn, enjoyed his "Irish Chief." They communicated well and loved to swap stories.

But as Iran-Contra gathered momentum on the Hill, and with his increasingly strained relations with Nancy, it was clear to me that Don would be leaving.

Senate Majority Leader Howard Baker took this shot while I was nominating Ron for President at the national convention in Dallas in 1984.

Since no one had been groomed to succeed him, and most of the old Reagan crowd were either in the private sector or elsewhere in the government, the supply from which to draw a replacement was mighty thin.

When Don's departure was the topic of speculation in Washington, I received a few press calls asking about rumors that I might be the next Chief of Staff.

After saying "No way," I decided that I had better start help-ing to find a replacement, lest I get an "I-need-you" call from Ron.

At the time, Carol and I were busily engaged in building a new house in the McLean, Virginia woods, and I was just getting es-tablished in the law firm. It would have been chaos if I went back into the government.

So I took out a long legal writing pad, as I do when confronted with difficult problems, and outlined the qualities and strengths needed in a Chief of Staff in the difficult days of Iran-Contra.

I concluded that we needed a person who might not be attain-able! A new "chief" would have to be personally compatible with the Reagans and with the "Reagan crowd" in and out of the White House. Further, he or she should have credibility with Congress and the media. In other words, he should be an "old Washington hand" who could skillfully steer the President through the rest of his term in the most productive way possible, politically and personally.

After listing the criteria, I tried to fit a person. At first, it seemed like the proverbial search for a needle in a haystack.

Then, a seemingly unattainable candidate struck me as just right: the former Senate Majority Leader, Howard Baker. The more I thought about it, the more excited I became. On a scale of one to ten, Howard was a "ten." Here was an experienced, re-spected Washington "hand," held in high regard by Congress, the media and the business community.

Then, realism struck me. Why would Howard leave a top law firm where he was making a lot of money? It was a position that still allowed him to spend time with his wife, Joy, and his family. I asked myself why he would even consider going to the White House to be beaten up on a daily basis?

Besides, I thought, Howard had been toying with running for President again. He hadn't run well in 1980 and might want vindication in 1988. Also, the conservatives might still be upset with Howard over his vote in favor of the Panama Canal Treaties.

But the more I thought about the "downside," the less worrisome it seemed. Howard had never been materialistic, so the money shouldn't be a problem, I thought. As to the Presidency, I thought I knew Howard pretty well. I suspected, without talking to him, that deep down he'd really like a "graceful exit" to avoid running for President. And the conservatives? They might grumble a bit, but most of them would go along with President Reagan's choice.

Armed with my case, I met with Ron and Nancy in the residence the morning after I finished my analysis. I opened by stating that the position had to be filled quickly. I said that I wanted to do anything I could to help, but I'd made heavy commitments in the private sector and just couldn't see my way clear to come into the White House. Besides, I said, I was looking at a possible run for the Presidency myself.

They both gave me a blank look. What I'd just said wasn't going down too well, I thought. Thank God I had an alternative plan. I told them of my "criteria" exercise and that Howard Baker, if we could get him, was a natural.

There was no reaction at all from Nancy. Bad sign! Ron said that it was his understanding that Howard was going to run for President. I told him that I didn't believe it and explained why.

By then, Nancy warmed a bit. Good sign! She asked how they could get in touch with him. I told them that Howard was in Florida visiting his grandchildren. I said that if the Reagans were interested, they should call him immediately.

Ron and Nancy both thanked me as I left, and Ron said he'd call right away.

Within a couple of hours, Ron called and excitedly told me that I was right — Howard *was* interested! Ron asked me what I thought the next step should be, and I suggested a quick meeting at the White House to make sure there was a clear meeting of the minds. I also said I'd attend if he wished. He did.

On the afternoon of February 27, 1987, Tom Loranger, my assistant, and I picked up Howard Baker on 15th Street near the White House. It was raining, and Howard looked like a forlorn character with his coat turned up and holding an umbrella. It says a lot about Washington that this lonely-looking figure, within about an hour, would be an international celebrity again and be engaged in a huge, spirited press conference in his law offices.

Of course, the meeting with the President turned out to be a formality. The rest is history. Howard Baker went on to do a magnificent job as Chief of Staff.

Although most pundits seemed happy to opine that the Iran-Contra scandal would neutralize the Reagan presidency, Ron not only survived but successfully negotiated the Intermediate Nuclear Force (INF) treaty with Gorbachev, a major step in ending the Cold War. That helped Ron to conclude his presidency on a very high note.

There's no question that Howard Baker played a major role in giving the Reagan Presidency a happy ending.

THE REAGAN PRESIDENCY

By objective standards, the Reagan presidency was a successful one.

On the economic side, he broke every rule and not only got away with it, but flourished.

As a fiscal conservative, and I thought Ron was one, too, I was taken aback when he not only did not propose a balanced budget, but simultaneously proposed an historic reduction in taxes and a dramatic increase in defense spending. He said that rebuilding our defense capability would be expensive, and he was right! I was worried that, together, these policies could be a recipe for fiscal trouble.

As it turned out, the trouble was short-term. The House, still controlled by the Democrats, wouldn't reduce domestic spending by a penny, so the defense increases fueled a sharp increase in the national debt. As a percentage of Gross Domestic Product — the usual yardstick — it grew during Ron's first term to levels well above those considered "normal." But, as the effects of his tax reductions kicked in and economic expansion went forward, that percentage came back down to "normal" levels.

The expansion began in November 1982, marking the end of the recession, and didn't stop for a minute during the rest of Ron's two terms in the White House.

On the foreign policy front, the Cold War was successfully concluded without any bloodshed, a remarkable accomplishment. Even though there were many factors contributing to this achievement, including the deterioration of the Soviet economy, I doubt very much if the Berlin Wall would have come down as quickly as it did if Ron Reagan had not been President of the United States.

Conclusion: A Personal View of Ronald Reagan

After Ron was elected President, the news media, as only they can do, described me as "the First Friend."

At first, I didn't pay much attention to my new moniker, but before long, I learned that one could pay a price for being perceived as being at the right hand of "the man."

It seemed that anyone with a Washington ax to grind would find his or her way to my door. For weeks after the 1980 election, the hallway outside my Senate office was lined with people looking for jobs or other favors. When the personnel apparatus in the White House started to function, the "Laxalt Personnel Department" saw a perceptible decrease in work!

On the plus side, we were able to place several Nevadans in the administration: Bob Broadbent of Boulder City and Hal Furman of Carson City went to the Department of the Interior; Reese Taylor of Carson City to the Interstate Commerce Commission; Bob Horton of Winnemucca to the Bureau of Mines; Cam Batjer of Carson City to the U.S. Parole Commission; Joe Brown of Las Vegas to the Foreign Claims Settlement Commission; Marybel Batjer of Carson City to the Department of De-

To Paul—
A favorite picture of me & my favorite fellas—
Fondly
Nancy

Having a chat with the President in the Oval Office shortly after his election. Nancy liked the shot enough to send it to me with a special inscription. *White House photo*

fense; James Stearns of Reno to the Securities Investment Protection Corporation; Todd Foley to the White House's Office of Public Liaison and William Wynn to the Department of Housing and Urban Development.

When I became General Chairman of the Republican Party, Frank Fahrenkopf of Reno became Chairman of the Republican

National Committee, where he quickly became a "star."

It was often said that Ron Reagan had a million acquaintances but very few friends. His staff when he was Governor and later as President never referred to him as "Ron." The only ones who called him by his first name were his Los Angeles and Hollywood friends. They usually called him "Ronnie."

From the time we first met, we got along. At the beginning, I was his "protector" when it came to national politicians, for he seemed half-afraid of them. Like most Hollywood types, he tended to be self-oriented. Most of his adult life had been spent with people who adored him as a screen actor. Rarely would he even inquire about what was going on in my life. The same was true of others.

Our bond was politics and our jobs. We'd rarely discuss family, recognizing the subject could be a minefield. In the later years of his presidency, however, he would often ask about my wife, Carol.

He and Nancy had a special bond. They truly loved and respected one another. At the beginning of our relationship, I felt her "adoring look" at his speeches was a bit much, but later realized she wasn't acting. She meant it!

Nancy was and is Ron's "Rock of Gibraltar." If he has a real friend in this world, it is Nancy. I've often thought that if it had not been for Nancy's drive and will, Ron never would have been President.

In my presence, they had their spats, but their differences were never fundamental and would quickly blow over.

Since 1994, Ron has been one of the many victims of Alzheimer's. Although he is physically strong, his memory has gradually faded away.

Nancy, to the very end, continues to be Ron's best friend.

CHAPTER 20

❖ *Laxalt v. The Sacramento Bee* ❖

THE BEE'S LIBELOUS ARTICLE

On November 1, 1983, my chief of staff, Ed Allison, came into my Senate office. From the troubled look on his face, I sensed that he had bad news.

He told me that the Sacramento Bee, the media powerhouse in the California capital, had just run a front-page story contending that during our family's ownership and control of the Ormsby House, up to $2 million had been skimmed (the illegal diversion of cash) from the operation; that somehow my political connections sidetracked any potential investigation; and that there was evidence of organized crime involvement in the business.

The first impulse of a politician who has been subjected to a media assault is to ignore it. Perhaps, the thinking goes, it will only be a 24-hour news story and then go away.

After all, the Sacramento Bee, a liberal bastion, had slammed Reagan for years. It was apparent to me that they were now attacking me to get at Ron just as the re-election campaign was getting under way.

Ed and I agreed that the piece was so extensive and potentially harmful that we didn't have the luxury to ignore it. We had to respond. Ed issued a statement denying the assertions of the story and characterizing it as ludicrous, since the hotel had struggled financially to the point that there wasn't anything to skim but debt.

For months, we fenced around with the Bee people, including C.K. McClatchy, its chief executive, without any positive results. Prior to filing my libel suit, I even traveled to Sacramento for a summit meeting with McClatchy, his editor and the investigative reporter who wrote the story.

I submitted language that I felt was due the Laxalt family, essentially stating that after a post-story investigation, there was no credible evidence of skimming nor any mob affiliations.

After submitting the language to McClatchy at the meeting, he asked for time to consider my request with his people. When they were out for more than an hour, my hopes rose that we could clean up this mess with a minimum of trouble and notoriety.

Finally, they came back and McClatchy informed me that our proposal was unacceptable, that they would issue a clarifying statement to the effect that the Bee "had never meant to state or imply that Laxalt participated in or had any knowledge of any alleged skimming operation."

That, of course, was insufficient as far as I was concerned, so we concluded the meeting with my telling them, "We'll see you in court."

I learned later that the investigative reporter raised hell about my offer, feeling that he was being "hung out to dry," and that McClatchy had to go along.

To say "see you in court" and to actually get there are two different things. For me to sue, I had a great deal of careful homework to do before embarking on this dangerous trip.

Although I hadn't done any libel work as a lawyer, I had followed the evolution of libel law closely. The existing law was that if I was a public person — and I certainly was at that point — in order to sue the Bee successfully for libel, I would have to prove not only that the story was false, but also that it was written with "actual malice" (i.e., it was knowingly false or written with reckless disregard as to whether it was false or not).

That difficult standard was established in the landmark libel case of 1964 known as Sullivan v. New York Times.

This placed a huge burden on libel plaintiffs. This is precisely what the U.S. Supreme Court, in one of its misguided moments, intended to do. They felt that the press should have that additional protection. Someday, the Court will reverse the Sullivan decision so that the malice requirement is not required. That is the law in Britain, and it should be the law here.

To make the assessment as to whether we could meet the malice requirement, I needed a libel law "pro." I found one in New York City, who was reported to be exceptionally knowledgeable and tough as nails – just the man to represent me.

After meeting the lawyer, Seymour Shainswit, he assured me that not only was there a sustainable libel case here, it was a very strong case. He must have sincerely believed this was true, because he was retained on a contingent fee basis. Under this arrangement, if we prevailed, by trial or settlement, Sy would receive a percentage of the total recovery. I'd be responsible for the costs associated with prosecuting the case.

Going "contingent" was the only way I could afford to go forward. On a straight per hour cost basis, the fee could easily have totaled several million dollars. On a Senate salary, that was out of the question. A contingent fee was mandatory.

I quickly learned that being responsible for "costs" was also far from being a free ride. As distasteful as it was, we would have to solicit contributions. To avoid violating any Senate rules or running afoul of the IRS, we created a trust as the vehicle for receipts and disbursements.

At that time, I was overloaded with my Senate responsibilities, so my daughter Michelle volunteered and did yeoman's work. She made the all-important Senate contacts for the trust fund and became my chief solicitor for funds. Thanks to her, this part of the effort was a great success. All in all, she collected some $800,000. I was mighty impressed and grateful.

I later met alone with C. K. McClatchy in my Senate office. He asked me to reconsider my refusal, making the case that my family was "beyond reproach" and that the prospect of a huge libel lawsuit was causing him problems.

I once again told him that the article was "a piece of shit," and he should know it. Further, I told McClatchy that he should stand up to his people, issue our statement, and we'd each have a Merry Christmas. He told me that he didn't think he could do that and left my office.

I had the distinct feeling then, and still do today, that he simply didn't have the guts to overrule his own people and do the right thing. What a shame! Had he done so, a lot of heartbreak could have been avoided.

After our complaint was filed in Nevada in September of 1984, the publicity around the country was extensive. It wasn't all that often that a politician took on a media giant.

The reaction from the media was interesting. The Nevada press, for the most part, was very supportive. Bob Brown, editor of the Valley Times in North Las Vegas, editorialized as follows:

"The story makes clear that there is no evidence that Mr. Laxalt was aware of any skimming going on. In other words, if there were skimming, it was Mr. Laxalt who was victimized.

"The paper's own story admits that there was never an investigation of the supposed skimming – purportedly because of Mr. Laxalt's prominence in Republican politics.

"Well, we can't help wonder just how, without an investigation, anyone could possibly know there actually was skimming, much less place even a ballpark dollar figure on it?"

About the suggestion that my political friends quashed any potential investigation, Bob opined, "Everyone knows that since Watergate the power of any President to sidetrack or play politics with an IRS probe has been virtually nil. Even if there were an attempt to do so by someone to help Sen. Laxalt, or save him some embarrassment, the leaks would be all over Washington in 10 minutes flat.

"So it seems to us that the contention that the alleged skimming at Ormsby House was never investigated because of Sen. Laxalt's political juice is so ridiculous that it falls of its own weight."

Since Bob Brown didn't always agree with me, I greatly appreciated his support.

In Washington, where I enjoyed generally good relations with the press, I didn't receive one critical remark or story about my suing the Bee. Notably the wire services, including Brendan Riley of the Associated Press, Jay Matthews of the Washington Post and Wally Turner of the New York Times, all reported the story objectively. One major reporter told me in confidence that he felt I'd been "screwed," and he wished me well.

It should also be pointed out that James Avance, Chairman of Nevada's Gaming Control Board, and an appointee of Democrat Governor Richard Bryan, wrote me a letter in December 1984, in which he said that the Bee's article caused the Board to conduct an "investigative review" of the allegations.

Mr. Avance said the investigation found that the Board "did not have information during the early 1970s which would justify an investigation of the charge of skimming at the Ormsby House."

He concluded by saying that the Gaming Control Board "has further determined that there is no justification to investigate those allegations any further."

It wasn't long into the battle before we came to the conclusion that we couldn't afford Sy Shainswit, even on a "cost" basis. His idea of reasonable costs, like suites in Las Vegas hotels, was a bit different than ours.

About that time, Senator Arlen Specter of Pennsylvania collared me in the Senate dining room and asked how the suit was going. I told him we were having attorney problems, whereupon he said, "Paul, you ought to hire Jim Beasley from Philadelphia. My son works for him. I don't think there's a better libel lawyer in the country." Arlen continued, "He's recently secured a huge libel judgment from the Philadelphia Inquirer."

Michelle and I met with Beasley and were impressed. He had a James Cagney flair about him, appeared to be competent and not overly self-confident. Jim had familiarized himself with our matter and was convinced that the article was actionable.

We decided to retain Beasley on a contingent fee basis. He would be compensated for a fee only if we prevailed. To pay the "costs," we continued to depend on the Senate-approved trust fund, with Michelle as its executive director. As noted earlier, we received contributions from all over the country.

BIPARTISAN SUPPORT

The reaction from my Senate colleagues from both sides of the aisle still pleases me. Ted Kennedy stuck his neck out by helping and caught hell from the McClatchy people, who reminded him that the Bee had supported the Kennedy clan dating back to the time when John entered national politics.

Other Democrats helped, too: Dan Inouye of Hawaii, Chris Dodd of Connecticut, Dennis DeConcini of Arizona, Sam Nunn of Georgia and Russell Long of Louisiana. All of them pitched in — at some political cost to them, I'm sure. Dan Inouye even defended his contribution on national television.

My fellow Republicans, with Barry Goldwater leading the charge, also helped greatly. Senator Ted Stevens of Alaska, a gutsy, honest and loyal individual, also stood foursquare with me throughout the suit.

Without my colleagues' support, and that of many others, we wouldn't have been able to sustain the libel suit. Even though the case was handled on a contingency basis, it was still expensive — more than a million dollars in costs.

Had attorneys' fees been charged on an hourly basis, the total tab would have been several million dollars.

I have always said that political differences should never turn personal. My friendship with Ted Kennedy proved my belief in that theory. His help in funding my libel suit against the liberal Sacramento Bee was a courageous move.

After hiring Beasley, we spent three years in the arduous process of litigation. Trying to be a cooperative client for Jim while still performing my duties as a U.S. Senator proved to be a challenge.

I still find it difficult to relate to modern day litigation. When I left the practice in the 1960s, very little time was spent on "discovery." There might be an occasional deposition or interrogatory, but that was about it. It seems now that litigation is consumed by discovery, very expensive discovery.

THE SUIT IS SETTLED

Finally, after all the pushing and pulling, the suit was settled in June 1987. Key to the settlement was an admission by McClatchy that pretrial discovery "had not shown that there was a skim" at the Ormsby House. That, alone, exposed the story for the garbage that it was.

McClatchy said that the story only alleged that Federal agents were investigating skimming allegations. Baloney! Had McClatchy admitted this and cleared Ormsby House at the Sacramento meeting back in 1984, the matter would have been quickly cleaned up. But instead, I'm confident, he felt he could "outgun" us with lawyers, and we would eventually dismiss the suit, as many libel plaintiffs do.

Under the settlement, we agreed that the question of our attorneys' fees and court costs would be left to a panel of former Federal judges. Our side selected Griffin Bell, former United States Attorney General under President Jimmy Carter, which surprised some of our Republican friends. McClatchy selected Judge Charles Renfrew, and Bell and Renfrew subsequently picked Judge Philip Tone.

Ironically and tragically, on the day before we announced at a Washington press conference that the suit was settled, my beloved Kathy, brother Mick's former wife, took her life.

Kathy had been secretly taped by an unscrupulous Bee agent who posed as a friend. In the portion in which the suit was discussed, she apparently felt that she had made harmful statements and after the interview brooded about it and went into a deep depression.

I was unaware of her condition and have often wondered whether she would have taken her life had she known of the settlement. We shall never know.

She was an unfortunate victim of the Bee's ruthless activity. Those responsible will have to live with that. The bastards!

On March 31, 1988, after an extensive review, the three-judge panel awarded us $647,452.52 in fees and costs. It was a sweet victory!

I issued a statement which said: "It is not impossible for a public servant to win the good fight against a wealthy and powerful newspaper chain." Griffin Bell said that he would have awarded even more money, but he felt the panel's decision was "fair."

Barry Goldwater, after hearing the news from Daughter Michelle, wrote her a letter in which he said:

"What a wonderful bit of news to hear from the boss girl herself about what the Sacramento Bee was made to do.

"One of the few times in my life I ever disagreed with your old man was when he didn't stick it right to that Sacramento Bee and if it meant having them go broke, hurrah. But anyway it was a good settlement and it brought justice to a place that needed it."

One is always asked after an ordeal such as this, "Would you do it again?" My answer: You bet I would! There's nothing more valuable, in my book, than one's reputation and the reputation of one's family as well.

I'm comforted by the fact that if my descendants ever do a computer check on Laxalt v. Sacramento Bee, they can take pride in the fact that I didn't surrender when the going got tough!

I rather think that the powers that be, at the Sacramento Bee and elsewhere, realized thereafter that falsely maligning a public official can be a dangerous endeavor.

CHAPTER 21

❖ *Leaving the Senate* ❖

LEAVING THE U.S. SENATE — EASIER SAID THAN DONE!
It's been said that it's often easier getting into the U.S. Senate
than getting out — at least getting out voluntarily.

In the old days, Senators usually died in office or were defeated. In Nevada's history, only Alan Bible, my predecessor, had
left office on his own.

The difficulty of getting out seemed to increase in direct pro-
portion to one's stature in the Senate. Two examples come to mind.

Ed Muskie of Maine was a powerhouse on Capitol Hill. He
had even made a respectable run for President in 1972 until, in the
snows of New Hampshire, he broke down on national television
over what he considered to be a vicious news story about his wife.

In the Senate, Ed became chairman of the powerful Budget
Committee.

In one of our frequent gym sessions in the late 1970s, Ed
often confided to me that he would like to retire from the Senate,
but pressure from his family, staff and constituents kept him in.

In the latter stages of the Carter Administration, I was astonished to learn, as were my colleagues, that he was going to resign
from the Senate to become Secretary of State.

After congratulating Ed, I asked, "Why?" With a wistful
smile, he looked down on me (he was 6'4" tall) and said, "Paul,

have you never heard of a graceful exit?"

Years later, Senator Lloyd Bentsen of Texas, formerly the influential chairman of the Finance Committee, announced that he, too, was leaving the Senate to become the Secretary of the Treasury in the Clinton Administration. Hardly anyone in the Senate could understand why.

At a going-away reception, I said, "Lloyd, is this another Muskie graceful exit?" "Yes," he said, "it sure is!"

When I was first elected to the Senate, I resolved that at the right time I would leave voluntarily. I did not want to be carried out or be defeated at the polls.

As my second term progressed, I privately decided that the end of my term in 1986 would be an appropriate time to leave the Senate. But there was one serious complication — there seemed to be no graceful way to exit!

I told the Reagans, in confidence, what I wanted to do. To say that my reception was "chilly" is an understatement. I pledged to them that if I decided to leave, I'd stay in Washington for at least the remainder of Ron's term. That seemed to mollify them, but not much.

Finally, I decided that I would set a "date certain" in order to settle the matter. I also resolved to decide at Marlette, our family mountain retreat in the Sierra Nevada, in August 1985.

Unfortunately, I announced my plan before leaving for Marlette, which left me open to the most intense personal lobbying I've ever experienced.

Staff, colleagues and friends were all over me. The arguments were essentially the same: "You're relatively young"; "You can't leave us now that we're in the midst of the 'Reagan Revolution'"; and "Another six years will pass quickly."

No one seemed particularly concerned about how I felt. Carol, however, was very supportive, indicating that whatever I decided would be fine with her.

The pressure to "stay on" was even more intense in Nevada than Washington. It came from close personal friends who had been politically allied with me for years.

We ended up having a "summit barbecue" at Marlette. Dick Wirthlin, the President's pollster for many years and a good friend of mine, agreed to conduct a survey and present the results to my friends.

Essentially, Dick found that chances of a successful reelection were excellent, and that a substantial reservoir of good will toward me existed in the state. Further, he found that if I left, chances for a Republican to succeed me were good.

This was vital information, for the last thing I wanted was to leave and have my seat captured by a Democrat. That result (God forbid) could spell the difference between Republican and Democrat control of the Senate.

The Reagans had raised this eventuality, too, but I tried to assure them that due in great part to the success of their administration, Nevada had become a safe Republican state. To have a respected expert such as Dick Wirthlin confirm that important point was very reassuring.

After all the presentations had been made, if a secret ballot had been taken that day at Marlette, my retiring from the Senate would have lost by a large margin.

This fact troubled me greatly. The period immediately thereafter was a frustrating time of indecision for me — a new experience. In the past, indecision about anything had not been a problem for me.

In this case, however, I'd feel at one moment as though I had no choice but to run again, then quickly feel the opposite way.

In the middle of one night in my mountaintop tent, I suddenly sat up, wide awake. It was a beautiful, star-filled, moonlit evening. A clear truth had struck me: "Damn it, Paul, cut out this constant change of mind. The fact is you don't want to serve another six years in the Senate. You've paid your dues. Now, it's time for you to do something else."

That did it! My mind was made up! I'd leave the Senate and be fully comfortable with the decision.

I wish this episode had a happier ending than it did.

After conferring with all kinds of political "pros," I decided to support as my successor, Jim Santini, who served Nevada in the House of Representatives as a Democrat from 1974-1982. Jim had run for the Senate in 1982, but lost after an ugly primary against the incumbent, Howard Cannon.

Before officially entering the 1986 Senate race, Jim switched parties and became a Republican, a move that his opponents described as "shameless opportunism."

While I was serving as chairman of the 1984 Reagan Presidential campaign, I asked Jim to be national chairman of the "Democrats for Reagan" effort. He declined. Looking back, I feel that if he had accepted the post, he could have easily overcome the "party-switching" issue.

During the campaign in 1986, Jim and his family worked their tails off, but the race was lost to then-Congressman Harry Reid. The party-switch, plus an excellent campaign by Harry, was too much for Jim to overcome.

Although my seat was lost to the Democrats, it did not mean the difference in control of the Senate. Republicans enjoyed a slight 53-47 majority before the election, but ended up on the short end of a 55-45 margin afterward.

As this book was being written, Harry Reid was narrowly elected to a third term in the Senate. He thus became the Minority Whip, the second ranking position among Democrats in the Senate.

EXPLORING A PRESIDENTIAL CAMPAIGN

It's been said, with some validity, that almost every U.S. Senator, at one time or another, thinks that he or she is destined to be President of the United States.

I can say that I didn't think in those terms in the first ten years of my Senate time. After all, most of that time was spent trying to get Ron Reagan elected and, after 1980, keeping him there.

But after Ron's reelection in 1984, from time to time people (principally conservatives) would ask me to consider seriously making a run. The thinking was that even though George Bush was Vice President and had served well, he would never enjoy the trust and confidence of most conservatives. These folks felt that because of my record and closeness with Ron that I was the "rightful heir." With Ron's blessing, I could secure the Republican nomination and sail through the general election so long as the Democrats continued to nominate McGovern-like liberals.

Bill Rusher, who was a moving force behind Goldwater's nomination in 1964, asked one day to have lunch with me in the Senate dining room. As I recall, it was near the time in mid-1986 when there was a Laxalt for President "boomlet" in the national press.

Bill said I should run. I thanked him for the compliment, but I told him that I'd prefer holding off making a decision until after I left the Senate in 1987, which would be well ahead of the Republican convention in August 1988. Bill and others warned me that holding off was hazardous, that presidential politics was requiring far more lead time and money than, say, in 1976 or 1980.

I felt, wrongly as it turned out, that with my experience and contacts from three Reagan campaigns, I could start later.

I should have been tipped off – had I been listening – when Lee Atwater, the young dynamo who wound up running George Bush's successful campaign, came to me in 1986, and said he wanted to be on my team, but that I had to make up my mind quickly. When I told Lee I wasn't prepared to do so, he soon signed up with the Bush campaign – a huge loss for me.

After leaving the Senate in January 1987 and settling into my new law firm, I decided that I had to "fish or cut bait." In analyzing the situation, I felt that I should enjoy substantial Reagan support if I chose to run. Further, my contacts in New Hampshire, the first primary state, would be helpful. Nackey Loeb, owner of the all-powerful Manchester Union Leader, would help, I reasoned. After all, she was an old friend from Nevada, and I had worked closely with her late husband, Bill, in the Reagan elections. Jerry Carmen, who was our top operative in New Hampshire, might also be available to help.

In addition, I thought, the California Reagan "Kitchen Cabinet" would be of great help, particularly in raising money. Holmes Tuttle, a fund-raising genius, was a close friend and should be eager to help, I told myself.

Before going any further, I decided that I had better find out where I stood with Ron. I felt I'd better give Ron a "heads up" so he wouldn't be blindsided.

Realistically, I knew he wouldn't take a position in the primary. He never had, not even when his own daughter, Maureen, ran for the U.S. Senate in California. Further, although we hadn't talked about it, I felt that aside from our close personal relationship, politically he probably had to support George Bush, who had served so loyally as his V.P.

When I told him I was considering running, he didn't seem the least surprised. After all, there had been press speculation to that effect. He wished me well, and that was about it. I didn't expect an endorsement, but he didn't discourage me either.

Much later, I sadly realized that I was wasting my time in talking to him. While he publicly professed neutrality, I learned that he had been committed to George Bush for some time. He felt that George had been a loyal, effective Vice President and had earned his support.

I also learned later that the Kitchen Cabinet members, with the exception of Charlie and Mary Jane Wick – God bless them – were also committed to George.

I never discussed the situation with Nancy, knowing how awkward it would be for her. But I learned that she was supportive of me and quietly communicated her feelings to her friends.

While this turn of events was disappointing, other people continued to urge me to go forward. Even though Ron might be committed, they said, he'd never go public during the primary, and we could simply smile whenever we were questioned as to whether Ron was supportive. Also, I was reminded that each election is brand new, and some of the old timers like the Kitchen Cabinet might not be a significant force this time.

Some of my Senate colleagues, such as Jake Garn, Orrin Hatch, Chic Hecht, Ted Stevens and Malcolm Wallop, joined by Congressmen Larry Craig (now Senator), Phil Crane, Dan Schaefer, Bob Smith and Barbara Vucanovich said that they would endorse me if I ran. They all did. Others, even though they had previously been pushing me to run, thinned out when decision time came.

The Bush people had done their homework. While I was contemplating, they were securing commitments.

Some of my long-time Nevada friends, such as Jerry Dondero, Ed Allison and Sig Rogich, strongly urged me to run. They contended that the race was "wide open," and that if I didn't give it a try, I would always regret it.

Finally, I decided to give it a shot, but on a strictly conditional basis. I had learned in the Reagan races that talk is cheap. What one needed were personal, public commitments and lots of money. Indeed, having adequate money in hand was absolutely essential.

We came to the conclusion that in order to make a credible

start in Iowa and New Hampshire, we'd need a minimum of $2 million. If we could bank that much money, I'd go.

A further and last condition was that I would be straight with the people. This was going to be a true exploratory effort, and the goal was a serious one.

In a crowded press conference at the National Press Club on April 28, 1987, with Carol at my side, I announced my candidacy for President of the United States. It was an exciting day for my family and friends, but not so for me.

My problem was that I knew full well how difficult it is to run for President, and that the coming months were going to be the most demanding challenge of my life.

This began the four most miserable months of my life. Even my combat time in Leyte was less vexing.

With Carol at the National Press Club in Washington where I announced the formation of my Presidential Exploratory Committee in April 1987.

Fortunately, we had a Learjet at our disposal, which we leased from my old friend, Jack Dreyfus. That helped take the sting out of the campaigning somewhat.

In that Learjet, we traveled all over the country, sometimes covering two or three states in a day. How we were able to do as much as we did, I still don't understand. We had no advance people to arrange schedules and events.

I usually flew with Doc Bodensteiner, a young staffer from Nevada, and Tom Loranger, my trusted chief of staff in the Senate, who had gone with me into the private sector.

We never knew for certain whether a scheduled event would

be held or not. Even if it was, it would usually be with a handful of people. All this should have been easily bearable, but my problem was that I was totally spoiled. To say the least, this was a bit different from the well-oiled, beautifully organized campaign trips I had taken with the President in 1984.

The scheduling was so grueling that I became chronically tired. Each appearance was hard work, mainly because within me I realized that we were gaining no traction with the voters.

Even the Nevada events were not satisfying, although we had excellent turnouts in Elko and Washoe Valley. I had the feeling, though I dared not express it, that they felt my campaign was not only a long shot but a loser. In fairness, I didn't know whether they actually felt that way or whether a certain paranoia about Nevada was settling in with me after many unpleasant incidents in the Bible Belt states in which people took sharp issue with Nevada's live-and-let-live philosophy. Some were so direct as to ask how I, coming from the "Sin State," could realistically aspire to be President.

Now, just a few years later, when some of those same states — such as Mississippi, Alabama and Missouri — have casino gambling, I wonder if they still consider Nevada the "Sin State." If they do, Nevada certainly has a lot of company these days.

Iowa was difficult, if not impossible, politically. Even though my friend Bud Hockenberg, a Des Moines lawyer, gallantly tried to organize a campaign for me, it was quickly apparent that Iowa was a non-starter for Laxalt.

This was apparent at a major Des Moines Republican gathering where all the candidates were required to appear. I ran into Bob Dole there, who was the acknowledged "star." He'd been in and out of Iowa for years and was practically a "hometown boy" as far as the folks there were concerned. His appearance ignited the crowd, although he felt that he'd been slighted when Bush was selected to speak at the lunch earlier that day.

I was scheduled near the end of the program, the sort of placement that "throwaway candidates" — those with no chance — were usually accorded. By the time I appeared, the crowd was numb from being shouted at for hours. They were polite, but far from enthusiastic. I left feeling, as I had before, that Iowa was a waste of time and energy for me.

As I went to the airfield in Des Moines for another trip somewhere, I ran into Joe Biden, the Senator from Delaware and a friend, who was running for President on the Democrat ticket.

He looked frazzled and dispirited and said, "Paul, what the —— are we doing here?" I confess that I didn't have an answer. (Before long, both of us dropped out and had no further need to campaign in Iowa.)

New Hampshire wasn't much better. Jerry Carmen, who hailed from New Hampshire and who had served in top positions in the Reagan Administration, was my campaign chairman. He and his family did their best to help, but it was apparent that we were too late.

Dole and Bush had the state well in hand as far as the moderate vote was concerned. Nackey Loeb of the Union Leader, was disappointing. She proved once again that personal friendship often doesn't translate into political support. After a few meetings with her, it was apparent that unless I embraced positions to the right of Genghis Khan, the Union Leader would not be in my corner. Naturally, she later became a staunch supporter of Pat Buchanan.

Nackey's response reminded me of the time when Chic Hecht was running for the U.S. Senate in Nevada. He went for help to a businessman who asked him what his positions were on various issues. Chic responded by saying, "Issues, shit! I thought you were my friend!"

For me, New Hampshire came to a head when one of my campaign operatives in the state suggested that I appear before a rubber plant to make some point (still lost on me) about condoms and AIDS. I put my foot down and said that I wouldn't embarrass myself in this manner.

Near the end of August, I left the campaign trail to spend a few hours at Marlette, my Sierra Nevada refuge. I hoped the clear air, blue skies and the company of old friends and family would clear my head.

Labor Day, the deadline I had imposed on Jerry Dondero to have $2 million in the bank, was just days away. Jerry was gathering information nationwide so that we could evaluate our money situation.

Jerry came up to Marlette and reported that we were short of our goal. We had raised about $1.2 million, but had less than $1 million in the bank. Nevertheless, he felt that we were gathering momentum, and that the deadline should be extended.

The summit conference with Jerry was short and sweet. Despite his heroic efforts, I said that I frankly was relieved we hadn't reached our goal; that the campaign wasn't going anywhere, anyway.

I decided we should announce the termination of the campaign immediately, and that we would refund the money collected thus far, less expenses. We did.

What went wrong? I suspect that in organizing my campaign much as I had Reagan's, I committed a fatal error, like a client representing himself in court. A cold, objective political analyst would have made a no-nonsense assessment of the political situation and told me that we were too late with too little to mount a respectable campaign, and that we shouldn't even begin.

CHAPTER 22

❖ *Life Beyond the Senate* ❖

A few months after Howard Baker left the Senate, he said to a reporter, "I'm happy to report there is life outside the Senate."

That was consoling news to those of us prepared to leave the comfort and security of the Senate for the uncertain waters of the private sector.

Dick Schweiker, who went to an insurance trade association after leaving the Senate, had told me that it took him a good year to adjust.

To have a leisurely lunch, to have dinner at home at a reasonable hour, not to have to "run" to the Senate floor for a vote, not to have your "schedule card" full of appointments from early morning until late at night, not to have the press constantly "in your face" — to have all those changes occur all at once was a major readjustment.

Before all that came into play, though, important decisions had to be made. First, where would we live? After all, I had made a commitment to the Reagans to stay nearby for the remainder of Ron's term. And, as desirable as Nevada is, we thus concluded that the Washington area, in terms of my commitment and work prospects and Carol's commitments to the Ford and National Theater boards, was where we should make our primary residence.

Then, the question was, "What would I do?"

There are a number of options for ex-Senators, such as law firms, trade associations, think tanks and academic institutions.

Joining Finley, Kumble

In the months before leaving the Senate, I was contacted by several law firms based in the Washington and New York areas, as was Louisiana Senator Russell Long, who was also leaving the Senate after 36 distinguished years of service. Russell, the son of the legendary Huey Long, was one of the most capable legislators I'd met in my years in the Senate. During our "recruitment," it felt like fraternity rushing.

We both decided to join the New York City-based law firm of Finley, Kumble, Wagner, Heine, Underberg, Manley, Myerson & Casey. The firm, which was quite profitable, had close to 2,000 employees, including 700 lawyers, and had offices in sixteen cities.

Russell and I decided to join them because they were large and entrepreneurial, would provide us with new offices in the office building adjacent to the recently-renovated Willard Hotel in Washington, and would pay us well. After many years in public service, the prospect of financial freedom was very appealing.

But we quickly learned that what glitters is not always gold. While sitting on Finley, Kumble's management committee, it was apparent to us, from the very beginning, that there were deep internal divisions within the firm. This was a fact that the leaders of the firm, with whom we had talked before joining, had been careful not to disclose to us. Had we known, we would have avoided them like the plague.

Trouble at the Law Firm

The longer we were there, the clearer the conflicts became. Lawyers tend to talk "out of school," much more than our colleagues in the Senate, who were quite close-mouthed about "family fights."

The law firm conflicts arose over how the profits should be distributed. At the time Senator Long and I signed on, the firm had grossed the huge sum of $165 million. In 1987, they expected to gross at least $200 million.

This rosy projection led to a bitter contest among the various main branches for a greater percentage of the profits. The lawyers in Florida and Los Angeles, in particular, felt the New York office had neglected them in the past. The Washington office, where we were based, was squarely in the middle.

As the months wore on, the battle intensified. Many of the money producers for the firm became deeply involved in the fight, spending more time on it than on lawyering. As a result, revenues dropped off sharply.

Matters came to a head in a nasty, confrontational meeting at the New York office. Present were the members of the management committee, including Russell and me. After hours of shouted recriminations ended inconclusively, Russell and I agreed that the pieces couldn't be put back together. And we were right.

In early 1988, Finley, Kumble et al., ignominiously went into bankruptcy.

The Washington branch had consisted of some 125 lawyers. They asked me to head the formation of a new firm, which I agreed to do, on the condition that after a reasonable period of time, I would leave to form my own company. Wisely, Russell Long refused to go along, deciding instead to form his own small law firm.

Our new firm was called Laxalt, Washington, Perito and Dubuc.

I eventually withdrew from the firm, mainly because I wanted to go out on my own, but also because of the firm's decision, over my objections, to represent the Communist government of

Angola. A few years after I left, this firm went under as well.

When the bankruptcy was concluded several years later, I settled for about $400,000, which, to say the least, delayed my early retirement. It was well worth the relief I experienced, however, from being "free at last."

STARTING OUR OWN BUSINESS

Since 1990 I have operated as the sole owner of The Paul Laxalt Group. From the outset, we have had loyal, well-paying clients. I am happy to say that the firm, from the beginning, has operated at a profit, and there has not been one cent of debt.

In these years, we have worked in the nebulous field of "governmental relations." The work consists mainly of guiding CEOs through the dangerous Washington waters.

From the beginning, I've been blessed with having Janene Assuras, my personal secretary, who unfortunately suffered a severe stroke in 1998, and Tom Loranger, my former top aide in the Senate, who came with me to the private sector. Elaine Christofferson, who also worked in my Senate office in Nevada, ably worked with us until the fall of 1998.

For five of his nine years in Washington, brother Peter (Mick) was in our group. An extremely capable lawyer, he was helpful in many areas. He finally decided, much to our regret, to return to Reno to be closer to his family.

Son John Paul served in the Department of the Interior's Bureau of Land Management during the Bush Administration. Thereafter, he came to our shop, where he handled various matters very capably. In 1997, he, too, returned to Nevada with his wife, Cindy, and their three children. I regretted his leaving, but understood that the "call of the West" was strong. He is now in an executive capacity in the Nevada state government.

Although we have no formal business connection, daughter

Michelle has officed with us since almost the beginning. We have associated on several matters. The experience has been productive and mutually satisfying.

Michelle has been recognized by her colleagues and by the Washingtonian magazine as one of the top lobbyists in town. She's a real pro in the toughest arena of all – Washington, D.C. As an admiring father, I marvel at how she is able to do her lobbying work, act as a radio talk show host, and raise three youngsters – all at once.

When asked, and I often am, what I do professionally in my present life, I say that I am a troubleshooter for various corporate CEOs. These CEOs have loads of legal, lobbying and accounting help. Nonetheless, they feel the need for experienced Washington help on a peer level. What they need more than anything is reliable intelligence: "What in the hell is really going on in that jungle called Washington, D.C.?" In some ways, it's the sort of help I gave Ron Reagan when he was President.

I've been blessed with top clients over the years, working with such great CEOs as Norm Augustine at Lockheed Martin (now retired), and John Snow at the railroad giant, CSX. Over the years, they were not only clients but became personal friends. Sure, we've run into a few jerks along the way, but only a few.

Personal Aspects of Life After the Senate

1976 was a vintage year for me. It heralded the beginning of Ron Reagan's first run for the Presidency. Far more importantly, it was the year Carol and I were married in a private ceremony in Reno, Nevada, with a few friends and family in attendance.

Since I took office in 1974, I had watched Carol "flower" from a small town woman into one who gradually became a personality on the Washington scene.

She refused to be intimidated by the complexities of Washington. Within days after her arrival, she had mastered the traffic maze that Mr. L'Enfant had created and knew her way around better than many cab drivers. To this day, she loves to act as a tour guide for our many Washington visitors.

Carol and I cutting the cake following our wedding – January 2, 1976.
Photo by Doc Kaminski

Her outgoing Italian personality, reflected in a great sense of humor, endeared her quickly to the social movers and shakers in Washington.

Carol was eventually asked to serve on the Boards of both Ford's and National Theaters, where she still faithfully serves. In fact, she is now an accomplished observer of the Washington theater scene.

Although frightened at first, she gradually became socially comfortable in any setting. One of my favorite recollections is from an event Carol and I attended at the White House in the early 1980s.

When Carol was growing up, her widowed mother, Anita Bernardini, like most, had to watch the family budget closely. Anita would regularly respond to her children's requests for what she considered to be "luxuries," by asking, "Who do you think I am, Mrs. Astor?"

One night at a White House dinner hosted by the Reagans, Carol was astounded when a friend said, "Senator and Mrs. Laxalt, I'd like you to meet a friend of mine. May I present Mrs. Astor." I'll never forget the joy in her voice when she excitedly communicated the news to her Mom. "Yes, Mom, there really is a Mrs. Astor!"

Her political outlet became the Republican Women's Federal Forum, which at its lunches attracts several hundred Republican women activists from the Washington area. It's an honor for Republican officeholders to be invited to speak at the Forum. Over the years, I've wondered at times whether the Forum hasn't made a "political junkie" out of my wife.

Carol reads avidly almost every political piece that appears in newspapers or magazines. It's also quite a treat to watch her debate our television when public figures with whom she disagrees appear on the screen. Poor Bill Clinton. He sure catches a lot of hell!

She has also worked wholeheartedly to develop positive relationships with the children and grandchildren. For a new wife in a "blended marriage," it wasn't easy, but it worked.

After our marriage, I was privileged to adopt her daughter, Denise, who now teaches first graders in Reno and tries to fill the gap for a number of "latch-key" kids. Her extended family is a source of pride to all of us. She's a selfless person, who is making a big contribution to the youngsters she teaches.

Denise

When I retired from the Senate, for a variety of reasons, it became clear that we would settle in Virginia. We had grown to love the Commonwealth over the years — its history, traditions and politics. We decided that Washington was the place for me to pursue my life in the private sector, and for Carol to continue doing her good work. Virginia, of course, is "next door."

During the Senate years, Carol and I lived in a small townhouse in Falls Church, Virginia. With the prospect of additional income after leaving the Senate, we shopped at some length for a new home, but we found none that met our requirements. We wanted a home with a combination of Virginia gentility and style and western informality. Most of the homes we looked at had elegant exteriors, but small rooms.

We finally decided to build our own. After acquiring a lot in the McLean, Virginia woods, we proceeded to take the perilous trip of building our own home without an architect.

With the invaluable help of a dedicated construction superintendent, John McDonald, we built a great house. We shamelessly plagiarized rooms in houses we had visited over the years.

For example, we always enjoyed the "Great Room" at George

Whittell's, and later Jack Dreyfus's "Castle" at Lake Tahoe with its two-story beamed ceiling, fireplaces at either end, and huge windows that, in the case of the Castle, overlooked Lake Tahoe.

With modifications, it was incorporated into our new house and has been the core of our entertainment area.

We went so far as to send for the specifications of the grand stairway in the Governor's Mansion in Carson City. It worked beautifully in the McLean house and offers an elegant "welcome" in the foyer.

Over the years, the house has served as a center for many activities. We've had several fund-raisers there for candidates. Annually, we host a Christmas party for our friends, and, of course, Carol thoroughly enjoys feeding the kids and grandkids when they're in town.

Carol should have been an events coordinator. She enjoys staging events and is in constant demand in the Washington area to help on various endeavors.

She's quite a farmer, too. The house sits on two acres, and I swear she has cultivated every square foot. As a result, we now have an oasis in the McLean woods, no more than a half-hour from the office in Washington.

Perhaps most importantly, we have plenty of room with plenty of privacy. After all those years of being in the public eye, it's a wonderful change for both of us. The best part, as far as I'm concerned, is that I share it with Carol.

We've also been blessed with finding our cabin in the Shenandoah Mountains overlooking the historic Civil War town of Front Royal, Virginia. It's one hour away by car from McLean.

Over the years, we have acquired adjoining lots so that the cabin now sits among six acres of woods. Here, too, we enjoy total privacy. We indulge the deer by feeding them cracked corn.

With the help of country friends from the Front Royal area

– Larry and Mary Donovan – the property has been easy to maintain.

And, of course, in the month of August it's Marlette Lake time. Our family property, which consists of about 100 acres, is in the heart of the Sierra Nevada at 8,300 feet, overlooking Lake Tahoe.

Our "Slice of Heaven on Earth" – Marlette Lake.
Special Collections, University of Nevada, Reno Library

For years, we have had a compound consisting of various tents for sleeping, eating, drinking and just plain "chilling out." It's an opportunity for family to get together, which we cherish, particularly the grandkids.

My campmates for years have been Bob Boucher, who lives in Carson City, and oversees the camp year round; Ollie Kinney, a retired Air Force Colonel from the Sacramento area; and Bob Smith, Carol's brother-in-law, who now lives in Arizona with Carol's sister, Gloria.

Unfortunately, two of our longtime campmates, Billy Budd and Swede Swanson, are no longer with us. We miss them greatly.

Swede's wife, Ruthe, a schoolmate at Carson High, was a loyal worker in each of my campaigns and served with Bill Sinnott in my Carson City Senatorial office. She, too, passed away prematurely. I often think of her.

Over the years, our group has learned to apportion camp duties, and for a bunch of "grumpy old men," we get along beautifully. A high point each year is when Father Caesar Caviglia barbecues a full lamb over our pit.

In addition to family and the regulars, several of our close Las Vegas friends such as Tom and Lyn Wiesner, Joe and Pam Brown and Barry and Sue Becker have spent a great deal of "Marlette time" with us. For a group of "city slickers," they're great campers and the best of company.

Marlette is almost a sacred place for me. It's where, as a young kid, I camped with Poppa Laxalt. It's where I made several serious personal and political decisions. No place on earth is as important to me.

Post-Senate Politics

Since leaving the Senate and public service, I've continued to have an interest in politics, although mainly as an observer rather than a participant.

Running a business a few blocks from Capitol Hill, I've learned first-hand what political fund-raising is like these days. In campaign years, I am deluged with requests for funds. Through the daily mail, not to mention the fax machine, we are bombarded with requests for money.

I now understand what people meant when they told me during my Senate years — particularly when I was General Chairman of the Party — that they were sick and tired of being "hustled" for money.

Campaign finance "reform" continues to be an issue the "out" party would love to support, while the "ins" give lip service to it, but privately don't want changes because they would diminish the huge advantages enjoyed by incumbents.

The longer I watch the system, the more I become concerned that our campaigns are being corrupted. When, as happens too often, requests for meetings with Senators or Representatives are first screened by campaign operatives, or when such a meeting is followed up by a request for a contribution, something is wrong.

I was involved peripherally in the 1988 and 1992 Bush campaigns and the 1996 Dole campaign. In time, several of us "old hands" concluded – correctly – that we were simply being "stroked," rather than being directly involved.

We should have known better. Unless you're a major fundraiser or are willing to spend, on a full-time basis, the time and energy to be on the inside of a campaign, you're really not entitled to a place at the table.

Yet, if the Bush campaign had listened to us in 1992, they would have had the candidate recognize how the recession was hurting millions of people and offer a plan for relief. Instead, he appeared not to give a damn.

In the Dole campaign, the strategists should have recognized that to beat an incumbent, you have to destroy his credibility. The Dole campaign had to prove that Bill Clinton – due to a lack of character – had forfeited the right to be President. If they had, the result would have been different.

In Nevada, at the local and state level, with great pride, I've seen former staffers run for and be elected to office. Each, so far as I know, continues to fly the banner of "conservatism" learned in my Senate office.

One of my long-time supporters, Kenny Guinn, ran for and

was elected Governor of Nevada in 1998. For years, I had attempted to have him seek office, but he repeatedly told me he and his wife, Dema, weren't ready. Last year, after having raised their family and achieving financial independence, he won a resounding victory. He'll be a great Governor and is off to a stunning start.

I am asked often if I regret leaving political office. I reply, "Not for a moment." As far as I'm concerned, my time in public service was concluded, and I was ready for the challenges of the private sector.

Each day, I count the blessings that I've had in my lifetime. I hope that Momma and Poppa Laxalt are pleased by what their "immigrant Basque family" has been able to accomplish in America. They should be.

What has happened to the Laxalts is a prime example of why the United States is called "the land of opportunity." Through their hard work and perseverance, our parents opened the door to that opportunity for each of their children, who have all been successful, not only in their various endeavors, but more importantly, in their lives as citizens in this "Sweet Promised Land."

This First Edition of
Nevada's Paul Laxalt
is limited to a printing of 5000 copies.

The paper is Finch Opaque Book
and the type is Centaur.

Designed by Jim Richards.

Printed by R. R. Donnelley & Sons Company
in the United States of America.